Release the Sun

Release the Sun

by
William Sears

Bahá'í
PUBLISHING

Bahá'í Publishing, 401 Greenleaf Avenue, Wilmette, IL 60091-2886

First edition published 1957. New edition 2003.
Reprinted 2016
Printed in the United States of America on acid-free paper ∞
ISBN 1-931847-09-6
060504034321

Cover Design by Robert A. Reddy
Book Design by Suni D. Hannan

Contents

Contents

Western map of Persia in the time of *Release the Sun*

Publisher's Preface

Release the Sun retells in vivid detail many of the events associated with the brief yet dramatic ministry of the Prophet-Herald of the Bahá'í Faith in Iran. Though the book has been available to English-speaking members of the Bahá'í Faith for some forty-five years, it was not widely available to the general public. Now, for the first time since the book's release in 1957, in this new, completely reedited edition, Bahá'í Publishing makes *Release the Sun* accessible to the general public.

A number of things about the new edition distinguish it from the first edition of the book. First, the narrative, which draws heavily from the stories found in *The Dawn-Breakers*—Nabíl-i-A'ẓam's monumental epic narrating the history of the earliest days of the Bahá'í Revelation—has been meticulously checked and rechecked to ensure its faithfulness to the details found in that work.

Second, a great number of notes referring to *The Dawn-Breakers* and its voluminous footnotes have been omitted for the sake of simplicity. This was done because the vast majority of notes were simply citations of *The Dawn-Breakers* and can be accessed quite readily through a number of excellent search engines that are freely available through the World Wide Web. Thus any reader who has access to the Web can easily search for and find the source of most of the quotations and extracts that appear in *Release the Sun*. Citations for those few extracts that do not come from *The Dawn-Breakers* appear in footnotes.

Third, while the epilogue and seven appendices of the first edition have been omitted, a glossary, bibliography, basic Bahá'í reading list, explanatory footnotes, and an index have all been added for the reader's convenience.

It is hoped that these changes will enhance the experience of the average Western reader, for whom the book was always intended but who has not had easy access until now to this dramatic and compelling story.

Preface to the First Edition

This book, *Release the Sun,* gives the early history of the Bahá'í Faith up through the hour of the martyrdom of its Herald, the Báb.

Professor Edward Granville Browne of Pembroke College, Cambridge University, wrote of this period in history, saying:

> "I am very anxious to get as accurate an account of all the details connected with the Bábí movement as possible, for in my eyes the whole seems one of the most interesting and important events that has occurred since the rise of Christianity . . . and I feel it my duty, as well as pleasure, to try as far as in me lies to bring the matter to the notice of my countrymen . . . for suppose anyone could tell us more about the childhood and early life and appearance of Christ, for instance, how glad we should be to know it. Now it is impossible to find out much . . . but in the case of the Báb it *is* possible. . . . So let us earn the thanks of posterity, and provide against that day now."*

This is an attempt to bring just such an account of the life of the Báb to the attention of the world. This same story has

---

* Edward Granville Browne, quoted by H. M. Balyuzi, in Lady Blomfield (Sitárih Khánum), *The Chosen Highway,* (Wilmette, IL: Bahá'í Publishing Trust, 1975), pp. v–vi.

been set down in everlasting language for the scholar in *The Dawn-Breakers*, written by Nabíl-i-A'ẓam, and in *God Passes By*, written by Shoghi Effendi Rabbani, the Guardian of the Bahá'í Faith.

Release the Sun does not present all of the drama of this epic, nor does it give, word for word, the exciting stories told during those memorable days. It merely offers a simplified version of a story too long neglected and overlooked by man in his search for peace of mind and satisfaction of soul.

William Sears
Wilgespruit, Transvaal, South Africa
September, 1957

A Note to the Reader

The system of transliterating Persian and Arabic names in this book is one of several that are currently in use. It differs from other systems in its use of accents ("á" and "í") instead of overlines ("ā" and "ī"), though there are other differences as well. This is the system of transliteration that Shoghi Effendi used for his English translation of the original Persian of *The Dawn-Breakers,* Nabíl-i-A'ẓam's history of the early days of the Bahá'í Faith, from which most of the stories in *Release the Sun* are drawn. To avoid confusion, we have opted to consistently transliterate most names and terms according to this system. Familiar place names such as "Baghdad" and "Tehran" are rendered as "Bag͟hdád" and "Ṭihrán," and "Qur'án" appears in place of the more familiar "Koran."

Release the Sun

Prologue

Prologue

A small whirlwind of dust moved quietly down the deserted street. It whipped a scrap of paper against a sleeping cat, frightening it out of the doorway into the house. Then all was motionless silence.

Suddenly, a young child hurried around the corner and raced down the empty street. His bare feet kicked up little puffs of dust from the hot earth.

"He's coming!" he cried out. "They're bringing him this way!"

People streamed from their houses with the panic of ants whose hill has been struck by a careless foot. The street was alive with thrilled and expectant faces. Their excitement increased as they heard the angry shouts of the approaching mob.

A river of men, women, and children flowed noisily around the corner. The young man they were following was overwhelmed by their insults. The mob cried out with delight. They knew he would not escape them. He was a captive. His guard pulled him along in front of the crowd by a long rope tied to an iron collar that was fastened about his neck. He was being taken to the authorities so that his death warrant might be signed.

When his steps faltered, the guard helped him on his way by jerking savagely on the rope or by planting a well-aimed kick. Occasionally, someone would dart out of the crowd, break through the guards, and strike the young man with a fist or a stick. Cheers of pleasure and encouragement accompanied each attacker. When a stone or a piece of refuse hurled from the mob struck the young captive in the face, both the guard and the crowd would burst into laughter.

"Rescue yourself, O great hero!" one of the pursuers called mockingly. "Break asunder your bonds! Produce for us a miracle!" Then he spat in derision at the silent figure.

The young man was returned to the barracks square. A short time later he was led to his place of execution. It was high noon in the public square of a sunbaked city.

The blistering summer sun glinted on the barrels of the raised rifles. The guns were pointed at the young man's breast. The soldiers awaited the command to fire and take his life.

Great crowds were still pouring into the public square. Thousands swarmed along the adjoining rooftops overlooking the scene of death. They were all hungry for one last look at this strange young man who had so troubled their country. He was either good or evil, but they were not sure which.

He seemed so young to die—only thirty. Now that the end had come, this victim of the mob's hatred did not seem dangerous at all. He gazed calmly as the hostile barrels of seven hundred and fifty cocked rifles were pointed at him.

I

The Promise of the Messiah

The Promise of the Messiah

This is the story of a modern search for the Holy Grail, the cup of everlasting life. It began in the land from which the three kings came to Bethlehem, guided by a bright star.

It was now the nineteenth century, and there was another sign in the heavens—a great fiery comet. Many were awed, many were frightened, and many were cheered, for both the East and the West were caught up in a millennial zeal.

In Persia (present-day Iran), home of the "three wise men," the excitement over the coming of a Messiah was greater than in any other land. In America and Europe, scholars wrote and spoke of the expected appearance of the promised Christ, but in Persia many people were actively searching for Him. They believed the Promised One to be already in their midst.

Among these devout searchers was Shaykh Aḥmad, a kindly, gentle man. At the age of forty he left his home and kindred in one of the islands of Bahrain to the south of the Persian Gulf and set out to unravel the mystery of the coming Promised One. An inner voice kept urging him on. Eagerly, he devoured everything written on the subject. He questioned the great religious and scientific authorities until he felt that at last he knew the truth.

He was now filled with an eagerness to unburden his soul. He began to search for someone with whom he could share his great secret—his certainty of the time and place for the appearance of God's new Messenger, who would fulfill all the promises given in the sacred books of the world's great religions.

Shaykh Aḥmad made his way on foot to the city of Shíráz in southern Persia. Often in his public talks he passionately extolled that city. Such was the praise he lavished upon Shíráz that his hearers, who were only too familiar with its mediocrity, were astonished at the tone of his language.

"Wonder not," Shaykh Aḥmad told them. "Before long the secret of my words will be made clear to you. A number of you will live to behold the glory of a day which all the prophets of old have foretold and have yearned to witness."

There was no one to whom Shaykh Aḥmad was able to pour out his knowledge in its entirety. He feared what the people might do to the one whose coming had set his heart on fire. He knew he must wait patiently until a kindred soul appeared with whom he could share his secret.

During those days a young man named Siyyid Káẓim was already on his way to visit Shaykh Aḥmad. He had heard of this great man and thought perhaps Shaykh Aḥmad himself might be the Promised One. Siyyid Káẓim lived near a famous tomb at Ardibíl, a city in northwestern Persia. One night in a dream he was told to arise and put himself under the spiritual guidance of Shaykh Aḥmad, whom he would find residing at Yazd.

Siyyid Káẓim began his journey from Ardibíl in the far north to Yazd in the heart of Persia at once. When he reached his destination, Shaykh Aḥmad greeted him affectionately. "I welcome you, O my friend! How long and how eagerly I have awaited your coming."

To him Shaykh Aḥmad confided all that he knew. He urged Siyyid Káẓim to kindle in every receptive heart the fire that burned so brightly in his own.

"You have no time to lose," Shaykh Aḥmad warned him. "Every fleeting hour should be fully and wisely used. Strive night and day to remove the veils of prejudice and orthodoxy that have blinded the eyes of men. For verily I say, the hour is drawing nigh."

By devoting special attention to his followers, Shaykh Aḥmad hoped to enable them to become the active supporters of the cause of the Promised One when He appeared.

Shaykh Aḥmad knew that the hour of his own death was approaching. He told his followers to continue to seek the truth through Siyyid Káẓim because he alone understood Shaykh Aḥmad's objective.

Shaykh Aḥmad died soon thereafter, and Siyyid Káẓim became the leader of his followers. Siyyid Káẓim also found that there was no one sincere enough or worthy enough to hear all that Shaykh Aḥmad had taught him. His followers were still tied to their homes, their families, their money, their businesses, their former beliefs. If the coming Promised One would exalt them and preserve all they held dear, then they were ready, nay eager, to accept. But if accepting His message meant forsaking all they cherished and perhaps even facing death, then their ears were deaf to the sweet music.

At long last Siyyid Káẓim found one young man in whom he could place his greatest trust. The youth's name was Mullá Ḥusayn. Such was the love and honor that Siyyid Káẓim bestowed upon Mullá Ḥusayn that some of his companions suspected that Mullá Ḥusayn might be the Promised One to whom their master was unceasingly referring, the One whom he so often declared was even now living in their midst, unrecognized by them all.

"You behold Him with your own eyes," Siyyid Káẓim told them, "and yet recognize Him not!"

Mullá Ḥusayn returned Siyyid Káẓim's great love and respect. At times he himself secretly wondered whether or not

Siyyid Káẓim might be the One they awaited. Mullá Ḥusayn, however, had a standard by which he planned to test whoever made such a stupendous claim. He would ask that a commentary be written on the story of Joseph, a certain chapter in the sacred scripture, and written in a style and language entirely different from the prevailing standards.

One day Mullá Ḥusayn privately asked Siyyid Káẓim to write such a commentary. Siyyid Káẓim refused.

"This is, verily, beyond me," he said. "He, that great One, who comes after me will, unasked, reveal it for you. That commentary will constitute one of the weightiest testimonies of His truth, and one of the clearest evidences of the loftiness of His position."

Mullá Ḥusayn asked Siyyid Káẓim why this chapter was called the "best of stories" in their holy book. Siyyid Káẓim replied, "It is not the proper occasion for explaining the reason." His words hinted that the future would unveil this truth.

Another among his followers felt that Siyyid Káẓim, in spite of his denials, was the One foretold. He went so far as to declare this publicly. Siyyid Káẓim was most displeased. He would have cast the speaker out of the company of his chosen followers had he not begged for forgiveness.

"My knowledge is but a drop compared with the immensity of His knowledge," Siyyid Káẓim asserted, "my attainments a speck of dust in the face of the wonders of His grace and power."

When Siyyid Káẓim made this forthright denial, still another of his followers was very distressed. He, too, had believed Siyyid Káẓim to be the great announced Figure. He prayed earnestly to God either to confirm the feeling in his heart or to deliver him from such a fancy. The manner in which he was assisted is recorded in his own words.

One day at the hour of dawn, this follower went to the house of Siyyid Káẓim, where he found him fully dressed in his best attire and about to leave. He asked the follower to accompany him.

At this time Siyyid Káẓim was residing in Karbilá, Iraq. He said, "A highly esteemed and distinguished Person has arrived. I feel it incumbent upon us both to visit Him." The two men began to walk through the streets of the city.

The sun had just appeared as the men reached a house where a youth stood as if he expected to receive them. His face revealed an expression of almost indescribable humility and kindliness. He quietly approached the visitors, extended his arms toward Siyyid Káẓim, and lovingly embraced him. His friendliness and affection contrasted strongly with the profound reverence that Siyyid Káẓim showed him. Siyyid Káẓim received the youth's expressions of affection and esteem speechlessly, his head bowed in humility.

The youth led the visitors to an upper chamber. A silver cup had been placed in the center of the room. After they were seated, their host filled the cup and handed it to Siyyid Káẓim, quoting a verse from the Qur'án: "A drink of a pure beverage shall their Lord give them."*

The follower was amazed when he saw Siyyid Káẓim quaff, without the least hesitation, that holy draft from a silver cup, the use of which is forbidden to the faithful according to the precepts of Islam. Each guest was given a drink from the cup, and no further words were spoken, such was the atmosphere of reverence and joy. Soon after, the visitors were escorted to the door and bidden farewell.

Three days later, that same young host arrived to take his seat amidst the assembled followers of Siyyid Káẓim. He sat close to the doorway and, with great modesty and dignity of bearing, listened to Siyyid Káẓim's discourse.

---

* Qur'án 76:21.

As soon as Siyyid Káẓim saw him, he immediately ended his discourse. One of his followers urged him to resume his talk about the coming of the Promised One.

"'What more shall I say?'" replied Siyyid Káẓim as he turned his face toward the young man. "'Lo, the Truth is more manifest than the ray of light that has fallen upon that lap!'"

The ray of sunlight to which Siyyid Káẓim referred had fallen upon the lap of that same youth he had so recently visited.

One of Siyyid Káẓim's followers asked, "Why is it that you neither reveal His name nor identify His person?"

Siyyid Káẓim indicated that if he were to divulge His name, both the Promised One of God and he himself would be put to death instantly.

Siyyid Káẓim had actually pointed with his finger to the ray of light that had fallen on that lap, and yet none of those who were present seemed to grasp its meaning.

Siyyid Káẓim became increasingly aware of the approach of the hour at which the Promised One was to be revealed. There is conclusive evidence that he referred time and again to this event. He was fond of saying, "I see him as the rising sun." He realized how thick the veils were that prevented even his own followers from seeing the truth. He kept warning them as John the Baptist had warned those who awaited Christ, "The kingdom of God is at hand."* With care and wisdom he gradually began to remove all the barriers that might stand in the way of their full recognition of that hidden Treasure when it appeared.

"Beware, beware lest after me the world's fleeting vanities beguile you," he cautioned them. "Renounce all comfort, all earthly possessions and kindred, in your quest of Him who is the Desire of your hearts and of mine. . . . detach yourselves from all earthly things, and humbly and prayerfully beseech

* Matthew 3:3.

your Lord to sustain and guide you. Never relax in your determination to seek and find Him. . . . Be firm till the day when He will choose you. . . . Well is it with every one of you who will quaff the cup of martyrdom in His path."

Siyyid Káẓim promised some of his followers that they would not only have the joy of seeing the coming Messenger of God face to face, but that they would see His Successor as well. He reminded them of the Qur'ánic prophecy "For soon after the first trumpet-blast . . . , there shall be sounded again yet another call, at which all things shall be quickened and revived."*

Repeatedly, Siyyid Káẓim told them that they would see not one, but two Messengers of God, the twin revelations promised in the Qur'án and the Bible for the "last days."

These two successive Messengers would be the fulfillment of the prophecy of the "second and third woe" mentioned in the Book of Revelation of St. John, which prophesies that the "third woe" would quickly follow the "second woe." They would also be the fulfillment of the two trumpet blasts mentioned in the Qur'án which in the "last days" would quickly follow each other.†

Siyyid Káẓim assured his followers that after the promised Dawn, the promised Sun would be made manifest. "For when the star of the Former has set," he said, "the Sun of the beauty of Ḥusayn‡ will rise and illuminate the whole world."

In the last year of his life, Siyyid Káẓim left the city of Karbilá to visit the holy shrines nearby. He stopped at a prayer-house beside the highway to offer his noonday devotions. He was standing beneath the shade of a palm when suddenly an Arab appeared. He approached Siyyid Káẓim and spoke to him.

---

* Qur'án 39:68.

† Revelation 11:4; see Qur'án 79:6–7.

‡ An allusion to the Imám Ḥusayn, The Third Imám of Shí'ah Islam.

"Three days ago I was shepherding my flock in this adjoining pasture," he told Siyyid Káẓim, "when sleep suddenly fell upon me. In my dream I saw Muḥammad . . . who addressed me in these words: 'Give ear, O shepherd, to my words. . . .'"

In this dream the Prophet instructed the shepherd to stay within the precincts of the prayer-house, saying that in three days a man, Siyyid Káẓim by name, would arrive accompanied by his friends. The shepherd was to tell him, "Rejoice, for the hour of your departure is at hand. . . . When you shall have . . . returned to Karbilá, there, three days after your return . . . you will wing your flight to Me. Soon after shall He who is the Truth be made manifest. Then shall the world be illuminated by the light of His face."

The thought of Siyyid Káẓim's approaching death saddened his companions. He comforted them with these words: "Is not your love for me for the sake of that true One whose advent we all await? Would you not wish me to die, that the promised One may be revealed?"

To his last breath, Siyyid Káẓim urged his followers to persevere in their search. He returned to Karbilá, and on the day he arrived he became ill. Three days later he died, just as foretold in the shepherd's dream.

2

The Search Begins

The Search Begins

Mullá Ḥusayn, Siyyid Káẓim's trustworthy disciple, was in the city of Iṣfahán at this time on a special mission for Siyyid Káẓim. He had been sent to win the support of an eminent religious leader. He was so successful in fulfilling his mission that the leader changed his views. In fact, he became so fond of Mullá Ḥusayn that he sent an attendant to find out where he was residing. The attendant followed Mullá Ḥusayn and saw him enter a room devoid of furniture, with but a single mat on the floor. He watched Mullá Ḥusayn offer his prayers and lie down on the mat with nothing to cover him from the cold but his cloak. The attendant reported this to his master, whose admiration for Mullá Ḥusayn then increased so greatly that he sent the attendant back to him with a gift of money.

However, Mullá Ḥusayn returned the money, saying, "Tell your master that his real gift to me is the spirit of fairness with which he received me, and the open-mindedness which prompted him, despite his exalted rank, to respond to the message which I, a lowly stranger, brought him. Return this money to your master, for I, as a messenger, ask for neither recompense nor reward. 'We nourish your souls for the sake of God; we seek from you neither recompense nor thanks.'* My prayer for your master is that earthly leadership may never hinder him from acknowledging and testifying to the Truth."

When Mullá Ḥusayn returned to Karbilá, Siyyid Káẓim was dead. Though his own heart was heavy, Mullá Ḥusayn cheered and strengthened the disconsolate followers of his beloved leader. He called them all together to renew their ardor and

* Qur'án 76:9.

asked them what the last wishes and instructions of their departed leader had been.

From their reluctant lips Mullá Ḥusayn extracted the following admissions: that repeatedly and emphatically Siyyid Káẓim had told them to leave their homes and scatter far and wide in search of Him to whose coming he had so often alluded; that the Object of their quest was now revealed, and the veils between them and Him could only be removed by a devoted search; and that nothing short of prayerful endeavor, purity of motive, singleness of purpose, and ceaseless search would ever lead them to Him.

"We acknowledge our failure," they told him.

"Why, then," Mullá Ḥusayn demanded, "have you chosen to tarry in Karbilá? Why is it that you have not dispersed, and arisen to carry out his earnest plea?"

To his entreaty they gave weak and evasive answers.

"Our enemies are many and powerful," one replied. "We must remain in this city and guard the vacant seat of our departed chief."

"It is incumbent upon me to stay and care for the children whom the Siyyid has left behind," another explained.

However, they all agreed to the leadership of Mullá Ḥusayn, saying, "Such is our confidence in you, that if you claim to be the promised One, we shall all readily and unquestionably submit."

"God forbid!" exclaimed Mullá Ḥusayn. "Far be it from His glory that I, who am but dust, should be compared to Him who is the Lord of Lords!"

Mullá Ḥusayn realized the futility of his efforts and spoke to them no more. He left and made his own plans to begin his quest for the Promised One.

Mullá Ḥusayn prepared for his search by withdrawing to spend forty days in retirement and prayer. His retreat was interrupted by the unexpected arrival of Mullá 'Alíy-i-Basṭámí and twelve other followers of Siyyid Káẓim. They had been stirred by Mullá Ḥusayn's words and had decided to follow his example and begin their own search as well. On several occasions Mullá 'Alí approached Mullá Ḥusayn to ask him where he was going and what his destination would be. Every time he neared Mullá Ḥusayn, he found him so deeply rapt in prayer that he felt it improper to venture a question. Mullá 'Alí decided to retire from society in the same manner and prepare his own heart for the quest. His companions followed his example.

As soon as the forty days were up, Mullá Ḥusayn left Karbilá. He was resolved never to cease his search until he was in the presence of the One he sought. The promises of Siyyid Káẓim stirred in his memory. Many were the prophecies that he turned over and over in his mind.

There was the Muslim tradition, "Verily, in the year sixty [1260 A.H./1844 A.D.] His Cause shall be revealed, and His name shall be noised abroad." There were also the traditions saying, "In His name, the name of the Guardian ['Alí] precedeth that of the Prophet [Muḥammad]"; "In [1260] the Tree of Divine guidance shall be planted"; and "The ministers and upholders of His Faith shall be of the people of Persia."

After his forty days of retirement, Mullá Ḥusayn set out at once for Persia, where he felt his search should begin. It was now the year 1260 A.H., and an inner prompting led him to the city of Bú<u>sh</u>ihr on the Persian Gulf. As he walked through the streets, his heart leaped with excitement, for something told him that this city had once felt the footsteps of the One he sought. He could feel the sweet savors of His holiness in Bú<u>sh</u>ihr. However, he did not remain there because something suddenly turned him like a compass needle to the east. He set out at once for the city of <u>Sh</u>íráz.

When he arrived at the gate of the city, he directed his brother and his nephew, who had accompanied him, to go to the mosque and await his return. He told them that he hoped to join them there for their evening prayer.

A few hours before sunset Mullá Ḥusayn's eyes fell upon a young man of radiant countenance. The youth advanced toward Mullá Ḥusayn and greeted him with a smile of loving welcome. He embraced Mullá Ḥusayn with tender affection as though he were an intimate and lifelong friend.

At first Mullá Ḥusayn thought him to be a follower of Siyyid Káẓim who, on being informed of his approach to S͟híráz, had come out to welcome him. Mullá Ḥusayn is reported to have recalled that memorable night as follows:

". . . He extended to me a warm invitation to visit His home, and there refresh myself after the fatigues of my journey. I prayed to be excused, pleading that my two companions had already arranged for my stay in that city, and were now awaiting my return.

"'Commit them to the care of God,' was His reply. 'He will surely protect and watch over them.'

"Having spoken these words, He bade me follow Him. I was profoundly impressed by the gentle yet compelling manner in which that strange Youth spoke to me. As I followed Him, His gait, the charm of His voice, the dignity of His bearing, served to enhance my first impressions of this unexpected meeting.

"We soon found ourselves standing at the gate of a house of modest appearance. . . . 'Enter therein in peace, secure,' were His words as He crossed the threshold and motioned to me to follow Him. His invitation, uttered with power and majesty, penetrated my soul. I thought it a good augury to be addressed in such words, standing as I did on the threshold of the first house I was entering in S͟híráz. . . . Might not my visit to this house, I thought to myself, enable me to draw nearer to the Object of my quest? As I entered the house and followed my

Host to His chambers, . . . a feeling of unutterable joy invaded my being. Immediately we were seated, He ordered a ewer of water to be brought, and bade me wash away from my hands and feet the stains of travel. . . . He then gave me to drink of a refreshing beverage . . . and Himself prepared the tea which He offered me."

Overwhelmed with these acts of extreme kindness, Mullá Ḥusayn arose to leave, observing that the time for evening prayer was approaching. "I have promised my friends to join them at that hour," he said.

With great courtesy, his host calmly replied, "You must surely have made the hour of your return conditional upon the will and pleasure of God. It seems that His will has decreed otherwise. You need have no fear of having broken your pledge."

Mullá Ḥusayn prepared himself for prayer, and his host stood beside him and prayed. While praying, Mullá Ḥusayn unburdened his soul and breathed the following prayer: "I have striven with all my soul, O my God, and until now have failed to find Thy promised Messenger. I testify that Thy word faileth not, and that Thy promise is sure."

It was about an hour after sunset when the host and his guest began to converse. "Whom, after Siyyid Káẓim, do you regard as his successor and your leader?" he asked Mullá Ḥusayn.

"At the hour of his death," Mullá Ḥusayn replied, "our departed teacher insistently exhorted us to forsake our homes, to scatter far and wide, in quest of the promised Beloved. I have, accordingly, journeyed to Persia, have arisen to accomplish his will, and am still engaged in my quest."

"Has your teacher," the host further inquired, "given you any detailed indications as to the distinguishing features of the promised One?"

Mullá Ḥusayn listed all of the things that Siyyid Káẓim had told him to look for in that beloved One of God. He would be of a pure lineage and of illustrious descent—a descendant of Fáṭimih, the daughter of Muḥammad. He would be between the ages of twenty and thirty. He would be endowed with innate knowledge. And he would be of medium height, free from bodily deficiency, and would abstain from smoking.

The host paused for some time. Then, with a vibrant voice, he declared, "Behold! All these signs are manifest in Me!"

He then considered each of the above-mentioned signs separately and conclusively demonstrated that each and all were indeed applicable to His person. Mullá Ḥusayn was greatly surprised and politely observed, "He whose advent we await is a Man of unsurpassed holiness, and the Cause He is to reveal, a Cause of tremendous power. Many and diverse are the requirements which He who claims to be its visible embodiment must needs fulfil. How often has Siyyid Káẓim referred to the vastness of the knowledge of the promised One! How often did he say: 'My own knowledge is but a drop compared with that which He has been endowed. . . .'"

Mullá Ḥusayn recalls, "No sooner had those words dropped from my lips than I found myself seized with fear and remorse, such as I could neither conceal nor explain. I bitterly reproved myself, and resolved at that very moment to alter my attitude and to soften my tone. I vowed to God that should my Host again refer to the subject, I would, with the utmost humility, answer and say: 'If you be willing to substantiate your claim, you will most assuredly deliver me from the anxiety and suspense which so heavily oppress my soul. I shall truly be indebted to you for such deliverance.'"

The name of Mullá Ḥusayn's host was Siyyid 'Alí-Muḥammad. This young man had spent several years working as a merchant for his uncle in the city of Bú<u>sh</u>ihr before coming to live with him in <u>Sh</u>íráz. As Mullá Ḥusayn looked upon the beautiful face of his host, what thoughts must have coursed through his mind, for in his name the name of the Guardian ('Alí)* preceded that of the Prophet (Muḥammad), He came from the land of Persia, and it was the year 1260 A.H. (1844 A.D.). Was not all of this foretold by Siyyid Káẓim?

Mullá Ḥusayn had two standards by which he hoped to determine the truth of whoever claimed to be that great Messenger. The first test was a treatise that he had composed himself. It dealt with the obscure and difficult teachings of Shaykh Aḥmad and Siyyid Káẓim. Whoever seemed capable of unraveling its mysteries would then be put to the test of revealing, without hesitating or reflecting, a commentary on the highly allegorical chapter of Joseph in the Qur'án.† Mullá Ḥusayn recalled the suspense of that moment in these words:

"I was revolving these things in my mind, when my distinguished Host again remarked: 'Observe attentively. Might not the Person intended by Siyyid Káẓim be none other than I?'

"I thereupon felt impelled to present to Him a copy of the treatise which I had with me. 'Will you,' I asked him, 'read this book of mine, and look at its pages with indulgent eyes? . . .'

"He graciously complied with my wish. He opened the book, glanced at certain passages, closed it, and began to address me. Within a few minutes He had, with characteristic vigour and charm, unravelled all its mysteries and resolved all its problems. . . . He further expounded to me certain truths which could be found neither in the reported sayings of the imáms of the Faith nor in the writings of Shaykh Aḥmad and Siyyid

* The son-in-law of the Prophet Muḥammad and first of the Twelve Imáms of Shí'ah Islam.

† The Súrih, or chapter, of Joseph tells the story of Joseph, the son of Jacob who, betrayed by his brothers and sold into slavery, was imprisoned in Egypt and later rose to rule the land. He is the same Joseph whose story is told in Genesis in the Bible.

Káẓim. These truths, which I had never heard before, seemed to be endowed with refreshing vividness and power.

"He then proceeded to say: 'Now is the time to reveal the commentary on the Súrih [Chapter] of Joseph.'"

It all happened just as Siyyid Káẓim had foretold it to Mullá Ḥusayn. Mullá Ḥusayn recalls that Siyyid 'Alí-Muḥammad "took up His pen and with incredible rapidity revealed the . . . first chapter of His commentary on the Súrih of Joseph. The overpowering effect of the manner in which He wrote was heightened by the gentle intonation of His voice which accompanied His writing. Not for one moment did He interrupt the flow of the verses which streamed from His pen. Not once did He pause till the Súrih . . . was finished. I sat enraptured by the magic of His voice and the sweeping force of His revelation. At last I reluctantly arose from my seat and begged leave to depart. He smilingly bade me be seated, and said: 'If you leave in such a state, whoever sees you will assuredly say: "This poor youth has lost his mind."'"

At that moment the clock registered two hours and eleven minutes after sunset. It was the eve of May 23, 1844.

"This night," Siyyid 'Alí-Muḥammad declared, "this very hour will, in the days to come, be celebrated as one of the greatest and most significant of all festivals. Render thanks to God for having graciously assisted you to attain your heart's desire. . . ."

Jesus first revealed His mission to simple fishermen. Now the Promised One of this age had given the first declaration of His mission to this humble Persian student, Mullá Ḥusayn. Never before in the history of the world's great religions have the exact words of such an unforgettable meeting been preserved by an eyewitness. Mullá Ḥusayn, however, has left in everlasting language a record of that first announcement by Siyyid 'Alí-Muḥammad, known to history as the Báb, or Gate.

Mullá Ḥusayn could never forget the inner peace and serenity that he had felt in the life-creating presence of the Báb. The historian Nabíl has recorded Mullá Ḥusayn's account of the encounter in the following words:

"I sat spellbound by His utterance. . . . All the delights . . . of Paradise . . . I seemed to be experiencing that night. Methinks I was in a place of which it could be truly said: 'Therein no toil shall reach us, . . . but only the cry, Peace! Peace!' Sleep had departed from me that night. I was enthralled by the music of that voice. . . . He then addressed me in these words:

"'O thou who art the first to believe in Me! Verily I say, I am the Báb, the Gate of God.'"

To Mullá Ḥusayn, the first to believe in Him, the Báb gave the title "Bábu'l-Báb," meaning Gate of the Gate. In that hour the Báb proclaimed that He was the One foretold in all the holy books of the past. He said that He had come to usher in a new era, a spiritual springtime in the hearts of humankind. His name—the Báb—means the Gate. His teaching, He said, would open the way to a new age of unity in which humanity would recognize one God and worship in one religion—the same religion that all of God's Prophets have taught from the beginning of time. It would be an age in which all people would live as brothers and sisters.

The Báb cautioned Mullá Ḥusayn not to tell a soul what he had seen and heard. In the beginning, He said, eighteen souls must spontaneously and of their own accord seek and accept Him and recognize the truth of His Revelation. When their number was complete, He would appoint each of the eighteen souls with a special mission and send them forth to accomplish their task.

Mullá Ḥusayn's long search was finally at an end. His own words can best describe the depth of that unique experience:

"This Revelation, so suddenly and impetuously thrust upon

me, came as a thunderbolt. . . . I was blinded by its dazzling splendour and overwhelmed by its crushing force. Excitement, joy, awe, and wonder stirred the depths of my soul. Predominant among these emotions was a sense of gladness and strength which seemed to have transfigured me. How feeble and impotent, how dejected and timid, I had felt previously! Then I could neither write nor walk, so tremulous were my hands and feet. Now, however, the knowledge of His Revelation had galvanised my being. I felt possessed of such courage and power that were the world, all its peoples and its potentates, to rise against me, I would, alone and undaunted, withstand their onslaught. The universe seemed but a handful of dust in my grasp. I seemed to be the Voice of Gabriel personified, calling unto all mankind: 'Awake, for, lo! the morning Light has broken. Arise, for His Cause is made manifest. The portal of His grace is open wide; enter therein, O peoples of the world! For He who is your promised One is come!'"

In such a state Mullá Ḥusayn left the Báb's house and joined his brother and nephew.

3

The Promise Is Fulfilled

The Promise Is Fulfilled

Mullá Ḥusayn was faithful to the Báb's instructions. He told no one of his discovery, even though a large number of Siyyid Káẓim's followers soon gathered about him. They recognized a new spirit in Mullá Ḥusayn's speech and marveled at it, unaware that the source of his knowledge and power flowed from the Báb, whose coming all of them were so eagerly awaiting.

"During those days," Mullá Ḥusayn states, "I was, on several occasions, summoned by the Báb to visit Him. . . . Every time I visited Him, I spent the entire night in His presence. Wakeful until the dawn, I sat at His feet fascinated by the charm of His utterance and oblivious of the world and its cares and pursuits. How rapidly those precious hours flew by! At each daybreak I reluctantly withdrew from His presence. How eagerly in those days I looked forward to the approach of the evening hour! With what feelings of sadness and regret I beheld the dawning of day!"

In the course of one of these nightly visits, the Báb addressed Mullá Ḥusayn in these words: "Tomorrow thirteen of your companions will arrive. To each of them extend the utmost loving-kindness. . . . Pray to God that He may graciously enable them to walk securely in that path which is finer than a hair and keener than a sword. . . ."

Some of these companions, the Báb told Mullá Ḥusayn, would become His chosen disciples. Others would be neither warm nor cold, while still others would remain undeclared until that future day when He for whom the Báb Himself was but the herald would appear.

The next morning Mullá 'Alí, one of Siyyid Káẓim's foremost disciples, arrived in Shíráz, accompanied by twelve companions. He soon noted the great change that had taken place in Mullá Ḥusayn. He was struck by the tranquil radiance of his face. The agitation and expectancy that had characterized his earlier search had vanished. Mullá 'Alí suspected the truth.

"How is it," Mullá 'Alí asked, "that we now see you teaching the people and conducting their prayers and devotions with the utmost tranquillity? Those evidences of agitation and expectancy seem to have vanished from your countenance. Tell us, we beseech you, the reason, that we too may be delivered from our present state of suspense and doubt."

Mullá Ḥusayn hinted that perhaps God, in His infinite mercy, had unlocked before his face the "Gate of His grace" and wished, according to His wisdom, to conceal that fact. Mullá 'Alí immediately understood the hint and, with tears in his eyes, begged Mullá Ḥusayn to reveal the identity of the One who had turned his agitation into peace and converted his anxiety to certainty.

Mullá Ḥusayn refused. "Beseech me not," he replied, "to grant you this favour." He urged Mullá 'Alí to trust in God, saying, ". . . He will surely guide your steps, and appease the tumult of your heart."

So great was the joy that shone from Mullá Ḥusayn's face that Mullá 'Alí could no longer bear to be deprived of that secret. By prayer and fasting he sought desperately to remove the veil that separated him from the Promised One. On the third night of his retirement, while rapt in deep prayer, Mullá 'Alí had a vision. There appeared before his eyes a light that moved off before him. Allured by its matchless beauty, he followed it in his vision until it led him to the Promised One.

Although it was the middle of the night, he rushed to Mullá Ḥusayn. His face was aglow with happiness. He threw himself into the arms of his friend. Mullá Ḥusayn realized at once that

Mullá 'Alí at last knew the truth. He knew where to find the Promised One.

Mullá Ḥusayn embraced Mullá 'Alí warmly and said, "Praise be to God who hath guided us. . . . !"

That very morning, at the break of day, Mullá Ḥusayn, followed by Mullá 'Alí, hurried to the residence of the Báb. At the entrance they were met by the Báb's much-loved servant, who immediately recognized them. He greeted them with these words:

"Ere break of day, I was summoned to the presence of my Master, who instructed me to open the door of the house and to stand expectant at its threshold.

"'Two guests,' He said, 'are to arrive early this morning. Extend to them in My name a warm welcome. Say to them from Me: "Enter therein in the name of God."'"

Mullá 'Alí's first meeting with the Báb did not differ greatly from Mullá Ḥusayn's first meeting with Him. The only difference was that the Báb had offered proofs of His mission for Mullá Ḥusayn to weigh and study; at this meeting, however, all such matters had been put aside, and a spirit of intense love and ardent fellowship prevailed. The entire room seemed to have been vitalized by the Báb's words. Everything in the room seemed to be vibrating with this statement: ". . . Verily, the dawn of a new Day has broken. The promised One is enthroned in the hearts of men. In His hand He holds the mystic cup, the chalice, of immortality. Blessed are they who drink therefrom!"

Each of Mullá 'Alí's twelve companions in turn, by his own efforts, sought and found the Báb. For some, the moment of truth came in their sleep. Others discovered it while awake, or during prayer or meditation. Like Mullá 'Alí, they and a few others eventually recognized the truth and, accompanied by Mullá Ḥusayn, attained the presence of the Báb. One by one, seventeen separate souls searched for the Báb, met Him, and accepted His teachings. The Báb named these individuals "Letters of the Living" and appointed them as His chosen disciples.

Among the seventeen Letters of the Living was one woman. She was known as Ṭáhirih the Pure. She accepted the Báb without ever actually attaining His physical presence. She saw Him in a dream and later had the opportunity to read some of His writings, then became a staunch believer and a courageous teacher, eventually sacrificing her life for her beliefs.

One night while conversing with Mullá Ḥusayn, the Báb said to him, "Seventeen Letters have thus far enlisted under the standard of the Faith of God. There remains one more to complete the number. . . . To-morrow night the remaining Letter will arrive and will complete the number of My chosen disciples."

The next evening as the Báb, followed by Mullá Ḥusayn, was returning to His home, a youth appeared. He was disheveled and dirty from traveling. He approached Mullá Ḥusayn, embraced him, and asked him if he had yet attained his heart's desire.

Mullá Ḥusayn tried to calm him. He advised him to rest for a while, promising to speak with him later. The youth, however, was agitated and refused to let the matter rest. He looked past Mullá Ḥusayn at the retreating figure of the Báb. Then, turning to Mullá Ḥusayn, he said, "Why seek you to hide Him from me? I can recognize Him by His gait. I confidently testify that none besides Him, whether in the East or in the West, can claim to be the Truth. None other can manifest the power and majesty that radiate from His holy person."

Mullá Ḥusayn marveled at these words. He pleaded with the youth to restrain himself, promising that the truth would be unveiled to him soon. Leaving him, Mullá Ḥusayn hurried to join the Báb. He told Him of his conversation with the young man.

"Marvel not at his strange behaviour," the Báb said. "We have in the world of the spirit been communing with that youth.

We know him already. We indeed awaited his coming. Go to him and summon him forthwith to Our presence."

Mullá Ḥusayn instantly recalled the Muslim tradition about the time of the end: "On the last Day, the Men of the Unseen shall, on the wings of the spirit, traverse the immensity of the earth, shall attain the presence of the Promised Qá'im,* and shall seek from Him the secret that will resolve their problems and remove their perplexities."

Now when this eighteenth disciple, or Letter of the Living, whom the Báb named Quddús (meaning "The Most Holy"), had accepted Him, the Báb addressed Mullá Ḥusayn, saying, ". . . Raise the cry: 'Awake! awake, for, lo! the Gate of God is open, and the morning Light is shedding its radiance upon all mankind! The promised One is made manifest; prepare the way for Him, O people of the earth! . . ."

The Báb gave a special message of assurance to Mullá 'Alí. "Your faith must be immovable as the rock, must weather every storm and survive every calamity. Suffer not the denunciations of the foolish and the calumnies of the clergy to afflict you, or to turn you from your purpose. . . . You are the first to leave the House of God, and to suffer for His sake. If you be slain in His path, remember that great will be your reward, and goodly the gift which will be bestowed upon you."

No sooner were these words uttered than Mullá 'Alí arose from his seat and set out to teach others about the Faith of the Báb.

True to the Báb's forewarnings, Mullá 'Alí was overtaken and brutally beaten just beyond the city's gate. He was the first to suffer for the new religion. He was also the first to bring news of the Báb to Ṭáhirih. In Najaf, Iraq, a starting point for Shí'ah Muslim pilgrimage and home to the Imám 'Alí's shrine, he was arrested for fearlessly proclaiming the Faith. He was bound with

* "He who shall arise," a title designating the Promised One of Islam.

chains and taken to Baghdád under sentence of death. He was cast into prison, tried again, and, still in chains, deported to Constantinople (now Istanbul). Some say he fell ill and died en route, others say he was martyred. No one knows what eventually befell this hero of God.

The Báb summoned all of the other disciples to His presence, and to each one He gave a special command and a special task. He spoke to all of them these parting words:

"O My beloved friends! You are the bearers of the name of God in this Day. . . . The very members of your body must bear witness to the loftiness of your purpose, the integrity of your life, the reality of your faith, and the exalted character of your devotion. . . .

"Ponder the words of Jesus addressed to His disciples, as He sent them forth to propagate the Cause of God. . . . 'Ye are even as the fire which in the darkness of the night has been kindled upon the mountain-top. Let your light shine before the eyes of men. Such must be the purity of your character and the degree of your renunciation, that the people of the earth may through you recognise and be drawn closer to the heavenly Father who is the Source of purity and grace. . . .'"

In this parting message to His disciples the Báb once again called their attention to the One who was soon to come after Him, the One for whom He was but the herald.

"I am preparing you for the advent of a mighty Day," He told them. ". . . The secret of the Day that is to come is now concealed. It can neither be divulged nor estimated. The newly born babe of that Day excels the wisest and most venerable men of this time, and the lowliest and most unlearned of that period shall surpass in understanding the most erudite and accomplished divines of this age. Scatter throughout the length and breadth of this land, and, with steadfast feet and sanctified hearts, prepare the way for His coming. Heed not your weaknesses and frailty; fix your gaze upon the invincible power of the Lord, your God, the Almighty. Has He not, in past days, caused Abraham, in spite of His seeming helplessness, to triumph over the forces of Nimrod? Has He not enabled Moses, whose staff was His only companion, to vanquish Pharaoh . . . ? Has He not established the ascendancy of Jesus, poor and lowly as He was in the eyes of men, over the combined forces of the Jewish people? Has He not subjected the barbarous and militant tribes of Arabia to the holy and transforming discipline of Muḥammad, His Prophet? Arise in His name, put your trust wholly in Him, and be assured of ultimate victory."

With such words as these the Báb quickened the faith of His disciples and launched the Letters of the Living on their mission. Each was assigned to return to his own native province to raise the call that the Gate to the Promised One had been opened, that His proof was irrefutable and His testimony complete. They were to refrain from mentioning the Báb's name and focus instead on His message, preparing the way for that Promised One of God prophesied in all of the world's great religions.

4

The Pilgrimage and the Proclamation

The Pilgrimage and the Proclamation

One morning at the hour of dawn, shortly after the Báb had launched his disciples on their mission, most of the disciples left Shíráz to carry out the teaching tasks He had given them. The first disciple, Mullá Ḥusayn, and the last, Quddús, remained with Him.

To these two the Báb disclosed His intention to go to Mecca. Just as Jesus had journeyed to Jerusalem, the stronghold of the Jews, to proclaim His mission, so did the Báb make plans to go on a pilgrimage to Mecca, the heart of the Muslim world. As the hour of His departure arrived, He called Mullá Ḥusayn to Him.

He Himself would visit Mecca and Medina, He told him, and there fulfill the mission with which God had entrusted Him. He had chosen Quddús to go with Him and would leave Mullá Ḥusayn behind to face the onslaught of a fierce and relentless enemy. He assured Mullá Ḥusayn, however, that until he had completely finished his work, no power on earth could harm him.

"The hosts of the invisible Kingdom, be assured, will sustain and reinforce your efforts. The essence of power is now dwelling in you, and the company of His chosen angels revolves around you. His Almighty arms will surround you and guide your steps. He that loves you, loves God. . . . Whoso befriends you, him will God befriend; and whoso rejects you, him will God reject."

The Báb, accompanied by Quddús, departed for the city of Búshihr on the Persian Gulf, where they boarded a boat. After two months of sailing on stormy seas, they landed on the coast of Arabia at Jiddah. A fellow passenger during this voyage has recorded the following:

"... From the day we embarked at Búshihr to the day when we landed ... whenever by day or night I chanced to meet either the Báb or Quddús, I invariably found them together, both absorbed in their work. The Báb seemed to be dictating, and Quddús was busily engaged in taking down whatever fell from His lips. ..."

Neither the storms that raged about them nor the sickness that seized the other passengers could disturb their serenity or interfere with their work.

The Báb entered the city of Mecca seated on a camel, as Christ had entered Jerusalem seated upon a donkey. Quddús refused to ride beside Him on the journey inland. He preferred, he said, to accompany Him on foot, holding the bridle of the camel and taking care of whatever needs the Báb might have. Each night, from sunset until dawn, Quddús sacrificed sleep and comfort to stand watch over the Báb to ensure His safety and comfort.

One day during His visit in Mecca, the Báb met a man named Muḥíṭ. The Báb recognized him as a distinguished follower of Shaykh Aḥmad who aspired to lead other followers of Shaykh Aḥmad. If Muḥíṭ were faithful to his master's instructions, he would now be energetically searching for the Promised One. The Báb spoke to him.

"Oh Muḥiṭ!" He said, "... Behold, we are both now standing within this most sacred shrine. ... He whose Spirit dwells in this place can cause Truth immediately to be known and distinguished from falsehood. ... Verily I declare, none beside Me in this day, whether in the East or in the West, can claim to be the Gate that leads men to the knowledge of God. ... Ask Me whatsoever you please; now, at this very moment, I pledge Myself to reveal such verses as can demonstrate the truth of

My mission. You must choose either to submit yourself unreservedly to My Cause or to repudiate it entirely. . . ."

This sudden, unexpected, and direct challenge unnerved Muḥíṭ. He claimed to believe in the Báb and even went so far as to swear his loyalty to Him. However, when the Báb, who was well aware of the poverty of Muḥíṭ's soul, offered to answer any questions and resolve any problems for him, Muḥíṭ hastily submitted some questions and then asked the Báb to send His reply in writing, claiming that he needed to leave immediately for Medina. Faithful to His word, the Báb promised to reveal His answer to the questions and deliver it to Muḥíṭ in Medina. Again Muḥíṭ pledged his loyalty to the Báb, assuring Him that no matter what happened, he would not leave Medina before receiving the Báb's response. The Báb kept His promise and prepared a written reply to Muḥíṭ's questions, delivering it to him in Medina. But Muḥíṭ was unmoved and refused to accept the precepts it contained. From that time on, his attitude toward the Báb and His followers was one of concealed and persistent opposition.

The Báb found no one in Mecca who would listen. They were all indifferent, antagonistic, or afraid. He made one last effort to awaken the people in that holy city of the Muslims. He wrote a letter to the sharif of Mecca, the custodian of the House of God, hoping that through him He might reach the hearts of the people.

In that letter, the Báb set forth in clear and unmistakable terms the distinguishing features of His mission and called upon the sharif to arise and embrace His Cause.

The sharif did not bother to read the letter or to share it with his friends, who were all too absorbed in their own affairs to respond to the call of the Báb.

Later, the sharif admitted his indifference. "I recollect that in the year '60," he said, "a youth came to visit me. He presented to me a sealed book . . . but [I] was too much occupied at that time to read [it]. A few days later I met again that same youth, who asked me whether I had any reply to make to his offer. Pressure of work had again detained me from considering the contents of that book. I was therefore unable to give him a satisfactory reply."

The Báb was treated exactly as Christ had been treated, with ridicule and contempt. It was the same as it had been in those days when Jesus accused the leaders of His day, saying, "Woe unto you, lawyers! for ye have taken away the key of knowledge: ye entered not in yourselves, and them that were entering in ye hindered."*

The people did not understand Him, no matter whether He spoke plain truths or in symbols. The historian A. L. M. Nicolas writes that the Báb, throughout His mission, had to act "as does a physician to children, who must disguise a bitter medicine in a sweet coating in order to win over his young patients. The people in the midst of whom he [the Báb] appeared were, and still are, alas, more fanatical than the Jews were at the time of Jesus. . . . Therefore, if Christ, in spite of the relative calm of the surroundings in which He preached, thought it necessary to employ the parable, Siyyid 'Alí-Muḥammad . . . was obliged to disguise his thought in numerous circuitous ways and only pour out, one drop at a time, the filter of his divine truths. He brings up his child, Humanity; he guides it, endeavoring always not to frighten it and directs its first steps on a path which leads it slowly but surely, so that, as soon as it can proceed alone, it reaches the goal preordained for it from all eternity."

Before leaving the cities of Mecca and Medina and completing His pilgrimage, the Báb visited the shrine of Muḥammad

---

* Luke 11:52.

and the resting-places of many holy men, pioneers and martyrs who had sacrificed their lives for the sake of God. He beseeched God to hasten the hour of His own martyrdom, which He knew was inevitable, and to accept His sacrifice so that all the peoples of the world might know the truth.

"The drops of this consecrated blood," He said, "will be the seed out of which will arise the mighty Tree of God, the Tree that will gather beneath its all-embracing shadow the peoples and kindreds of the earth. Grieve not, therefore, if I depart from this land, for I am hastening to fulfil My destiny."

5

The Persecution Begins

The Persecution Begins

After the Báb's pilgrimage to Mecca and Medina in Arabia He returned with Quddús to Búshihr in Persia. A short time later He sent Quddús on to Shíráz to bring greetings and instructions to His family and to the believers there. The Báb also sent some of His writings to be shared with them. He bade Quddús farewell with the greatest kindness.

"The days of your companionship with Me," He told him, "are drawing to a close. . . . In this world of dust, no more than nine fleeting months of association with Me have been allotted to you. . . .

"The hand of destiny will ere long plunge you into an ocean of tribulation. . . . In the streets of Shíráz, indignities will be heaped upon you, and the severest injuries will afflict your body. You will survive . . . and will attain the presence of Him who is the one object of our adoration and love. . . ."

When Quddús arrived in Shíráz he began to speak everywhere of the wondrous days he had spent with the Báb. He aroused the whole city with his inspired words. He became very friendly with an elderly mullá named Ṣádiq and gave him a copy of one of the Báb's writings.

Mullá Ṣádiq regularly preached and led the congregation in prayer at a local mosque. He was so taken with the theme and the language of the Báb's message that he resolved steadfastly to carry out all of its instructions. Among these instructions was the specific direction to include the following additional words in the traditional Islamic call to prayer: "I bear witness that He whose name is 'Alí Qabl-i-Muḥammad [a reference to the Báb] is the servant of Baqíyyatu'lláh [meaning "the Remnant of God," a reference to the Promised One yet to come]."

Mullá Ṣádiq carried out this particular instruction one day, astounding the congregation and creating an uproar. Word quickly spread among the populace, and public order was seriously threatened. Protests poured into the office of the governor of the province, Ḥusayn Khán.

"This disciple [Quddús] claims that his teacher is the author of a new revelation and is the revealer of a book which he asserts is divinely inspired," the governor was told. "Mullá Ṣádiq . . . has embraced that faith, and is fearlessly summoning the multitude to the acceptance of that message. . . ."

The governor ordered the arrest of both Quddús and Mullá Ṣádiq. They were delivered to him in handcuffs. The commentary that the Báb had written for Mullá Ḥusayn on the night He had announced His mission was turned over to the governor. It had been seized from Mullá Ṣádiq, who had been reading it aloud to an excited congregation. Ḥusayn Khán ignored Quddús because of his extreme youth. He directed his questions to Mullá Ṣádiq, who was older.

"Tell me," he asked Mullá Ṣádiq, referring to the Báb's commentary, "if you are aware of the opening passage . . . wherein the Siyyid-i-Báb addresses the rulers and kings of the earth in these terms: 'Divest yourselves of the robe of sovereignty, for He who is the King in truth, hath been made manifest! The Kingdom is God's, the Most Exalted. Thus hath the Pen of the Most High decreed!'"

The governor's wrath increased. "If this be true, it must necessarily apply to my sovereign, Muḥammad Sháh, . . . whom I represent as the chief magistrate of this province. Must Muḥammad Sháh, according to this behest, lay down his crown and abandon his sovereignty? Must I, too, abdicate my power and relinquish my position?"

Mullá Ṣádiq replied without hesitation, saying that if the words spoken by the Báb were true and if He were indeed a

Messenger of God, then the abdication of the king and others like him could not matter very much. It could not in any way alter God's purpose or change His sovereignty.

Ḥusayn Khán was extremely displeased with the answer. He cursed Mullá Ṣádiq and Quddús. He ordered his attendants to strip Mullá Ṣádiq of his garments and to scourge him with a thousand lashes. Then he commanded that both men's beards should be burned, their noses be pierced, and that a cord should be passed through this incision so that they could be led through the streets of Shíráz.

"It will be an object lesson to the people of Shíráz," Ḥusayn Khán declared, "who will know what the penalty of heresy will be."

Mullá Ṣádiq was so advanced in age that no one believed he could possibly survive such torture. Yet he was calm and self-possessed. He raised his eyes to heaven and offered a prayer.

"O Lord, our God! We have indeed heard the voice of One that called. He called us to the Faith—'Believe ye on the Lord your God!'—and we have believed. O God, our God! Forgive us, then, our sins . . . and cause us to die with the righteous."*

An eyewitness to the torture of Mullá Ṣádiq has given the following testimony:

"I was present when Mullá Ṣádiq was being scourged. I watched his persecutors each in turn apply the lash to his bleeding shoulders and continue the strokes until he became exhausted. No one believed that Mullá Ṣádiq, so advanced in age and so frail in body, could possibly survive fifty such savage strokes. We marvelled at his fortitude when we found that, although the number of strokes . . . already exceeded nine hundred, his face still retained its original serenity and calm. A smile was upon his face as he held his hand before his mouth. He seemed utterly indifferent to the blows that were being show-

---

* Qur'án 3:193.

ered upon him. When he was being expelled from the city, I succeeded in approaching him, and asked him why he held his hand before his mouth. . . .

"He emphatically replied: 'The first seven strokes were severely painful; to the rest I seemed to have grown indifferent. I was wondering whether the strokes that followed were being actually applied to my own body. A feeling of joyous exultation had invaded my soul. I was trying to repress my feelings and to restrain my laughter.'"

"'I can now realise," Mullá Ṣádiq said, "'how the Almighty Deliverer is able, in the twinkling of an eye, to turn pain into ease, and sorrow into gladness. Immensely exalted is His power above, and beyond the idle fancy of His mortal creatures.'"

Both Mullá Ṣádiq and Quddús withstood their torture with great fortitude. For Quddús, this was but the beginning of greater suffering to come. Exhausted and bleeding, both he and Mullá Ṣádiq were driven out of Shíráz. They were warned at the city gates that if they ever returned, they would both be crucified.

Mullá Ṣádiq and Quddús were the first followers of the Báb to suffer severe persecution on Persian soil.*

---

* Although Mullá 'Alí was attacked outside of Shíráz, his sufferings, intense as they were, cannot compare with the cruel and unusual punishment of Mullá Ṣádiq and Quddús. Furthermore, Mullá 'Alí's greatest suffering occurred beyond Persian territory, in Iraq.

6

The Gentle Arrest

The Gentle Arrest

Ḥusayn Khán's anger was not satisfied by the punishment he had inflicted on Mullá Ṣádiq and Quddús. He now directed his attack on the Báb Himself. He sent a mounted escort to Búshihr and ordered them to arrest the Báb and bring Him back in chains to Shíráz. This spectacle, he felt, would dampen the enthusiasm of the people for His Cause.

The guards set out at once to make the arrest. As they were marching across the wilderness en route to Búshihr, they met a horseman. It was the Báb, who, to their great surprise, had come to meet them. The leader of the escort has himself related the incident:

". . . As we approached him, he saluted us and enquired as to our destination. I thought it best to conceal from him the truth, and replied that in this vicinity we had been commanded by the governor* of Fárs to conduct a certain enquiry."

"The governor has sent you to arrest Me," He said. He told the escort to do with Him as they pleased.

The leader of the escort was caught off guard by the Báb's statement and by His apparent willingness to subject Himself to the indignities and possibly life-threatening harm that Ḥusayn Khán would have in store for him.

The leader of the escort was very taken with the Báb. He did not want Him to fall into the hands of the governor. He pretended not to recognize the Báb and ordered his men to move on.

"I tried to ignore him, and was preparing to leave," he reported, "when he approached me and said: 'I swear by the righ-

* Ḥusayn Khán.

teousness of Him who created man. . . . that all My life I have uttered no word but the truth, and had no other desire except the welfare and advancement of My fellow-men. . . . I know you are seeking Me. I prefer to deliver Myself into your hands, rather than to subject you and your companions to unnecessary annoyance for My sake.'"

The leader pleaded with the Báb, urging Him to flee from Ḥusayn Khán. He did not want to be a party to the brutality that the governor was planning against Him. He called Ḥusayn Khán "ruthless" and "despicable" and a "remorseless wolf" and begged the Báb to escape to the city of Mashhad in the province of Khurásán, where friends of the leader could protect Him.

But the Báb refused, saying, ". . . deliver me into the hands of your master. Be not afraid, for no one will blame you." Then, as if to assure the commander and his men, the Báb explained that until His last hour on this earth arrived, no person could possibly harm Him or interfere with the plan of Almighty God.

The leader bowed his head in consent and carried out the Báb's wishes. He ordered his escort to permit the Báb to ride on ahead of them as though they were a guard of honor rather than a party of arrest. They continued in this fashion until they reached Shíráz.

People turned around in the street to watch them and to marvel at this unusual spectacle. The escort, which had been commanded to bring the Báb back in chains, had returned Him instead with every sign of the respect due to royalty.

Ḥusayn Khán was furious. He rebuked the Báb publicly. In abusive language, he denounced His conduct and ridiculed His claim to be the author of a new revelation, berating Him for disgracing Islam and the Qur'án.

The Báb's gentle manners and courtesy only added to the governor's anger. The historian Nicolas writes, "We know that the Báb especially commended politeness and the most refined courtesy in all social relations. 'Never sadden anyone, no matter whom, for no matter what,' he enjoined." "... I have taught the believers in my religion," He says Himself, "never to rejoice over the misfortune of anyone.'"

Lovingly, but firmly, the Báb reminded Ḥusayn Khán that his duty as governor of the province of Fárs was to determine the truth about the affairs in his region and not to make decisions without first investigating personally.

These words further inflamed the governor's rage. He repaid the Báb's courtesy by turning to his attendant and commanding him to strike the Báb in the face.

The blow was so violent that the Báb's turban fell to the ground. The governor ordered the Báb to remain confined within the home of His uncle, Ḥájí Mírzá Siyyid 'Alí, until there was a decision about what to do with Him. He instructed the uncle to be prepared to surrender the Báb to the governor's office at a moment's notice.

For a while, the Báb led a life of comparative peace. During this period His followers met Him in secret in His uncle's home. One such visitor was a well-known scholar and clergyman named 'Abdu'l-Karím.

'Abdu'l-Karím was from the village of Qazvín. He was a merchant, but so great was his longing to know about God that he had given up his business and devoted his life to studying every branch of learning. Because of his great thirst for knowledge, he had soon eclipsed his fellow students. One day he was elevated to the status of teacher. He had qualified himself to speak as an authority on the sacred scriptures of Islam. He was told that he need no longer attend classes, for he now knew as much as the wisest doctor of Islam. Therefore he, 'Abdu'l-Karím, could now teach others.

At first 'Abdu'l-Karím was elated. But that night, as he began to think about things, his heart was troubled. If he were considered to be among the wisest of all, who was there on earth who really knew anything at all about Almighty God?

He knew he was still a victim of cares and worries, of temptations and doubts. Who was he to lead others? He was overcome with a sense of unworthiness. He struggled with these thoughts until dawn, neither eating nor sleeping. He prayed, "Thou seest me, O my Lord, and thou beholdest my plight . . . I am lost in bewilderment at the thought of the multitude of sects into which Thy holy Faith hath fallen. I am deeply perplexed when I behold the schisms that have torn the religions of the past. Wilt Thou guide me in my perplexities, and relieve me of my doubts?" 'Abdu'l-Karím anguished over the answer to this question.

He relates, "I wept so bitterly that night that I seemed to have lost consciousness. There suddenly came to me the vision of a great gathering of people, the expression of whose shining faces greatly impressed me. A noble figure, attired in the garb of a siyyid,* occupied a seat on the pulpit facing the congregation. He was expounding the meaning of this sacred verse of the Qur'án: 'Whoso maketh efforts for Us, in Our ways will We guide them.' I was fascinated by this face. I arose, advanced towards him, and was on the point of throwing myself at his feet when that vision suddenly vanished. My heart was flooded with light. My joy was indescribable."

'Abdu'l-Karím had consulted a man known throughout the city for his spiritual insight. This man had immediately recognized the siyyid in the vision as Siyyid Káẓim and had told 'Abdu'l-Karím where to find him. 'Abdu'l-Karím had set out at once for Karbilá. There he had found Siyyid Káẓim. He had been standing, addressing a crowd, just as 'Abdu'l-Karím had seen him in his dream. He was speaking those very same words. 'Abdu'l-Karím spent an entire winter in close companionship with Siyyid Káẓim, who spoke constantly of the coming Messenger.

* "Chief," "lord," "prince"; a descendant of the Prophet Muḥammad.

"The promised One," he would openly and repeatedly declare, "lives in the midst of this people. The appointed time for His appearance is fast approaching. Prepare the way for Him, and purify yourselves so that you may recognize His beauty." Siyyid Káẓim said the new Messenger of God would not be recognized until after his death. He implored his followers to arise and seek Him without rest.

On the day when 'Abdu'l-Karím parted from Siyyid Káẓim, he told him, "Rest assured, O 'Abdu'l-Karím, you are one of those who, in the day of His Revelation, will arise for the triumph of His Cause. You will, I hope, remember me on that blessed Day."

'Abdu'l-Karím returned to his home in Qazvín to await that wonderful day. A few years passed with no sign of the Promised One's coming, but 'Abdu'l-Karím's heart was assured.

He returned to his business as a merchant, but each night he would come home and withdraw to the quiet of his room. He would beseech God with all of his heart, saying, "Thou hast, by the mouth of an inspired servant of Thine, promised that I shall attain unto the presence of Thy Messenger and hear Thy Word. How long wilt Thou withhold me from my promise?" Each night he would renew this prayer and would continue his supplications until the break of day.

One night in February 1840, 'Abdu'l-Karím was deep in prayer, almost in a trance-like state, when something extraordinary occurred. "There appeared before me a bird, white as snow, which hovered above my head and alighted upon the twig of a tree beside me," he has related. "In accents of indescribable sweetness, that bird voiced these words: "'Are you seeking the Manifestation, O 'Abdu'l-Karím? Lo, the year '60.'* Immediately after, the bird flew away and vanished." The

* "The year '60" refers to 1260 A.H., or A.D. 1844.

memory of the beauty of that vision lingered long in 'Abdu'l-Karím's mind.

A few years went by, but 'Abdu'l-Karím did not forget the message of the bird, and it was always on his mind. Then word came of a wondrous person living in the city of Shíráz. He left for Shíráz immediately.

He continued to treasure within his heart the strange message conveyed to him by the bird. When he subsequently attained the presence of the Báb and heard from His lips those same words, spoken in the same tone and language as he had heard them in his vision, he realized their significance.

'Abdu'l-Karím burst into tears and threw himself at the Báb's feet in a state of profound ecstasy, much to the astonishment of his companions. The Báb lovingly took him in His arms, kissed his forehead, and invited him to be seated by His side. In a tone of tender affection, He succeeded in appeasing the tumult of 'Abdu'l-Karím's heart.

In spite of Ḥusayn Khán's close supervision, many such great figures came to visit the Báb. Stories of conversions similar to that of 'Abdu'l-Karím caused great excitement in Shíráz. Both the famous and the lowly were willing to take whatever risk was necessary to gain His presence. People met in groups on the street to discuss Him, some blaming, some approving.

Ḥusayn Khán was infuriated at his helplessness and inability to stem the flow of the Báb's rising popularity.

7

The Enchantment of the King's Messenger

MULLÁ ḤUSAYN came to visit the Báb in Shíráz. Immediately, strong voices were raised against him.

"He again has come to our city," they clamored; "he again has raised the standard of revolt, and is, together with his chief, contemplating a still fiercer onslaught against our time-honoured institutions!"

So grave and menacing was the situation, that the Báb instructed Mullá Ḥusayn to return to his home province of Khurásán. He also dismissed all the rest of His companions in Shíráz, except for 'Abdu'l-Karím, whom He kept with Him to help transcribe His writings.

The Báb's disciples—the Letters of the Living—spread throughout the length and breadth of Persia, fearlessly proclaiming the regenerating power of the newborn Revelation.

Soon the fame of the Báb spread far beyond the circle of His disciples. It reached the authorities. They became alarmed at the enthusiasm with which the people everywhere were embracing His message. This was no longer merely a local matter. People from every social stratum were passionately inquiring and then accepting the Báb's teachings. A historical account states that the followers of the Báb were "ardent, brave, carried away, ready for anything; they were fanatical in the true and noble sense of the word; that is to say that every one . . . thought himself of no importance, and burned with a desire to sacrifice his life-blood and his belongings for the cause of Truth."

The same flood of persecution that surrounded Jesus now gradually engulfed the Báb. The combined opposition of church and state unleashed what historians have called the most appalling wave of hatred imaginable. Soon the sands of Persia were stained by a freely given red river of human martyrdom.

The officials arranged great public debates in Shíráz and invited the governor, the clergy, the military chiefs, as well as the people to attend. They thought that in this manner they would discredit the young Prophet.

However, the Báb spoke such profound truths on these occasions that, day by day, the crowds that followed Him greatly increased in number. His purity of conduct at an age when physical passions are most intense impressed the people who met Him. His words were in perfect harmony with His personal conduct. He was possessed of extraordinary eloquence and daring. A French historian and diplomat to Persia at that time, Comte de Gobineau, writes, "From his first public appearances, they [the mullás of Shíráz] sent to him their most able Mullás to argue with him and confuse him. . . . instead of benefiting the clergy, they contributed quite a little to spread and exalt, at their own expense, the renown of this enthusiastic teacher."

The Báb unsparingly exposed their vices and their corruption. Like Jesus, He proved the infidelity of the religious leaders toward their own beliefs. He shamed them publicly and defeated them with their own holy book in His hand.

Gobineau says further that the Báb was "of extreme simplicity of manner, of a fascinating gentleness, those gifts further heightened by his great youth and his marvellous charm, he drew about himself a number of persons who were deeply edified. . . . He could not open his lips (we are assured by those who knew him) without stirring the hearts to their very depths."

Sir Francis Younghusband writes in *The Gleam* of the Báb's "wonderful charm of appearance. Men were impressed by his knowledge and his penetrating eloquence of speech. . . . As soon as he ascended the pulpit there was silence."*

* Sir Frances Younghusband, *The Gleam*, p. 194.

Another historical document states, "By the uprightness of his life the young Siyyid [the Báb] served as an example to those about him. He was willingly listened to when . . . he condemned the abuses evident in all classes of society. His words were repeated and elaborated upon and they spoke of him as the true Master and gave themselves to him unreservedly."

These impressions of the Báb did not come from His followers and sympathizers alone. Comte de Gobineau states in his history that "even the orthodox Muḥammadans who were present [at these meetings when the Báb spoke] have retained an indelible memory of them and never recall them without a sort of terror. They agreed unanimously that the eloquence of 'Alí-Muḥammad was of an incomparable kind, such that, without having been an eyewitness, one could not possibly imagine."

Soon all of Persia was stirring with stories about the Báb. The people eagerly hungered for more news. A wave of enthusiasm swept over the country. Leading government and religious figures either attended these meetings in person or delegated their most able representatives to inquire into the truth of the matter.

The *Journal Asiatique* states that the Faith of the Báb had many followers "in all classes of society, and many among them were of important standing; great lords, members of the clergy, military men and merchants had all accepted this doctrine."

Those in authority began to ask searching questions. Finally, the Crown itself became interested. Muḥammad S͟háh, the king, decided to investigate. He felt that he should find out whether the reports about this remarkable young man were true. So he summoned his prime minister to consult with him about who they might send on such an assignment.

The king and the prime minister chose someone in whom they both had the greatest confidence. His name was Siyyid Yaḥyá. He would later be given the name "Vaḥíd," meaning "Peerless," by the Báb.

Vaḥíd was known to be the most learned, eloquent, and influential of all the king's subjects. If anyone could silence the Báb, it would be he. The great leaders of Persia all testified to his knowledge and wisdom. His father was one of the most celebrated religious doctors of that age, and now Vaḥíd had followed in his father's footsteps and had even eclipsed him. His fame and popularity were known throughout the land. He was admitted to be outstanding among all the leading figures of Persia. Whenever he was present at a meeting, he was invariably the chief speaker. Furthermore, Vaḥíd, because of his wisdom, was frequently consulted by the government in times of trouble.

He was living at that time in Ṭihrán as an honored guest of the king; therefore the king and his prime minister thought immediately of Vaḥíd when they sought an honest person to send on this important mission. The king was very disturbed. He wanted to know what political significance the rise of this new religion might have, so he sent careful instructions.

"Tell him from us," the king commanded, "that inasmuch as we repose the utmost confidence in his integrity, and admire his moral and intellectual standards, and regard him as the most suitable among the divines of our realm, we expect him to proceed to Shíráz, to enquire thoroughly . . . , and to inform us of the results of his investigations. We shall then know what measures it behoves us to take."

Vaḥíd had been wanting to investigate the Báb's claims firsthand anyway and assured the king of his readiness to comply with his request, then set out immediately for Shíráz.

On his way to Shíráz, Vaḥíd decided what questions he would ask the Báb. These questions, he felt, would test the Báb's knowledge to the utmost. Upon the answers that He gave would rest, in Vaḥíd's opinion, the truth or falsehood of His claim to be a Messenger of God.

When Vaḥíd arrived in Shíráz, he met an intimate friend whose name was 'Aẓím, who had already met the Báb. He asked 'Aẓím whether he was satisfied with his interview with the Báb.

"You should meet him," 'Aẓím replied, "and seek independently to acquaint yourself with His Mission. As a friend, I would advise you to exercise the utmost consideration in your conversations with Him, lest you, too, in the end should be obliged to deplore any act of discourtesy towards Him."

Vaḥíd arranged to meet the Báb, who welcomed him with affection. For nearly two hours Vaḥíd courteously directed question after question at the Báb. He pointed out the most obscure and perplexing passages of holy scripture. He dwelled on many mysterious prophecies and traditions of Islam. He spoke at great length of certain difficult and vague metaphysical themes.

The Báb listened patiently to Vaḥíd's learned and detailed references, quietly noting his questions. Then He began to speak, giving brief but persuasive answers to each of Vaḥíd's questions. The conciseness and clarity of His replies excited Vaḥíd's admiration and wonder. He suddenly felt ashamed of his long and showy display of learning. His feeling of personal superiority vanished, and he was embarrassed by his own presumptuousness and pride. Vaḥíd felt so abased that he hurriedly asked permission to leave and told the Báb, "Please God, I shall, in the course of my next audience with You, submit the rest of my questions and with them shall conclude my enquiry."

Vaḥíd withdrew. As soon as he left the Báb he hastened to the home of his friend 'Aẓím and told him what had happened during the first interview to cause his own deep humiliation. 'Aẓím reminded Vaḥíd of his earlier advice and urged him not to forget it a second time.

Vaḥíd was confident that his inquiry into the Faith of the Báb would end with the second interview. He had his questions clearly in mind. They were direct and to the point this time. He would be polite, as 'Aẓím suggested, but firm.

However, when Vaḥíd entered the Báb's presence and began to speak with Him, he found himself discussing things that had nothing whatsoever to do with his inquiry. To his great surprise, all the questions that he had intended to submit to the Báb had disappeared from his memory. Then later, to his even greater surprise, he found that the Báb was answering the very questions he had momentarily forgotten. He spoke with the same brevity and lucidity that had so excited his admiration before.

"I seemed to have fallen fast asleep," Váḥíd later observed. "His words, His answers to questions which I had forgotten to ask, reawakened me. A voice still kept whispering in my ear: 'Might not this, after all, have been an accidental coincidence?' I was too agitated to collect my thoughts. I again begged leave to retire."

Vaḥíd returned to 'Aẓím again and told him what had happened. 'Aẓím spoke frankly to this most learned of the Persians. "Would that schools had been utterly abolished," he said, "and that neither of us had entered one! Through our little-mindedness and conceit, we are withholding from ourselves the redeeming grace of God, and are causing pain to Him Who is the Fountain thereof. . . ."

Pride in his own knowledge had been like a curtain that separated Vaḥíd from the Báb. 'Aẓím entreated him, "Will you not this time beseech God to grant that you may be enabled to attain His presence with becoming humility and detachment, that perchance He may graciously relieve you from the oppression of uncertainty and doubt?"

This third and final interview has been reported in detail by Vaḥíd not only for the king and prime minister, but also for posterity. Vaḥíd states, "I resolved that in my third interview with the Báb, I would, in my inmost heart, request Him to reveal for me a commentary on the Súrih of Kawthar.*

"Should he . . . reveal this commentary in a manner that would immediately distinguish it in my eyes from the prevailing standards . . . I would then be convinced of the Divine character of His Mission, and would readily embrace His Cause. If not, I would refuse to acknowledge Him.

"As soon as I was ushered into His presence, a sense of fear, for which I could not account, seized me. My limbs quivered as I beheld his face, I, who on repeated occasions had been introduced into the presence of the Sháh and had never discovered the slightest trace of timidity in myself, was now so awed and shaken that I could not remain standing on my feet.

"The Báb, beholding my plight, arose from His seat, advanced towards me, and, taking hold of my hand, seated me beside Him.

"'Seek from Me,' He said, 'whatever is your heart's desire. I will readily reveal it to you.'

"I was speechless with wonder. Like a babe that can neither understand nor speak, I felt powerless to respond. He smiled as He gazed at me and said: 'Were I to reveal for you the commentary on the Súrih of Kawthar, would you acknowledge that My words are born of the Spirit of God? Would you recognise that My utterance can in no wise be associated with sorcery or magic?'

"Tears flowed from my eyes as I heard Him speak these words. All I was able to utter was this verse of the Qur'án: 'O our Lord, with ourselves have we dealt unjustly: if Thou forgive us not and have not pity upon us, we shall surely be of those who perish.'"

---

* Qur'án 108. Kawthar is said to be a river in paradise.

Then the Báb called for his pen-case and some paper. He began to reveal the commentary that Vaḥíd's inmost heart had requested, though Vaḥíd had not breathed a word of this desire.

No less than two thousand verses were revealed by the Báb on that occasion. The bewildering rapidity with which they were written was no less remarkable than their matchless beauty and profound meaning. Even more startling to Vaḥíd was the fact that this explanation that the Báb gave was the one that he himself had arrived at through private meditation. He had believed himself to be the only person who had reached this hidden meaning, and he had never made it known to anyone.

Vaḥíd's report of this interview communicates his sense of wonder: "How am I to describe this scene of inexpressible majesty? Verses streamed from His pen with a rapidity that was truly astounding. The incredible swiftness of His writing, the soft and gentle murmur of His voice, and the stupendous force of His style, amazed and bewildered me. He continued in this manner until the approach of sunset. He did not pause until the entire commentary . . . was completed. He then laid down His pen and asked for tea. Soon after, He began to read it aloud in my presence. My heart leaped madly as I heard Him pour out, in accents of unutterable sweetness, those treasures enshrined in that sublime commentary.

"I was so entranced by its beauty that three times over I was on the verge of fainting. He sought to revive my failing strength with a few drops of rose-water which He caused to be sprinkled on my face. . . . when He had completed His recital, the Báb arose to depart."

With a scribe, Vaḥíd devoted three days and three nights to transcribing the newly revealed commentary. He and the scribe verified all of the traditions in the text and found them to be entirely accurate.

Vaḥíd discharged his responsibility to the king, writing a detailed and personal account of his investigation of the Báb.

He summed up his investigation by saying, "Such was the state of certitude to which I had attained that if all the powers of the earth were to be leagued against me they would be powerless to shake my confidence in the greatness of His Cause."

Vaḥíd himself did not return to the capital. He began to summon the people to accept the new Messenger of God. Such was his enthusiasm and fervor that other learned doctors decided Vaḥíd must have suddenly lost his mind. A history of the times states that Vaḥíd "wrote without fear or care a detailed account of his observations to . . . the chamberlain in order that the latter might submit it to the notice of the late king, while he [Vaḥíd] himself journeyed to all parts of Persia, and in every town and station summoned the people from the pulpit-tops in such wise that other learned doctors [leaders] decided that he must be mad, accounting it a sure case of bewitchment."*

When it was reported to the king that Vaḥíd had investigated the Báb, found His Cause to be the truth, and had accepted it himself, the king was greatly troubled. He spoke confidentially to his prime minister.

"We have been lately informed," he said, "that Siyyid Yaḥyáy-i-Dárábí [Vaḥíd] has become a Bábí.† If this be true, it behoves us to cease belittling the cause of that Siyyid."

Ḥusayn Khán, at whose home Vaḥíd had stayed during his interviews with the Báb, attacked him openly. To him also the king sent an imperial command that read, "It is strictly forbidden to any one of our subjects to utter such words as would tend to detract from the exalted rank of Siyyid Yaḥyáy-i-Dárábí. He is of noble lineage, a man of great learning, of perfect and consummate virtue. He will under no circumstances incline his ear to any cause unless he believes it to be conducive to the

* 'Abdu'l Bahá, *A Traveler's Narrative,* pp. 7–8.

† Follower of the Báb.

advancement of the best interests of our realm and to the well-being of the Faith of Islám."

Vaḥíd, acknowledged as the most outstanding of the leaders of Persia, selected as his personal messenger by the king himself, embraced the Faith of the Báb and began to teach it. To Ḥusayn Khán, the governor, who challenged him, asking if he had fallen under the enchantment of the Báb's magic spell, Vaḥíd replied, "No one but God . . . is able to captivate the heart of Siyyid Yaḥyá [Vaḥíd]. Whoso can ensnare his heart is of God, and His word unquestionably the voice of Truth."

Vaḥíd was but one of many illustrious figures who were being attracted to the Faith of the Báb. The prime minister and the people of the royal court tried to belittle each of these new believers in the eyes of the king.

One day as the king was riding on horseback, an old man named Ḥájí Siyyid Javád crossed the street in front of him. Undisturbed by the king's presence, the old man approached him and greeted him cheerfully. The king was very much taken with the old man's courtesy, dignity, and manner. He replied to the greeting and invited the old man to come and visit him at the palace.

Before they had returned to the royal residence, those close to the king began whispering to him, "Does not your Imperial Majesty realise that this Ḥájí Siyyid Javád is none other than the man who, even prior to the declaration of the Siyyid-i-Báb, had proclaimed himself a Bábí, and had pledged his undying loyalty to his person?"

The king knew they were jealous and envious of the attention he had bestowed upon the old man. He was displeased with them and at the same time confused by their constant backbiting.

"How strange!" he exclaimed. "Whoever is distinguished by the uprightness of his conduct and the courtesy of his manners, my people forthwith denounce him as a Bábí and regard him as an object worthy of my condemnation!"

Because of the king's orders, Ḥusayn Khán could no longer openly express his hatred of Vaḥíd; therefore, he began quietly undermining Vaḥíd's friendship with the king. In the days to come this treachery would lead to Vaḥíd's death in his native town of Nayríz.

8

The Avenging Hand of God

The Avenging Hand of God

The few months that the Báb spent as a prisoner in the house of his maternal uncle, Ḥájí Mírzá Siyyid 'Alí, were to be His last days of friendship and tranquillity. They were now drawing rapidly to a close.

What memories must have stirred in His mind as He shared those last free hours with His family and friends! This uncle had shown great love for the Báb throughout His entire life. In His infancy, the Báb lost His father, and was brought up by this same uncle. Anxious to give Him every advantage, Ḥájí Mírzá Siyyid 'Alí had placed the Báb under the care of a tutor while He was still a child.

Those days have been preserved for history through the words of that tutor: "The sweetness of His utterance still lingers in my memory. I felt impelled to take Him back to His uncle . . . to tell him how unworthy I felt to teach so remarkable a child.

"I have brought Him back to you," the tutor told Ḥájí Mírzá Siyyid 'Alí, "and commit Him to your vigilant protection." He suggested that the boy not be treated as a mere child, for in Him he discerned evidences of a mysterious power, and He had no need of teachers.

The Báb's uncle scolded Him and said, "Have you forgotten my instructions? Have I not already admonished You to follow the example of Your fellow-pupils, to observe silence, and to listen attentively to every word spoken by Your teacher?"

The little boy promised to obey faithfully, but it was impossible to restrain His superior mind and intelligence. The tutor said frankly, "Day after day He continued to manifest such remarkable evidences of superhuman wisdom as I am powerless to recount."

A well-known Muslim cleric went to the home of the Báb's uncle at this time. He has given the following account of that visit:

"... In the early morning I heard a tiny, sweet little voice in the next room, which I found to be a prayer room. It was a little child's voice in prayer—such prayers, such a voice, such devotion that I became absolutely enraptured. ... I waited patiently until dawn. ... And then that little child came, and I saw he was the little child between seven and eight years of age—and he it was who had been chanting in the prayer room. As soon as I gazed upon the child I saw such illumination, and on his face an expression so beautiful, that I felt I could not find throughout the whole human race one like him."*

The Muslim cleric followed the boy to the tiny school that He attended. He could not forget that face. He went to the tutor and inquired about the child.

"What do you think of this boy?" he asked.

The tutor spoke with great feeling. "What are you asking me? This child seems to be ready to proclaim, to give out a message to the world. What can I say about this child! You see that this child comes to my school as a pupil, but in reality he is my teacher and I am his pupil. During classtime he says so many wonderful things and goes into so many deep and important questions that I have never heard anything like it in all my life. When the children go out to play one sees him sitting there, reading most important writings. If the children come and insist that he go and play with them he slips away and returns to his work."†

The tutor's admiration for this little boy increased the cleric's interest and wonder. He returned to the home of the Báb's

---

* Ḥájí Siyyid Javád, quoted in Jináb-i-Avárih, "Heralds of the New Day," *Star of the West*, vol. 14, no. 9 (Dec. 1923), pp. 271–272.

† Ibid.

uncle and told him what the tutor had said. The uncle then confided to the cleric a dream that he had had about his nephew when the Báb was five years old.

He had dreamed that a pair of balancing scales hung down from heaven. On one side of the scales was one of the Prophets. On the other side, which was empty, this child was placed by an invisible hand. Then the side with the child weighed down the other, and the Prophet seemed to be going up while the little boy was coming down.

The Báb's uncle was finally persuaded to take the boy out of school. With the greatest of love and care the uncle raised the child. When He was seventeen the Báb left Shíráz for Búshihr, where He engaged in business for His uncle as a merchant. During this time He won the esteem of all the merchants with whom He had contact because of His integrity and religious devotion.

An eyewitness who met the Báb in those days has said, "I often heard those who were closely associated with Him testify to the purity of His character, to the charm of His manners, to His self-effacement, to His high integrity, and to His extreme devotion to God. A certain man confided to His care a trust, requesting Him to dispose of it at a fixed price. When the Báb sent him the value of that article, the man found that the sum which he had been offered considerably exceeded the limit which he had fixed. He immediately wrote to the Báb, requesting Him to explain the reason. The Báb replied: 'What I have sent you is entirely your due. There is not a single farthing in excess of what is your right. There was a time when the trust you had delivered to Me had attained this value. Failing to sell it at that price, I now feel it My duty to offer you the whole of that sum.'"

When the Báb was twenty-two, He married. He and His wife had one child, a son, whom they named Aḥmad. Sadly, the child died the year before the Báb proclaimed His mission.

He wrote movingly of the passing of Aḥmad, whom He loved dearly.

"O God, my God!" He said. "Would that a thousand Ishmaels were given Me, this Abraham of Thine, that I might have offered them, each and all, as a loving sacrifice unto Thee. . . . Grant that the sacrifice of My son, My only son, may be acceptable unto Thee. Grant that it be a prelude to the sacrifice of My own, My entire self, in the path of Thy good pleasure. Endue with Thy grace My life-blood which I yearn to shed in Thy path. Cause it to water and nourish the seed of Thy Faith. Endow it with Thy celestial potency, that this infant seed of God may soon germinate in the hearts of men, that it may thrive and prosper, that it may grow to become a mighty tree, beneath the shadow of which all the peoples and kindreds of the earth may gather. . . ."

The wife of the Báb understood His mission from the very beginning. The Báb confided to her the secret of His future sufferings. He unfolded to her eyes the significance of the events that were soon to take place and told her not to disclose this secret to anyone. He counseled her to be patient and resigned to the will of God.

To lighten the burden of her woes in the days to come, He entrusted her with a special prayer. The reading of this prayer, He promised, would remove her difficulties.

"In the hour of your perplexity," He directed her, "recite this prayer ere you go to sleep. I Myself will appear to you and will banish your anxiety."

These peaceful days within the circle of His family were now at an end. He would soon be caught up in a whirlwind of adversity that would not cease until it had carried Him swiftly to the field of martyrdom.

The governor of the province of Fárs, Ḥusayn Khán, exerted every effort to embarrass and degrade the Báb in the public's eyes. He was outraged because Vaḥíd's acceptance of the Báb had, for a time, tied his hands. He could not afford to offend the king, yet he could not bear to see the Báb moving about, once again free and unmolested. The sight of the constant stream of followers and friends who were once more entering His house enraged him.

The Báb was very courageous in proclaiming His Faith. He sent a message to one of the leading figures of the city of Zanján, saying, "He whose virtues the late siyyid [Siyyid Káẓim] unceasingly extolled, and to the approach of whose Revelation he continually alluded, is now revealed. I am that promised One. . . ."

Ḥusayn Khán decided to use spies to watch the Báb for evidence of the slightest mistake on His part. The governor sent repeated letters to the prime minister, Ḥájí Mírzá Áqásí, expressing his grave concern at the huge numbers of people who were embracing His Cause. The prime minister responded promptly to the governor's entreaties. He told Ḥusayn Khán that he was sick and tired of the turmoil in Shíráz.

He ordered Ḥusayn Khán to have done with the Báb by having him killed immediately and secretly.

One of Ḥusayn Khán's agents came to him with the news that the people gathered about the Báb were now so numerous as to constitute a public menace. The spy reported, "The eager crowd that gathers every night to visit the Báb surpasses in number the multitude of people that throngs every day before the gates of the seat of your government. Among them are to be seen men celebrated alike for their exalted rank and extensive learning. Such are the tact and lavish generosity which his maternal uncle displays in his attitude towards the officials of your government that no one among your subordinates is inclined to acquaint you with the reality of the situation."

Ḥusayn Khán's anger was now directed not only at the Báb and His companions, but also at his own untrustworthy assistants. The spy suggested a plan.

"If you will permit me," he said, "I will . . . surprise the Báb at the hour of midnight and will deliver, handcuffed, into your hands certain of his associates who will enlighten you concerning his activities, and who will confirm the truth of my statements."

The governor refused. "I can tell better than you what the interests of the State require. Watch me from a distance; I shall know how to deal with him."

Ḥusayn Khán summoned the chief constable and ordered him to go immediately to the house of the Báb's uncle. There he was to secretly scale the wall, climb up to the roof, and from there suddenly enter the home. Then he was to arrest the Báb immediately and bring Him and any of His visitors to Ḥusayn Khán. He was also to confiscate whatever books and documents he could find.

"I swear by the imperial diadem of Muḥammad Sháh," Ḥusayn Khán exclaimed, "that this very night I shall have the Siyyid-i-Báb executed together with his wretched companions. Their ignominious death will quench the flame they have kindled, and will awaken every would-be follower of that creed to the danger that awaits every disturber of the peace of this realm. By this act, I shall have extirpated a heresy the continuance of which constitutes the gravest menace to the interests of the State."

Later that night the chief constable, as instructed, broke into the house, arrested the Báb, and seized all documents. He ordered the Báb and His companions to accompany him to the seat of the government.

The Báb was calm and unruffled. He knew the hour of separation had struck. He quoted words from the chief constable's holy book: "That with which they are threatened is for the morning. Is not the morning near?"*

---

* Qur'án 11:83.

The chief constable did not understand that by those words the Báb foretold the beginning of suffering on both sides. He conducted the Báb and His friends into the street, where he put them under guard.

As they were approaching the marketplace, they heard cries of excitement. People were rushing frantically from the city as though fleeing some terrible calamity.

The constable was filled with dread as an awesome sight passed before them. A long train of coffins was being hurried through the streets. Each coffin was followed by a procession of men and women shrieking in anguish. The chief constable inquired as to what had happened.

"This very night," he was told, "A plague of exceptional virulence has broken out. We are smitten by its devastating power. Already since the hour of midnight it has extinguished the lives of over a hundred people. . . . The people are abandoning their homes, and in their plight are invoking the aid of the Almighty." An outbreak of cholera was wreaking havoc.

The chief constable rushed his prisoners through the streets to the home of the governor. The house was deserted, except for an old man who served as doorkeeper. The governor and his family had fled.

The doorkeeper explained, "Two of his Ethiopian maids and a man-servant have already fallen victims to this scourge, and members of his own family are now dangerously ill." In his despair, the governor had abandoned his home and fled with the rest of his family to a garden on the outskirts of Shíráz.

The chief constable decided to take the Báb to his own home. He would keep Him and His friends there until he received further instructions from the governor.

As he approached his home, he heard the sound of weeping. He became terrified. As he rushed forward, he remembered those words the Báb had spoken such a short time before: "That with which they are threatened is for the morning, is not the morning near?" The constable found that his own son had been stricken with cholera and was very near death.

In despair, he threw himself at the Báb's feet and implored Him to forgive his transgessions and misdeeds and save the life of his son.

"I adjure you," he begged, clinging to the hem of His garment, "by Him who has elevated you to this exalted position, to intercede in my behalf and to offer a prayer for the recovery of my son. Suffer not that he, in the prime of youth, be taken away from me. Punish him not for the guilt which his father has committed. I repent of what I have done, and at this moment resign my post. I solemnly pledge my word that never again will I accept such a position even though I perish of hunger."

The Báb, who was preparing to offer a prayer at dawn, directed the chief constable to take some of the water that He had been using to wash His face. He told him to give it to his son to drink.

The chief constable followed the Báb's instructions, and his son recovered. As soon as the constable saw the signs of recovery in his son, he sat down and wrote a long letter to Ḥusayn Khán. He told the governor the entire story of that night of panic and begged him to cease his attacks on the Báb.

"Have pity on yourself," the constable wrote, "as well as on those whom Providence has committed to your care. . . ."

The governor replied that the Báb should be immediately released and given freedom to go wherever He might please. He insisted, however, that the Báb leave the city of Shíráz at once. If he could not triumph over Him personally, he could at least drive Him out from the circle of His friends.

As a result of his actions, Ḥusayn Khán brought the days of his own peace and prestige to an end. History records that as soon as the king learned of these events, Ḥusayn Khán was dismissed from office. From the day of his dismissal, he fell victim to many misfortunes. No one was willing to come to his assistance. In the end his plight was so tragic that he was unable to earn his daily living. Sunk in misery and shame, he languished until his death.

The Báb Himself foretold the governor's downfall. In a letter written to the king, He said of Ḥusayn Khán, ". . . his cruelty has drawn the punishment of heaven. . . ."

The Báb was obedient to Ḥusayn Khán's decree. He made plans to leave Shíráz at once. Thus in the summer of 1846 He bade farewell to His native town, to His family, and to His friends.

He left His family in the care of His uncle, Ḥájí Mírzá Siyyid 'Alí. He embraced His uncle lovingly in parting, promising, "I will again meet you amid the mountains of Ádhirbáyján, from whence I will send you forth to obtain the crown of martyrdom. I Myself will follow you, . . . and will join you in the realm of eternity."

9

The Kindly Governor

The Kindly Governor

The Báb departed Shíráz for Iṣfahán, a city noted for its learned clergy. Here He found that the first one to have embraced His teachings was a humble sifter of wheat. As soon as he had heard the Báb's message, he accepted it and devoted his life to teaching others. A few years later, when he heard that some of his fellow believers were sacrificing their lives for their beliefs, he left his work, arose, and, sieve in hand, hurried through the bazaars of Iṣfahán.

"Why leave so hurriedly?" his friends asked.

"I have risen to join the glorious company of the defenders of Shaykh Ṭabarsí!" he replied. "With this sieve . . . I intend to sift the people in every city through which I pass. Whomsoever I find ready to espouse the Cause I have embraced, I will ask to join me and forthwith to the field of martyrdom."

Such was the devotion of this youth that the Báb referred to him in writing with great love, saying that although Iṣfahán was a city distinguished by the religious fervor of its inhabitants, the learning of its clergy, and by the eager expectation shared by high and low alike of the coming of the Promised One, when the Messenger of God appeared, the learned, the wise, and the religious rejected Him. Of all the inhabitants of that seat of learning, only one person—a sifter of wheat—was found to recognize the Truth.

This, the Báb said, was the fulfillment of the prophecy of the Promised One that says, "The lowliest of the creatures shall become the most exalted, and the most exalted shall become the most debased."

As the Báb approached the city of Iṣfahán, He wrote a letter to the governor of the province, Manúchihr Khán. The letter was so courteous and friendly and of such exquisite penmanship that it immediately attracted the governor's attention. Unlike Ḥusayn Khán, he was not opposed to knowing more about this visitor. He decided to take the Báb under his protection until he could investigate the truth of His claim.

Manúchihr Khán instructed the head imám of Iṣfahán, the foremost religious authority of the province, to meet the Báb and to welcome Him into his own home. He told him to treat the Báb with great kindness and consideration.

The imám sent his brother to meet the Báb at the city gate. When the Báb approached his house, the imám went out to welcome Him personally and ceremoniously brought Him inside. From that very first night, he fell under the spell of the Báb.

The Báb's presence in Iṣfahán caused even more excitement than it had caused in Shíráz. An unceasing stream of visitors and friends flowed from every quarter of the province to the house of the head imám. Some came out of mere curiosity, others to gain a deeper understanding of His message. Some came, as they had to Jesus, to seek healing for their sicknesses and ailments.

The governor himself, Manúchihr Khán, came one night to visit the Báb. He asked Him to write a commentary about the specific mission that the Prophet Muḥammad had come to earth to discharge.

The Báb instantly took up His pen and began to write. In less than two hours He filled about fifty pages with an explanation of the origin, the character, and the pervasive influence of Islam. The governor was deeply impressed with the originality, vigor, and accuracy of that commentary. With masterly insight the Báb once again expressed the central theme of His mission: that the people had looked for the arrival of the Day of the Promised One, and now that Day had come. He argued with such force and courage that those who heard Him were awed.

The governor was enthusiastic. "Hear me!" he called to the people present at that meeting. "Members of this revered assembly, I take you as my witnesses. . . . I solemnly testify to my belief in the reality of the superhuman power with which this Youth is endowed, a power which no amount of learning can ever impart."

With these words the governor brought the meeting to a close.

The clerics of the region plotted to undermine the Báb's growing influence. They firmly believed that unless they arose to stem the tide of this popular enthusiasm for the Báb, the foundations of their own livelihood and future would be swept away.

At first they refrained from outright hostility. Instead, they began circulating wild rumors and base accusations concerning the Báb's teachings. They made certain that these false rumors reached Ṭihrán, the capital of Persia, and were especially made known to the prime minister, Ḥájí Mírzá Áqásí.

The prime minister was already fearful that the king might be inclined to befriend the Báb because of Vaḥíd's acceptance of Him. He knew that such a friendship between the king and the Báb might easily lead to his own downfall. He was even more afraid that the governor of Iṣfahán, Manú<u>ch</u>ihr <u>Kh</u>án, might try to arrange an interview between them, as the governor enjoyed the king's complete confidence. Ḥájí Mírzá Áqásí knew, therefore, that he must prevent such a meeting. He wrote a strongly worded message to the head imám of Iṣfahán and lashed out at him for playing host to the Báb.

"We have expected you to resist with all your power every cause that conflicts with the best interests of the government and people of this land," he said. "You seem instead to have befriended, nay to have glorified, the author of this obscure and contemptible movement."

The prime minister wrote to all of the other clerics of Iṣfahán as well. Although he had previously ignored them, now he showered his attention and favors upon them. He made lavish promises to them. They knew what he wanted, and by his gifts to them, he welded them together against the Báb.

The head imám refused to change his respectful attitude toward the Báb. However, he did take steps to lessen the ever-increasing number of people who thronged each day to visit the Báb. Another cleric began preaching against Him from the pulpit in shocking language.

When Manúchihr Khán heard of what was happening in Iṣfahán, he immediately had the Báb brought into the safety of his own home. This protective gesture by the governor further inflamed the clerics of Iṣfahán. They called for a great gathering of all their numbers. Once assembled, they issued a written document, which was signed and sealed by virtually all the religious leaders of the city. It declared the Báb a heretic and condemned Him to death. About seventy of the leading members of the clergy set their seal to this document.

Two of the clerics refused to sign it. It was an abusive document, they said. The head imám did not sign it because he feared the governor's wrath. Instead of signing it, he wrote on the document a statement saying that he could find no fault with the Báb's character or person. Then he added, "The extravagance of his claims, however, and his disdainful contempt for the things of the world, incline me to believe that he is devoid of reason and judgment."

As soon as the governor learned of the clerics' plan to execute the Báb, he conceived a plan of his own. He issued immediate instructions for the Báb to leave for Ṭihrán accompanied by five hundred horsemen of the governor's own mounted bodyguard. At sundown they were to proceed toward Ṭihrán. He gave further orders that at various points along the way, one hundred of the soldiers should return to Iṣfahán. To the captain of the last hundred, a man in whom the governor placed complete confidence, he gave instructions to send back twenty of the one hundred soldiers at every further mile post. Of the remaining twenty, ten should be dispatched to the town of Ardistán to collect taxes. The final ten, all of whom should be the captain's most trusted men, were to return in disguise with the Báb by an unfrequented route to the governor's home in Iṣfahán. All of this was to take place before dawn the next day.

The instructions were carefully carried out. In order to ensure the safety and comfort of the Báb upon His return, the governor, Manúchihr Khán, had Him occupy his own private apartment. In fact Manúchihr Khán served the meals himself and personally waited on the Báb at all times for a period of four months.

Three orders to slay the Báb had already been issued. One by the prime minister, one by Ḥusayn Khán, and one by the clerics of Iṣfahán. Each order had failed. It had been exactly as the Báb had told the military escort of Ḥusayn Khán when they had come to arrest Him on the way from Búshihr:

"No one knows the mystery of My Cause; no one can fathom its secrets. . . . Until My last hour is at hand, none dare assail Me, none can frustrate the plan of the Almighty."

One day, while the Báb was seated in the governor's private garden, Manúchihr Khán approached Him. He said, "The almighty Giver has endowed me with great riches. . . . Now that I have, by the aid of God, been led to this Revelation, it is my ardent desire to consecrate all my possessions to the furtherance of its interests and the spread of its fame."

Manúchihr Khán had already devised a plan. "It is my intention," he told the Báb, "to proceed, by Your leave, to Ṭihrán, and to do my best to win to this Cause Muḥammad Sháh, whose confidence in me is firm and unshaken. I am certain that he will eagerly embrace it, and will arise to promote it far and wide.

"I will also endeavour to induce the Sháh to dismiss the profligate Ḥájí Mírzá Áqásí, the folly of whose administration has well-nigh brought this land to the verge of ruin. . . .

"I hope," he concluded, "to be enabled to incline the hearts of the rulers and kings of the earth to this most wondrous Cause. . . ."

The Báb was deeply moved. He expressed the hope that God would reward Manúchihr Khán's noble intentions. He said, "So lofty a purpose is to Me even more precious than the act itself. Your days and Mine are numbered, however; they are too short to enable Me to witness, and allow you to achieve, the realisation of your hopes. . . ."

The Báb told Manúchihr Khán that the Faith of God would not be spread by the kings and rulers of the world. Instead, He said, it would triumph through the efforts of the poor, the persecuted, and the lowly. The blood these humble people would shed in the path of their Lord and their sacrifice and suffering would preserve and strengthen the Faith of God. The Báb made Manúchihr Khán a promise as a reward for his love and service.

". . . God," He said, "will, in the world to come, place upon your head the crown of immortal glory, and will shower upon you His inestimable blessings." He then told Manúchihr Khán that his life on this earth would come to an end in exactly three months and nine days.

As the days of his life drew to a close, the governor spent more and more time with the Báb.

He admitted to the Báb that he felt an indefinable joy pervading his soul, but he felt apprehensive for the Báb. He dreaded the thought of leaving Him to the mercy of his successor, Gurgín Khán. He was certain Gurgín Khán would discover the Báb's presence in his house and would mistreat Him grievously.

"Fear not," the Báb assured him. He quoted from the Qur'án, saying,

". . . Of My own will have I chosen to be afflicted by My

enemies, 'that God might accomplish the thing destined to be done.'"*

Manú<u>ch</u>ihr <u>Kh</u>án was satisfied with these words. His heart was refreshed. He knew now that he had not spent his own days on earth in vain. He had met and believed in the Promised One. His ears had not been stopped by his own learning, nor had his eyes been blinded by his own wealth. Serene and confident, he died three months and nine days later after a slight fever.

Mír Muḥammad-Ḥusayn, the brother of the imám who so bitterly persecuted the Báb and His followers in Iṣfahán, did not escape the avenging finger that so remorselessly sought out these persecutors. He was expelled from Iṣfahán and, despised, wandered from one village to another. He finally contracted a loathsome disease from which he sickened and died, a disease so foul-smelling that his own wife and daughter could not bear to attend him.

Almost immediately, Gurgín <u>Kh</u>án, Manú<u>ch</u>ihr <u>Kh</u>án's successor, was informed of the Báb's presence in the governor's residence. Gurgín <u>Kh</u>án verified it, then sent an urgent letter to the king. In it he said that four months earlier many in Iṣfahán believed that the Báb had been sent to the imperial court for questioning. But, in truth, the Báb remained in Iṣfahán, secretly living as a guest in the home of Gurgín <u>Kh</u>án's predecessor. "Whatever it pleases your Majesty to decree," he wrote, "I unhesitatingly pledge myself to perform."

The king was still convinced of the loyalty of his dear friend Manú<u>ch</u>ihr <u>Kh</u>án. He felt certain that the governor had been waiting for a favorable occasion when he could arrange a meeting between himself and the Báb. Now his sudden death had interfered with that plan.

---

* Qur'án 8:42.

The king, therefore, decided to carry out what he believed to have been the wish of his friend, the governor. He would meet the Báb at last.

10

The King's Summons

The King's Summons

Muḥammad Sh͟áh, king of Persia, was torn between two conflicting desires. He wanted to meet the Báb. He was anxious to see in person this young man who could win over to His Faith someone as learned and gifted as Vaḥíd as well as a man of such nobility, stature and wealth as Manúc͟hihr K͟hán. He was eager to know more of this young Prophet who could so powerfully affect such illustrious people. Yet he was alarmed at the same time. He was frightened of what might happen if the Báb gained too much popularity. His prime minister, Ḥájí Mírzá Áqásí, constantly warned him to beware of the Báb. The priests at court spoke of the Báb in the same manner as the religious authorities had spoken of Jesus in His time, suggesting He was a political revolutionary and that He would undermine the state and destroy the king's influence over his subjects.

The king wavered. He blew hot and cold. Prompted by the prime minister, he at one time issued instructions to do away with the Báb, then later withdrew them. Now, thinking it would have pleased his friend, the late Manúc͟hihr K͟hán, the king again expressed his eagerness to meet the Báb in person. So he summoned the Báb to the capital city of Ṭihrán. The historian Nicolas writes, "The Sh͟áh, whimsical and fickle, forgetting that he had, a short time before, ordered the murder of the Reformer [the Báb], felt the desire of seeing, at last, the man who aroused such universal interest. . . ."

The king ordered the prime minister to escort the Báb in disguise and under guard to the capital. He also instructed the party to avoid passing through any villages or towns. "Beware," he warned him, "lest anyone discover his identity or suspect the nature of your mission. No one but you, not even the members of his escort, should be allowed to recognise him. Should anyone question you concerning him, say that he is a merchant whom we have been instructed to conduct to the capital and of whose identity we are completely ignorant."

The king said he wished to protect the Báb from His enemies in this manner. In reality, the prime minister had arranged the plan for an entirely different reason. He wanted the Báb to remain in disguise and hidden because he feared the influence that He might exercise upon the inhabitants of the cities through which He passed if people recognized Him.

Late one night, in accordance with the king's instructions, the Báb set out for Ṭihrán.

En route to the capital, the Báb's guards discovered His identity in spite of the precautions and became His supporters. His irresistible charm, combined with His compelling dignity and loving-kindness, won them over and transformed them. In their eagerness to serve and please Him they spoke up as the party neared the old city of Qum. They told the Báb they would gladly ignore their orders and take Him there so He could visit its holy shrine.

The Báb replied that He preferred to go by way of the country, for the city was unholy. The people of Qum paid tribute to the shrine with their lips while with their acts they heaped dishonor upon it. Outwardly they reverenced, but inwardly they disgraced.

The prime minister sent a message that intercepted the party one day's journey from Ṭihrán and commanded the guard not to take the Báb to Ṭihrán, but to the village of Kulayn instead. There the guard was to hold the Báb and await further instructions. The prime minister was determined that the Báb should never reach the capital. He continually warned the king of the danger of religious revolt and suggested that the Báb was a dangerous threat to the peace of the realm.

The prime minister's influence over the king was inordinate. Comte de Gobineau, the French historian and diplomat, writes, "His disposition naturally weak, [the king] had become very melancholy and, as he craved love and could not find it in his family either with his wives or children, he had centered all his affection upon the aged Mullá [Ḥájí Mírzá Áqásí], his tutor. He had made of him his only friend, his confidant, then his first and all-powerful minister, even his god!" The *Journal Asiatique* states that the prime minister gained such power over the king that one could truly say that the prime minister was the real sovereign. P. M. Sykes, in *A History of Persia,* states, "Ḥájí Mírzá Áqásí, who had been its virtual ruler for thirteen years, 'was utterly ignorant of statesmanship . . . yet too vain to receive instruction . . . brutal in his language; insolent in his demeanour; indolent in his habits; he brought the exchequer to the verge of bankruptcy and the country to the brink of revolution."

To ensure the security of his own position, Ḥájí Mírzá Áqásí finally persuaded Muḥammad Sháh to send the Báb to a remote fortress called Máh-Kú in the northwestern corner of Persia. According to one historian, the king had been suffering from illness for some time. The Báb had promised to heal him if He were permitted to come to Ṭihrán. However, Ḥájí Mírzá Áqásí feared that if the Báb should bring about such a cure, the king would no longer be under his thumb.

He induced the king to write to the Báb as follows: "Much as we desire to meet you, we find ourself unable, in view of our immediate departure from our capital, to receive you befittingly in Ṭihrán. We have signified our desire that you be conducted to Máh-Kú. . . ."

The Báb had written earlier to the king asking for an audience with him. He had requested permission to come to the capital so that before the king and all the religious leaders of the land, He might present the proofs of His mission. He agreed to leave the decision of its truth or falsehood entirely in the hands of the king. He said that He would accept the king's judgment as final and, in case of failure, was ready to sacrifice His head.

Both the prime minister and the king had originally welcomed this letter. They were convinced that once the Báb faced the religious leaders of the land, they could humiliate Him and divest Him of all prestige. However, when they received the news of His overwhelming victories in debate at Shíráz, and especially when word came of the conversion of both Vaḥíd and Manúchihr Khán to His Faith, they were no longer eager, or even willing, to have Him at the capital.

When the king's message reached the Báb, telling Him of His transfer to the prison of Máh-Kú, He knew whose hand was behind the cruel order.

"You summoned Me from Iṣfahán to meet the doctors [religious leaders] and for the attainment of a decisive settlement," He wrote the prime minister. "What has happened now that this excellent intention has been changed for Máh-Kú and Tabríz?"

With these words, the Báb foreshadowed the suffering He was to face in the northern city of Tabríz, where He would be summoned from prison, once to be beaten and a second time to be slain.

Thus the king broke his promise to meet the Báb. A royal party including the young son of the king, Prince Farhád Mírzá, left with the king and the prime minister for a lovely park in the neighborhood of Ṭihrán. While there, the prince approached the prime minister and asked him, "Ḥájí, why have you sent the Báb to Máh-Kú?"

The prime minister replied, "You are still too young to understand certain things, but know that, had he come to Ṭihrán, you and I would not be, at this moment, walking free from care in this cool shade."

The historical document *Journal Asiatique* records, "As the order of the prime minister Ḥájí Mírzá Áqásí became generally known, it was impossible to carry it out. From Iṣfahán to Ṭihrán, everyone spoke of the iniquity of the clergy and of the government towards the Báb; everywhere the people muttered and exclaimed against such an injustice."

The Báb was ordered to proceed first to the city of Tabríz. He refused to accept the funds provided by the government for the expense of the journey. All of the allowances that were given to Him by the prime minister, the Báb bestowed upon the poor. For His own needs He used the money that He had earned as a merchant in Bú<u>sh</u>ihr and <u>Sh</u>íráz.

Rigid orders were given to avoid entering any of the towns on the journey to Tabríz. When the party at last approached the gate of the city, the leader of the escort, Muḥammad Big, approached the Báb.

"The journey from Iṣfahán," he said, "has been long and arduous. I have failed to do my duty and to serve You as I ought. I crave Your forgiveness, and pray You to vouchsafe me Your blessings."

"Be assured," the Báb replied, "I account you a member of My fold. They who embrace My Cause will eternally bless and glorify you, will extol your conduct and exalt your name."

The rest of the guards followed the example of their chief and, with tears in their eyes, bade the Báb a last affectionate farewell. Reluctantly, they delivered Him to the soldiers of the governor of Tabríz.

II

The Tumult in Tabríz

The Tumult in Tabríz

The news of the Báb's arrival at Tabríz caused great excitement. Huge crowds set out to meet Him at the gate, eager to extend their welcome to Him. The officials into whose custody the Báb had been delivered refused to allow the people to draw near and receive His blessing.

One youth, however, was unable to restrain himself. He ran barefoot through the gate of the city, past the officials, rushing well over a mile toward the Báb. He approached the horsemen who were marching in advance and joyously welcomed them.

"Ye are the companions of my Well-Beloved," he cried, "I cherish you as the apple of my eye."

They granted the youth permission to meet the Báb. As soon as the young man's eyes fell on Him, a cry of exultation broke from his lips. He fell upon his face and wept profusely. The Báb dismounted from His horse, put His arms around the young man, wiped away his tears, and embraced him.

Of all the believers of Tabríz on that day, only that youth succeeded in reaching the Báb and being blessed by His hand. All of the others had to content themselves with seeing Him from afar. A mere glimpse would have to satisfy their longing.

An immense crowd of people thronged the gate of the city to witness the Báb's entry. Some were merely curious, while others were earnestly trying to find out if the Báb were in truth such a wondrous figure as they had been told. Still others were moved by their faith and devotion and sought to attain His presence so they could assure Him of their loyalty.

As He walked along the streets of Tabríz, cries of welcome rang out on every side. The great majority of those who saw

Him shouted aloud, *"Alláh-u-Ákbar,"* the traditional Muslim invocation meaning "God is most great!" They cheered the Báb on His way.

So great was the clamor that His arrival raised that a crier was sent out among the people to warn them of the danger of continuing this behavior.

"Whoever shall make any attempt to approach the Siyyid-i-Báb," the people were warned, "or seek to meet him, all his possessions shall forthwith be seized and he himself condemned to perpetual imprisonment."

The Báb was confined in Tabríz, at first in one of the city's chief houses, then later in a room of the Citadel, a fortress-like structure. A detachment of soldiers stood guard at the entrance. In spite of strict orders from their superiors, these soldiers soon became His friends. They were entirely obedient to the Báb's instructions and permitted whomever He wished to visit Him. They were in reality a protection against the onrush of the multitude who thronged about the house, the Báb said, but they were powerless to prevent those whom He desired to meet from attaining His presence.

This same detachment of soldiers who now guarded and protected Him would, on a future day in a mysterious manner, be chosen to discharge the volley that would cause His death; but only after another squadron of soldiers would find themselves powerless to kill Him, an event the historian Nicolas describes as "unique in the annals of the history of humanity."

One day shortly after the Báb's arrival in Tabríz, a noted merchant of the city who was named Ḥájí 'Alí-'Askar went to see Him. Ḥájí 'Alí-'Askar was warned by his friends not to go, but he refused to heed their counsel and made his way to the house where the Báb was imprisoned. Nothing could keep Ḥájí 'Alí-'Askar from the Báb's presence, even if it meant giving up his life.

In the days past, he had journeyed many miles with Mullá Ḥusayn, the first follower of the Báb. They had taught the Báb's message together in many towns. Time after time, Ḥájí 'Alí-'Askar would complain bitterly to Mullá Ḥusayn of his own earlier failure to meet the Báb in Shíráz. This was a source of great sorrow to Ḥájí 'Alí-'Askar.

"Grieve not," Mullá Ḥusayn had told him. "The Almighty is no doubt able to compensate you in Tabríz for the loss you have sustained in Shíráz." Mullá Ḥusayn spoke very confidently. "Not once," he said, "but seven times, can He enable you to partake of the joy of His presence, in return for one visit which you have missed."

Now that the Báb was in Tabríz, Ḥájí 'Alí-'Askar would allow nothing to keep them apart. As he approached the door of the house in which the Báb was confined, he was immediately arrested along with the friend who accompanied him.

A command was sent from the Báb to the guards: "Suffer these visitors to enter, inasmuch as I Myself have invited them to meet Me."

This message silenced the guards at once. Ḥájí 'Alí-'Askar and his friend were ushered into the Báb's presence. He greeted them affectionately and made them welcome. He gave them many instructions to carry out, assuring them that whenever they wished to visit Him, no one would bar their way.

Ḥájí 'Alí-'Askar said, "Several times I ventured to go to Him [the Báb] in order to ascertain His wish regarding certain details connected with the commission with which He had entrusted me. Not once did I encounter the slightest opposition on the part of those who were guarding the entrance of His house. . . .

"Not until the time of my visit to the Báb in Tabríz, when, despite adverse circumstances, I was, on several occasions, admitted into His presence, did I recall those words of Mullá

Ḥusayn and marvel at his remarkable foresight. How great was my surprise when, on my seventh visit to the Báb, I heard Him speak these words: 'Praise be to God, Who has enabled you to complete the number of your visits and Who has extended to you His loving protection.'"

An eyewitness has related the following: "During the first ten days of the Báb's incarceration in Tabríz, no one knew what would next befall Him. The wildest conjectures were current in the city.

"One day I ventured to ask Him whether He would continue to remain where He was or would be transferred to still another place."

The Báb answered, saying that for a period no less than nine months, He would remain confined in "the Open Mountain," alluding to the prison of Máh-Kú. From there, He said, He would be transferred to "the Grievous Mountain," alluding to the prison of Chihríq. Both of these prisons were located in the remote northwestern corner of Iran, among the mountains of the province of Ádhirbáyján.

Five days after the Báb made this prediction, He was transferred to the castle of Máh-Kú and placed under the custody of its warden, 'Alí Khán.

The people of Tabríz must have watched with saddened hearts as the Báb departed from their city. Perhaps many were confused by His apparent helplessness and docility and turned away as the people had turned away from Christ. They may have whispered among themselves as they had whispered in Jerusalem when Christ was delivered in turn to Caiaphus and Pilate. If this was the Promised One, why was He subjected to the whims of men?

12

The High Stone Prison

The High Stone Prison

The Báb was delivered into the custody of 'Alí Khán, the warden at Máh-Kú, where He was imprisoned inside a four-towered stone fortress, high on the summit of a mountain. Below the fortress, to the west, flowed the river Aras, called Araxes by the Greeks, forming the boundary between Persia and Russia.

The prime minister, Ḥájí Mírzá Áqásí, had chosen Máh-Kú for the Báb's imprisonment for several reasons. It was a wild and inhospitable region inhabited by Kurdish people, who had always been the bitter enemies of the Persians. The prime minister had bestowed many favors upon this rebellious region, and he felt it was now under his complete control. Ḥájí Mírzá Áqásí thought that imprisoning the Báb would cut Him off permanently from His followers and would separate Him from their activities. In this way, His Cause would be stifled at its birth and soon extinguished. Few, if any, would ever try to penetrate that unfriendly country.

The plan was a failure. The hostility of the native people of Máh-Kú was gradually softened by the Báb's gentle manner and His loving influence. Their opposition to His teaching melted when they saw the wisdom of His words. Each morning they would come from the village of Máh-Kú and gather on the road below the prison, calling out to the Báb to ask for His blessings on their daily work.

The Báb Himself writes of those early days in Máh-Kú, "My companions are two men and four dogs." Yet despite this isolation His teachings reached the multitudes who gathered outside. He would dictate to Siyyid Ḥusayn of Yazd, who had been brought with Him in captivity from Tabríz and made excursions into town to buy provisions for the Báb. On a quiet day, the people at the foot of the mountain could hear the Báb's voice clearly. An eyewitness of those days has said, "Mountain and valley re-echoed the majesty of His voice. Our hearts vibrated in their depths to the appeal of His utterance."

For the first two weeks the prison warden, 'Alí Khán, did his best to discourage such practices, but he was unable to dampen the people's enthusiasm. He refused to permit any of the villagers to enter the Báb's presence. Nor would he allow any of the Báb's followers who came to the mountain to remain in the village of Máh-Kú even for one night. Ḥájí Mírzá Áqásí had warned 'Alí Khán of the danger of falling under the spell of the Báb's charm. The prime minister considered the Báb an agitator who should be treated accordingly, and 'Alí Khán was determined not to let down his guard.

However, as time went on, 'Alí Khán found himself increasingly helpless to resist his growing attraction to the Báb. During the nine months of the Báb's imprisonment from the summer of 1847 until April 1848, his hostility was transformed from enmity to devotion.

One day he went to the Báb. "A poor man, a shaykh,* is yearning to attain Your presence," he said. "He lives in a masjid† outside the gate of Máh-Kú. I pray You that I myself be allowed to bring him to this place that he may meet You. By this act, I hope that my evil deeds may be forgiven, that I may be enabled to wash away the stains of my cruel behaviour toward Your friends."

'Alí Khán's request was granted. From that moment on, he tried by every means in his power to make up for his past ha-

* Venerable old man; man of authority; elder, chief, professor, superior of a dervish order, and so forth.

† Mosque.

tred. He did all he could to soften the rigor of the Báb's imprisonment. At night he would still close the gate of the village, but in the daytime those whom the Báb wished to see were allowed to visit Him, converse with Him, and receive His instructions.

A. L. M. Nicolas writes, "All the historians . . . tell us that in spite of the strict orders to keep the Báb from communicating with the outer world, the Báb received great numbers of disciples and strangers in His prison." Another source reports, "So great multitudes continued to come from all quarters to visit the Báb, and the writings which emanated from His inspired pen during this period were so numerous that they amounted in all to more than a hundred thousand verses."

During this nine-month period in Máh-Kú, the Báb composed the monumental repository of His laws, a book known as the Persian Bayán. In it the Báb defines His mission as twofold: to call men back to God and to announce the coming of the Promised One of all ages and religions. This great Messenger of God, He said, would appear soon after Himself. The station of this Messenger yet to come was so exalted, the Báb told His followers, that if one were to hear a single verse from Him and recite it, it would be better than reciting the entire Bayán a thousand times.

The Báb urged His followers to remember these words and to seek and find this great Figure upon His own passing. He implied that His Faith and that of the One to come after Him were identical; they were one Faith: The Báb was the Herald, and the One yet to come was the Author. This truth was now in the stage of seed, but in the day of Him who was yet to come, its perfection would become apparent and would blossom and bear marvelous fruit.

Repeatedly, the Báb told His followers that He was but the preparation for that great Day of God promised in all the scriptures of the world's great religions. Christ had warned His disciples of the last days in these words: "Watch therefore: for ye know not what hour your Lord doth come."* The Báb echoed this warning, saying, "Be awake on the day of the apparition of Him Whom God will manifest. . . ."

The Báb's constant prayer during those months of captivity in Máh-Kú was that He might be able to prepare the soil of men's hearts for the coming of this great world Shepherd. "O my God!" He said, ". . . Through him destroy all tyrants . . . annihilate, through his justice, all forms of oppression. . . ."

The Báb said that He spoke of His own suffering only so that it might serve as an example to His followers so that they would not act toward Him whom God shall make manifest as the believers in the Qur'án acted toward the Báb.

"Of all the tributes I have paid to Him Who is to come after Me," the Báb wrote while at Máh-Kú, "the greatest is this, My written confession, that no words of Mine can adequately describe Him, nor can any reference to Him in my Book, the Bayán, do justice to His Cause."†

The Báb left no question whatsoever in the minds of His followers as to His own station: He was the Dawn, and the One to come was the Sun. "Were He to appear at this very moment," proclaimed the Báb, "I would be the first to adore Him, and the first to bow down before Him."‡

The historian Nicolas writes that when the Báb was asked for proofs of His mission, His answer was admirable for its precision and clarity. Nicolas found His explanations new and original and His literary work of profound interest.

---

* Matthew 24:42.

† The Báb, quoted in Shoghi Effendi, *The World Order of Bahá'u'lláh,* p. 62.

‡ The Báb, quoted in Bahá'u'lláh, *Epistle to the Son of the Wolf,* p. 171.

For the nine months that the Báb was imprisoned in the fortress at Máh-Kú, He wrote prolifically. His followers came from all parts of Persia to visit Him. After they had stayed for three days the Báb encouraged them to return to their homes and continue the work of teaching and consolidating the Faith. Not only was the Báb able to meet His followers in spite of the isolation imposed upon Him by the prime minister, but, more important, He was given the time and opportunity to set down in permanent form the fundamental truths of His Mission.

In His solitary chamber the Báb was not permitted to have even a lighted lamp. The winter was so severe that the water with which He washed Himself would freeze in drops on His face.

During this time Mullá Ḥusayn decided to visit the Báb at Máh-Kú. He had been teaching the Cause industriously in the city of Mas͟hhad. Mas͟hhad is where the Eighth Imám is buried, making the city the greatest center of pilgrimage in all of Persia. Half of the city derived its living from the flow of pilgrims coming to visit the shrine. All these people were now joined together against this teacher who might possibly deprive them of their livelihood. To denounce abuses of religion might be all right in some other city, but it was not acceptable in Mas͟hhad, where everyone of every class was thriving on them. It was all very well for the Promised One to come, and undoubtedly He had the right, but He certainly was a public nuisance. Mullá Ḥusayn was told plainly, by actions as well as words, that it might be very thrilling to undertake the conquest of the world with the Báb, but there was a big risk involved—not to mention fatigue and danger—especially now, while everyone was enjoying perfect peace in a fine city where business was good and one could earn a living with ease and security.

Mullá Ḥusayn left Mashhad. He yearned for the pure, holy presence of the Báb. He told his friends, "I have vowed to walk the whole distance that separates me from my Beloved. I shall not relax in my resolve until I shall have reached my destination."

'Alí Khán saw Mullá Ḥusayn approaching Máh-Kú one morning at sunup. He went out to greet him, bringing a horse so that he might finish the final stage of his journey in ease.

Mullá Ḥusayn refused the mount, vowing to complete the entire journey to visit the Báb on foot.

When Mullá Ḥusayn reached the prison gate, he saw the Báb standing at the threshold. The Báb stretched forth His arms and affectionately embraced him.

One day as they stood together on the roof of the prison looking out over the mountains of Ádhirbáyján, the Báb turned toward Mullá Ḥusayn and quoted a prophecy, saying, "'Shíráz will be thrown into a tumult; a Youth of sugar-tongue will appear. I fear lest the breath of His mouth should agitate and upset Baghdád.'"

The meaning of this verse was concealed, He told Mullá Ḥusayn, but it would be revealed in the year 1853. He then related to Mullá Ḥusayn many things that would happen in the future and told him not to disclose them to anyone.

As the Báb bade His last farewell to Mullá Ḥusayn, He said to him, "You have walked on foot all the way from your native province to this place. On foot you likewise must return. . . . your days of horsemanship are yet to come. You are destined to exhibit such courage, such skill and heroism as shall eclipse the mightiest deeds of the heroes of old."

The Báb instructed Mullá Ḥusayn to visit the believers in each of the villages on his way home and to convey to them the Báb's love and affection. ". . . Inflame their hearts anew with the fire of the love of the Beauty of God," He told him, "and . . . endeavour to fortify their faith in His Revelation."

"A few days after your departure from this place," the Báb said, "they will transfer Us to another mountain. Ere you arrive at your destination, the news of Our departure from Máh-Kú will have reached you."

The Báb's prediction soon came to pass. Those who had been sent by the prime minister to watch secretly and report what was taking place at Máh-Kú sent back alarming news. People who had once been unfriendly were now showing the greatest respect and love for the Báb. In fact, people were coming from everywhere to visit Him. Even 'Alí Khán, the warden, was enchanted and was treating the Báb as a guest rather than as a prisoner.

Both fear and rage impelled the prime minister to issue an order for the instant transfer of the Báb to the castle of Chihríq, which the Báb called "the grievous mountain."

Mullá Ḥusayn was in Tabríz when the news of the Báb's transfer to Chihríq reached him.

The Báb said farewell to the people of Máh-Kú. Their hearts were heavy at the sad sight of His departure. The One they had come to love so much was now going out of their lives forever. During His nine months of captivity among them, they had recognized to a remarkable degree the power of His personality and the greatness of His character.

13

The Scourging at Tabríz

THE SCOURGING AT TABRÍZ

THE BÁB was subjected to a closer and more rigorous confinement at Chihríq. The prime minister gave strict and explicit orders to the warden, Yaḥyá Khán, who was the king's brother-in-law. He told Yaḥyá Khán that no one was to be allowed to enter the Báb's presence. There were to be no exceptions to this rule. The prime minister specifically warned him not to follow the example of 'Alí Khán, who had gradually been led to disregard the orders he had received.

Yet, in spite of the emphatic nature of the order, Yaḥyá Khán found himself powerless to obey it. He, too, soon became fascinated with his Prisoner and completely forgot the duty he was expected to perform. Love for the Báb claimed his entire being, and he would have preferred to be slain rather than to cause Him the slightest discomfort.

The villagers who lived in Chihríq were initially even more hostile toward the Báb and His followers than the people of Máh-Kú had been, yet even they fell under the transforming influence of the Báb. The spirit that He radiated was a life-creating thing. It changed hate into love, enemies into friends.

This is confirmed by the historian Lord Curzon in the following extract from *Persia and the Persian Question:* "His qualities were so rare in their nobility and beauty, His personality so gentle and yet so forceful, and His natural charm was combined with so much tact and judgment, that after His Declaration He quickly became in Persia a widely popular figure. He would win over almost all with whom He was brought into personal contact, often converting His gaolers to His Faith and turning the ill-disposed into admiring friends."

The size of the crowds who had visited Him at Máh-Kú was now dwarfed by the number of those who flocked to Him at Chihríq. Yaḥyá Khán would not refuse admittance to anyone who wished to see Him. So many sought His presence that there was no room to accommodate them all. They had to be housed an hour's distance away.

M. Mochenin, who was on duty for a foreign organization in that region, writes in his memoirs, "The multitude of hearers was so great that the court was not large enough to hold them all; most of them stayed in the streets and listened with religious rapture. . . ."

Whatever provisions were required for the Báb were purchased in old Chihríq and brought to the prison. One day some honey was purchased for Him. The price seemed exorbitant. He refused it and said, "Honey of a superior quality could no doubt have been purchased at a lower price. . . . It behoves you in all your transactions to follow in My way. You must neither defraud your neighbour nor allow him to defraud you." He insisted that the purchase be returned and replaced with a honey better in quality and cheaper in price.

During those days a dervish walked all the way from India to seek the Báb. As soon as he met Him, he embraced His Faith. He told the following story:

"In the days when I occupied the exalted position of a ***navváb****** in India, the Báb appeared to me in a vision. He gazed at me and won my heart completely. I arose, and had started to follow Him, when He looked at me intently and said: 'Divest yourself of your gorgeous attire, depart from your native land, and hasten on foot to meet Me in Ádhirbáyján. In Chihríq you will attain your heart's desire.' I followed His directions and have now reached my goal."

---

* Nabob—a provincial governor of the Mogul empire in India, or a person of great wealth or prominence.

This fulfilled the words of the Islamic tradition that prophesies, "On the last Day, the Men of the Unseen shall, on the wings of the spirit, traverse the immensity of the earth, shall attain the presence of the promised Qá'im, and shall seek from Him the secret that will resolve their problems and remove their perplexities."

This was but one of many remarkable events that followed upon each other in swift succession. They caused the turmoil in Chihríq to eclipse that of Máh-Kú. A continuous stream of seekers and followers flowed back and forth through the old fortress. Men of distinguished merit, eminent members of the clergy, and even government officials were openly and rapidly embracing the Faith of the Báb.

One of the most outstanding literary figures of Persia, who was also a high government official, accepted the Báb's message and devoted both his person and his pen to spreading His teachings. He was surnamed Dayyán, meaning "One Who Rewards," or "Judge," by the Báb. Previously, Dayyán had vehemently denounced the Báb and His message. Then one night he had a dream, which he thought he would use to test the Báb. He wrote to the Báb, saying, "I have conceived three definite things in my mind. I request you to reveal to me their nature." A few days later he received a reply penned by the Báb that described the dream and revealed exactly what Dayyán had had in mind. The accuracy of that reply brought about his complete conversion. Though Dayyán was not accustomed to walking, he went on foot up the steep and stony path to meet the Báb. This meeting stirred in him a fiery spiritual ardor that lasted to the end of his life.

The Báb knew that the hour of His deeper affliction was approaching. He told all of His followers who had gathered in Chihríq to disperse and return home to their most important work, which was teaching the Báb's message to others. He instructed the believer from India to return to his native land

and work unceasingly for the spread of the Faith there. He obeyed the Báb at once, and alone, clad in simplest attire, staff in hand, he went down the mountainside and walked all the way back to his home in India, teaching in every village along the way.

Calmly, the Báb waited for the inevitable edict of Ḥájí Mírzá Áqásí. It was not long in coming. When the news of all these startling events reached the capital, the prime minister was violently angry. He had failed again. He knew he must not fail a third time. He demanded that the Báb be transferred at once from the prison at Chihríq to the city of Tabríz. Strict orders were given to avoid any contact with those towns to which the Báb's influence had already spread. He was to be brought to Tabríz by an indirect and unsuspected route that would take Him through the village of Urúmíyyih (now Rezā'īyeh).

However, no matter where the Báb was sent, He was always received in virtually the same way. On His arrival in Urúmíyyih, the prince Malik Qásim Mírzá ceremoniously received Him and gave the Báb a guard of footmen to hold back the gathering crowd. The people were crushing against each other in their eagerness to catch a glimpse of so marvelous a prisoner.

Arrangements were made one day for the Báb to go to the public bath in Urúmíyyih. The prince, having heard wondrous tales about his guest, was anxious to test the Báb's power and courage. He ordered his groom to offer the Báb one of his wildest horses to ride.

The groom feared that the Báb might suffer harm from this untamed animal. He secretly approached the Báb and tried to convince Him not to mount this steed, which had already thrown off the best of horsemen.

"Fear not," the Báb replied. "Do as you have been bidden, and commit Us to the care of the Almighty."

The villagers had learned of the prince's plan. They filled the public square the next morning, eager to witness the test and see what would happen to the Báb.

The unruly horse was brought from his stable. The frightened groom cautiously gave the bridle to the Báb.

The Báb quietly stepped toward the animal. Gently, He caressed the steed and then slowly placed His foot in the stirrup. The horse stood motionless as the Báb mounted. He rode the animal to the public bath. All along the way, people tried to rush in from every side to marvel at such a miracle and offer their allegiance to Him. On His return from the bath He again mounted the same horse and was once again acclaimed by the townspeople.

As soon as the Báb left the public bath, the people of Urúmíyyih rushed to take away every drop of water that He had used.

When the Báb was told that many people had spontaneously arisen to accept His Faith because of these remarkable events, which they considered a miracle, He calmly quoted the Qur'án, saying, "Think men that when they say, 'We believe,' they shall be let alone and not put to the proof?"*

This comment was fully justified by the attitude of these same people of Urúmíyyih when they later heard the news of the dreadful treatment which the Báb had suffered at Tabríz. Hardly a handful of those who so eagerly proclaimed their belief in His Cause on that day would remain faithful. Miracles, the followers of His Faith were to learn, are but a secondary proof and are of value only to those who witness them; of themselves, miracles have no lasting value. It was now as it had been in the time of Christ, for when Jesus miraculously healed the ten lepers, only one remained to thank Him. He said, "Were there not ten cleansed? but where are the nine?"†

Tales of what had happened in Urúmíyyih raced ahead of the Báb and His escort, causing a great wave of enthusiasm

* Qur'án 29:2.

† Luke 17:7.

across all of Persia. Tabríz, in particular, was in the throes of the wildest excitement. Word of the Báb's coming ignited people's imaginations and aroused fierce animosity in the religious leaders.

Such was the public fervor that the authorities decided to confine the Báb in a place outside the gates of the city. Precautions were taken, warnings were published, restrictions were enforced, yet all of these only served to aggravate a situation that had already become critical. The Báb had captured the people's fancy, and nothing the officials or clergy could do was able to diminish their ardor.

The prime minister, Ḥájí Mírzá Áqásí, issued an order from the capital. He demanded that all the leading religious dignitaries and government officials hold an immediate gathering. His words made clear the grave nature of this crisis. The religious leaders, he said, must decide at once upon the most effective measures for extinguishing the fire that the Báb had kindled. They must bring the Báb's power over the public to an abrupt end. There must be no mistakes. The Báb must be summoned before this important gathering, and there He must be humiliated in a manner that would permanently undermine His influence.

The Báb was well aware of the prime minister's intentions. On the second night after His arrival in Tabríz, the Báb told His friends that the next day, in the presence of the heir to the Persian throne, the assembled religious leaders, and the notables of Tabríz, He would publicly proclaim His mission.

The meeting was arranged according to the prime minister's plan. It took place in the governor's residence. An officer of the army was sent to bring the Báb into the presence of the gathering. Already a multitude thronged the outside entrance. They pressed forward in such large numbers that a passage had to be forced through the crowd before the Báb could enter.

When He came into the hall, He saw that every seat was occupied except one, which had been reserved as the seat of honor for the heir to the throne, the king's son. The Báb courteously greeted the assembly. He knew they planned to humiliate Him by making Him stand. Without the slightest hesitation He walked to that seat of honor and sat down.

A silence, long and intense, fell over the gathering. At last the stillness was broken by the presiding officer of the gathering.

"Whom do you claim to be?" he asked the Báb, "and what is the message which you have brought?"

It was the story of Christ retold. When Jesus was taken before the high priests and elders for their preplanned investigation, He was asked, "Art thou the Christ?" He replied, "I am."* There could no longer remain any doubt of His mission.

In like manner, with similar words, the Báb replied to this assembly, which also wished to hear Him condemn Himself by making the same staggering claim. Three times He repeated it in their presence.

"I am," exclaimed the Báb, "I am, I am the Promised One! I am the One whose name you have for a thousand years invoked, at whose mention you have risen, whose advent you have longed to witness, and the hour of whose Revelation you have prayed God to hasten. Verily I say, it is incumbent upon the peoples of both the East and the West to obey My word and to pledge allegiance to My person."

A hush fell over the hall. A witness to that stirring event has written, "Immediately after He had declared Himself to be the promised One, a feeling of awe seized those who were present. They had dropped their heads in silent confusion. The pallor of their faces betrayed the agitation of their hearts."

* Mark 14:61–62.

It was recorded of that meeting that "The majesty of His gait, the expression of overpowering confidence which sat upon His brow—above all, the spirit of power which shone from His whole being, appeared to have for a moment crushed the soul out of the body of those whom He had greeted."

At last, unable to bear the tension any longer, a member of the assembly arose and arrogantly reprimanded the Báb, calling Him a "wretched and immature lad of Shíráz."

The Báb turned to the presiding officer. "Your Honour," He said, "I have not come hither of My own accord. I have been summoned to this place."

"Hold your peace, you perverse and contemptible follower of Satan!" the presiding officer retorted.

The Báb serenely responded, "Your Honour, I maintain what I have already declared."

The authorities asked no truly sincere questions about the Báb's mission or His teachings. Instead, they indulged in a series of insulting and flippant questions that had nothing to do with His Faith but were designed solely to humiliate their prisoner.

After patiently bearing their abuse and insults throughout the session, the Báb quoted their own holy book to them, saying, "Far be the glory of thy Lord, the Lord of all greatness, from what they impute to Him, and peace be upon His Apostles! And praise be to God, the Lord of all the worlds!"* Immediately afterward, He arose and summarily ended the gathering by leaving the hall abruptly.

The religious authorities at once began to spread the most unfavorable and false reports of the Báb's part in that trial. They said His answers to their inquiries were both childish and unsatisfying, that they were not even the replies of a sane man, let alone those of a promised Redeemer.

---

* Qur'án 37:180.

Fortunately for history, two European scholars, following much investigation, preserved an unbiased account of those proceedings. The first was Dr. T. K. Cheyne, a Christian clergyman and student of that period. He has written, ". . . As for the Muslim accounts [of that trial], those which we have before us do not bear the stamp of truth: they seem to be forgeries. Knowing what we do of the Báb, it is probable that he had the best of the argument, and that the doctors and functionaries who attended the meeting were unwilling to put up on record their own fiasco."

The second scholar was Professor Edward G. Browne of Cambridge University. He characterized the questions that these religious leaders had asked the Báb as "frivolous and even indecent." He writes of the trial, "That the whole examination was a farce throughout, that the sentence was a foregone conclusion, that no serious attempt to apprehend the nature and evidence of the Báb's claim and doctrine was made, and that from the first to last a systematic course of browbeating, irony, and mockery was pursued appear to me to be facts proved no less by the Muḥammadan than by the Bábí accounts of these inquisitorial proceedings."

Even the presiding officer at that gathering, Ḥájí Mullá Maḥmúd, was displeased with the way the priests had conducted the meeting. He did not wish to have his name associated with it.

"How shameful is the discourtesy of the people of Tabríz!" he said. "What could possibly be the connection between these idle remarks and the consideration of such weighty, such momentous issues?"

A. L. M. Nicolas, referring to an earlier inquisition of the Báb by similarly hostile religious leaders, says they conditioned their belief in His truth on His ability to explain three miracles to them: First they asked how a human being could be immediately transported from one part of the world to another very distant point. Next they asked how one person could be in sixty different places at one instant. Then they asked how the heavens could revolve rapidly during the reign of a tyrant and slowly during that of an Imám.

"It was the solution of these insanities," says Nicolas, "that they proposed to the Báb! I shall not dwell on them any longer. . . . one will easily understand the emptiness and arrogance of all these minds."

The Báb was brought to the home of Mírzá 'Alí-Aṣghar, the ranking clergyman and head of the religious court in Tabríz. There He was given over to the governor's bodyguard for a humiliating punishment. However, the guard refused, preferring not to become involved in a matter that he viewed as solely the concern of the clergy.

Mírzá 'Alí-Aṣghar himself was thus forced to inflict the punishment on the Báb with his own hands.

Just as Jesus had fallen under the scourge of Pontius Pilate following His examination in the judgment hall where He proclaimed Himself as the Redeemer of men, the Báb, too, was subjected to the same indignity following a similar trial and the same great proclamation. Eleven times the rod of the bastinado was applied to His feet. At one point He was struck across the face with one of the blows, which caused a great wound.

Afterward Dr. Cormick, an English physician who was residing in Tabríz, was called to treat the Báb for a few days and, along with two Persian doctors, to determine whether He was sane. This was to help the authorities decide whether or not to put Him to death. Dr. Cormick set down in writing his impressions of the Báb gained from those meetings:

". . . the Báb was aware of my having been sent with two other Persian doctors to see whether he was of sane mind or merely a madman. . . . With this knowledge he was loth to answer any questions put to him. To all enquiries he merely regarded us with a mild look, chanting in a low melodious voice some hymns, I suppose. . . . He only once deigned to answer me, on my saying that I was . . . willing to know something about his religion, as I might perhaps be inclined to adopt it. He regarded me very intently on my saying this, and replied that he had no doubt of all Europeans coming over to his religion. Our report to the Sh́áh at that time was of a nature to spare his life. . . . He was a very mild and delicate-looking man . . . with a melodious soft voice, which struck me much. . . . In fact his whole look and deportment went far to dispose one in his favour. . . ."

The Báb was not released after His scourging. He was marched back under heavy guard to the prison of Chihríq. However, He left behind Him in Tabríz the memory of a great victory. News of His momentous declaration spread rapidly throughout the country. Many who had been opposers became followers. Many, pointing a finger at the cruel behavior of the religious leaders, recalled a well-known Islamic prophecy about the Promised One that said most of His enemies would be the Islamic religious authorities.

To those who felt great anguish because of the cruelties inflicted upon the gentle Báb, these words of His brought comfort: "Be patient . . . for verily God hath vowed to establish Thy glory in every land, amongst all who dwell on earth."

The trial in Tabríz had enabled the Báb to set forth clearly and emphatically the fundamental features of His Faith in the presence of the most illustrious Persian dignitaries. It had also enabled Him to destroy, in brief and convincing language, the arguments of His enemies.

Just as Jesus had said, "My teaching is not mine, but his who sent me,"* the Báb, too, made it plain that His message

* John 7:16.

was an outpouring from One far greater than Himself. His purpose was to proclaim the Word of God as a Messenger of God. The people were free to believe or not, as they chose.

When the Báb returned to the prison-fortress of Chihríq, He wrote a bold and moving letter denouncing the treacherous prime minister, Ḥájí Mírzá Áqásí. It foretold his downfall, which was soon to come. This was written as a warning to all such leaders who, refusing the truth themselves, had shut the door in the face of those whose destiny they held in their power.

The Báb gave the letter to one of His disciples and told him to deliver it into the hands of Ḥájí Mírzá Áqásí personally. The letter was titled the "Sermon of Wrath." It began with the words "O thou who hast disbelieved in God and hast turned thy face away from His signs!"

From that hour forth, the dreadful consequences that had already befallen so many who had persecuted the Báb and His followers began to descend upon the ringleaders of His affliction at Tabríz.

The head of the religious court, Mírzá 'Alí-Aṣghar, who with his own hands had scourged the Báb in the prayer-house, was despised and feared by a people who had sickened of his leadership and who prayed to be delivered from his evil ways. In less than a year Mírzá 'Alí-Aṣghar was struck with paralysis. After enduring excruciating pain, he died a miserable death in abject circumstances. Following his death, the functions of his office were permanently abolished in Tabríz. The very name of the institution that had been associated with his name became abhorred by the people.

The king himself, Muḥammad Sháh, did not escape retribution. He had been weak enough to listen to the malevolent promptings of his prime minister, Ḥájí Mírzá Áqásí, and had refused to meet the Báb in spite of His personal letter requesting such an audience. The king instead had banished the Báb to a remote mountain prison. No sooner had he agreed to issue that order than he was afflicted with an abrupt reversal of fortune. Several parts of his kingdom broke out in revolt. His health declined rapidly. Finally, at the early age of forty, he fell a victim to a complication of maladies that the Báb had foretold would in the end devour him.

The prime minister, Ḥájí Mírzá Áqásí, who had been the chief conspirator in the outrages committed against the Báb, was made the major target of this avenging wrath. Scarcely a year and six months from the moment he first came between the Báb and the king and prevented their meeting, he was hurled from power. While the Báb was still in the prison to which Ḥájí Mírzá Áqásí had condemned Him and from which He had sent the "Sermon of Wrath," the prime minister was dismissed in disgrace from his post, stripped of all of his dishonestly acquired property and riches.

C. R. Markham's *A General Sketch of the History of Persia* says, "Ḥájí Mírzá Áqásí, the half-crazy old Prime Minister . . . was sedulously collecting wealth for himself at Ṭihrán, at the expense of the wretched country. The governorships of provinces were sold to the highest bidders, who oppressed the people in a fearful manner."

When knowledge of the enormity of his graft and thefts became known, he had to flee for shelter from the anger of his countrymen. Ḥájí Mírzá Áqásí had expelled the Báb from His home and banished Him to a far place; now he, in turn, was expelled from his native country and banished to Iraq, where he fell a victim to disease and gnawing grief shortened his life.

History has recorded these words of the last days of Ḥájí Mírzá Áqásí: ". . . He met his death in circumstances of abject poverty and unspeakable distress."

14

The Massacre at the Fort of Shaykh Ṭabarsí

The Massacre at the Fort of Shaykh Ṭabarsí

Muḥammad Sháh was dead. The new ruler was the seventeen-year-old Náṣiri'd-Dín Sháh. Ḥájí Mírzá Áqásí was toppled from power and replaced by the new prime minister, Mírzá Taqí Khán.

The young king was even less friendly than his father. The new prime minister was more ironhearted in his rule, and his hatred for the Báb was more implacable than that of Ḥájí Mírzá Áqásí. He unchained a combined assault by the civil and religious powers against the Báb and His leading disciples. He was determined not to make the mistake the former prime minister had made in waiting too long.

The news of the Báb's triumph over His examiners at Tabríz spread rapidly throughout Persia. It awakened a new zeal in the hearts of His supporters, who redoubled their efforts to spread His teachings. It enkindled a corresponding reaction among His enemies. Encouraged by the new prime minister, persecutions unprecedented in their violence swept over the nation, engulfing the staunchest of the Báb's followers. This brief but triumphant period may well be the bloodiest and most dramatic in the rise of the new religion.

No story of the life of the Báb would be complete unless it told about His disciples, the Letters of the Living, who sacrificed everything in life, proving their love and devotion for His Cause. Some preceded the Báb in death, some followed shortly after. Almost every one of His chief followers was struck down during this raging period of persecution.

Quddús was imprisoned in the town of Sárí, and Mullá Ḥusayn set out to rescue him. A messenger had come from the Báb to Mullá Ḥusayn bearing the Báb's turban.

"Adorn your head with My green turban, the emblem of My lineage," the message said, "and, with the Black Standard unfurled before you, hasten to . . . lend your assistance to My beloved Quddús."

Mullá Ḥusayn immediately left Mashhad in the eastern province of Khurásán and headed for Sárí in the northern province of Mázindarán. His small party marched under a black banner, which Mullá Ḥusayn raised up so that all who wished to join him would know that he and his companions were followers of the Báb.

That emblem waved continuously over his small band for eleven months. It summoned all who gazed upon it to renounce the world and embrace the Cause of God. Black was the color of the standard that, according to the Prophet Muḥammad, would herald the arrival of the Promised One.

Mullá Ḥusayn and his party arrived at a junction on the high road to Mázindarán. They camped under the shadow of a big tree by a running stream for a few days.

"We stand at the parting of the ways," he told his companions. "We shall await His decree as to which direction we should take."

One day a fierce gale arose and struck down a large branch from the tree. Mullá Ḥusayn observed, "The tree of the sovereignty of Muḥammad Sháh has, by the will of God, been uprooted and hurled to the ground."

On the third day after he had made that prediction, a messenger arrived from Ṭihrán reporting the death of the king. The next day Mullá Ḥusayn and his companions decided to leave for Mázindarán.

Pointing toward Mázindarán, Mullá Ḥusayn said, "This is the way that leads to our Karbilá," alluding to the tragic martyrdom of the Imám Ḥusayn in A.D. 680 at Karbilá in Iraq. "Whoever is unprepared for the great trials that lie before us, let him now repair to his home and give up the journey."

Several times Mullá Ḥusayn repeated that warning. Then he declared, "I, together with seventy-two of my companions, shall suffer death for the sake of the Well-Beloved. Whoso is unable to renounce the world, let him now, at this very moment, depart, for later on he will be unable to escape."

Twenty of his companions chose to turn back, feeling unable to withstand the trials to which Mullá Ḥusayn alluded. The others continued the journey toward the town of Bárfurúsh (now known as Bábul).

The news of their coming alarmed the Sa'ídu'l-'Ulamá, the chief religious leader of that city. Nicolas says in his history that all the clerics of Bárfurúsh were exasperated with the followers of the Báb because of the many conversions that Quddús had brought about in their city—as many as three hundred in one week. The Sa'ídu'l-'Ulamá told the town crier to summon all the people to the mosque at once so he could deliver an important sermon.

When an immense throng had gathered, the Sa'ídu'l-'Ulamá ascended to the pulpit. He flung his turban to the ground, tore open the neck of his shirt, and angrily began to incite the people to arise against Mullá Ḥusayn and his party.

"Awake," he cried, "for our enemies stand at our very doors, ready to wipe out all that we cherish as pure and holy in Islám! . . . It is the duty of all the inhabitants of Bárfurúsh, both young and old, both men and women, to arm themselves against these contemptible wreckers of Islám. . . ." "To-morrow, at the hour of dawn, let all of you arise and march out to exterminate their forces."

The entire congregation arose in response to this appeal and made every preparation for the dawn, arming themselves with any weapon they could find or devise.

The next morning immediately after offering his morning prayers, Mullá Ḥusayn called his companions together and told them to abandon all of their possessions.

"Leave behind all your belongings," he urged them, "and content yourselves only with your steeds and swords, that all may witness your renunciation of all earthly things, and may realise that this little band of God's chosen companions has no desire to safeguard its own property, much less to covet the property of others."

Instantly, all obeyed. They unburdened their horses without a word. A prominent merchant who had joined the band had brought with him a satchel full of turquoise, which was undoubtedly his most treasured posession. Yet, at a word from Mullá Ḥusayn, he was the first to cast aside his satchel as an example to the others. He hurled it to the side of the road without a backward glance.

A short distance outside of Bárfurúsh, Mullá Ḥusayn and his companions encountered a multitude of people who blocked their way. In the face of the uproar from this angry populace, some of the companions began to unsheathe their swords.

"Not yet," Mullá Ḥusayn told them, "not until the aggressor forces us to protect ourselves must our swords leave their scabbards."

The mob, armed with guns, swords, axes, scythes, spades, and any other weapon they could create, moved forward toward that small group and met them on the road about three or four miles outside of town. They had set out from Bárfurúsh at the break of day, determined to meet and slay Mullá Ḥusayn's party and to plunder their possessions. The Sa'ídu'l-'Ulamá had retreated to the safety of his home after inciting the others to attack.

This was but one of a series of similar onslaughts that were taking place throughout the country, all encouraged by the prime minister, Mírzá Taqí Khán. The following historical report indicates the gravity of the situation: "The minister with the utmost arbitrariness, without receiving any instructions or asking permission, sent forth commands in all directions to punish and chastise the Bábís. Governors and magistrates sought a pretext for amassing wealth, and officials a means of acquiring profits; celebrated doctors [of religion] from the summits of their pulpits incited men to make a general onslaught; the powers of the religious and the civil law linked hands and strove to eradicate and destroy this people."

This was to be the first of three occasions on which the followers of the Báb withdrew to a chosen retreat, erected defenses, and defied further pursuit. They would fight for their lives with determined skill and strength, but they would not attack. Even in the midst of a fierce conflict they would not drive home an advantage or strike an unnecessary blow.

E. G. Browne, in his *Year Among the Persians,* writes that on one of these occasions even the women took part, and when their shelter was attacked, like the Carthaginian women of old, they cut off their long hair and bound it around their makeshift weapons to afford them the necessary support. "The desperate resistance offered by the Bábís must therefore," he says, "be attributed less to the strength of the position which they occupied than to the extraordinary valour with which they defended themselves."

Separated as they were from the Báb, their imprisoned leader, His followers did not yet understand His clear teaching on the matter of physical violence and warfare. Therefore they followed after the pattern of their previous religious teaching: Do not attack, but defend. In the book *A Traveler's Narrative,* 'Abdu'l-Bahá states, "In towns where these Bábís were but a limited number, all of them with bound hands became food for the sword, while in cities where they were numerous, they arose in self-defense in accordance with their former beliefs, since it was impossible for them to make inquiry as to their duty. . . ."*

* 'Abdu'l-Bahá, *A Traveler's Narrative,* p. 22.

His followers had not yet read the Báb's statement that ". . . The slaying of a soul is outside the religion of God; . . . and if anyone commands it, he is not and has not been of the Bayán, and no sin can be greater for him than this."

The mob poured down upon Mullá Ḥusayn and his companions and opened fire as they neared. Six of the defenseless party were struck down by that first blast.

Mullá Ḥusayn's companions pleaded with him. "Beloved leader," one of them exclaimed, "we have risen and followed you with no desire except to sacrifice ourselves in the path of the Cause we have embraced. Allow us, we pray you, to defend ourselves, and suffer us not to fall so disgracefully a victim to the fire of the enemy."

"The time is not yet come . . ." Mullá Ḥusayn replied.

A bullet struck another companion in the chest and killed him instantly. This companion was a man of humble and loving disposition. His devotion to the Báb was deep and sincere. He had walked on foot beside Mullá Ḥusayn all the way from Khurásán. At the sight of this much-loved companion fallen dead at his feet, Mullá Ḥusayn could no longer remain silent.

"Behold, O God, my God, the plight of Thy chosen companions, and witness the welcome which these people have accorded Thy loved ones. Thou knowest that we cherish no other desire than to guide them to the way of Truth and to confer upon them the knowledge of Thy Revelation. Thou hast Thyself commanded us to defend our lives against the assaults of the enemy. Faithful to Thy command, I now arise with my companions to resist the attack which they have launched against us."

Unsheathing his sword, Mullá Ḥusayn spurred on his horse and pursued the person who had slain his companion. His opponent took refuge behind a small tree, afraid to face him. He held his musket in front of his body to shield himself as Mullá Ḥusayn swept down upon him and, with a single, sweeping stroke of his sword, cut through the trunk of the tree, the barrel of the musket, and the body of his opponent.

This astonishing feat struck terror into the hearts of that unruly mob. Thus on the plain of Bárfurúsh the words the Báb had spoken to Mullá Ḥusayn at Máh-Kú began to come true: ". . . Your days of horsemanship are yet to come. You are destined to exhibit such courage, such skill and heroism as shall eclipse the mightiest deeds of the heroes of old."

The historian Nicolas states that "pain and anger redoubled the strength of Mullá Ḥusayn who with one single blow of his weapon cut in two the gun, the man and the tree."

Mullá Ḥusayn forced his way through the ranks of the retreating mob, heedless of the bullets that rained about him as he passed. Any who tried to attack him were struck down with a single stroke of his sword. He galloped his horse toward Bárfurúsh, riding straight to the residence of the Sa'ídu'l-'Ulamá. Three times Mullá Ḥusayn circled the house, calling for him to come out.

"Let that contemptible coward, who has incited the inhabitants of this town . . . and . . . concealed himself behind the walls of his house, emerge from his inglorious retreat," he cried out. "Let him, by his example, demonstrate the sincerity of his appeal and the righteousness of his cause. Has he forgotten that he who preaches a holy war must . . . himself march at the head of his followers, and by his own deeds kindle their devotion and sustain their enthusiasm?"

The mob surrendered and fled in panic, crying, "Peace, peace!"

That afternoon, after peace was at last restored, Mullá Ḥusayn addressed the people of Bárfurúsh: "O followers of the Prophet of God [Muḥammad] . . . ! Why have you risen against us? Why deem the shedding of our blood an act meritorious in the sight of God? Did we ever repudiate the truth of your faith? Is this the hospitality which the Apostle of God has enjoined his followers to accord to both the faithful and the infidel?"

Mullá Ḥusayn shamed the people of Bárfurúsh with his words. Then he assembled his companions, and they went to the village caravansary to camp for the night.

The Sa'ídu'l-'Ulamá came out of hiding as soon as Mullá Ḥusayn departed with his friends. He immediately planned an attack on them at the caravansary.

That evening at sunset, Mullá Ḥusayn gathered his companions together. He asked whether anyone among them would be willing to arise and risk his life for the sake of God and ascend to the roof of the caravansary to sound the call to prayer. This would demonstrate to the people that Mullá Ḥusayn and his companions were not enemies, but friends—lovers of Islam.

A youth gladly responded. Yet no sooner had the melodious opening words of "God is Most Great!" echoed over the countryside than a bullet struck him, killing him instantly.

"Let another one among you arise," Mullá Ḥusayn urged them, "and, with the selfsame renunciation, proceed with the prayer which that youth was unable to finish."

Another young man climbed to the roof and began to chant the words "I bear witness that Muḥammad is the Apostle of God." His testimony was cut short by another bullet, which struck him down.

Although Muḥammad Himself had commanded that all should honor their guests even if they are unbelievers, still these companions who were lodged for the night in the village caravansary were being slain for observing His sacred call to prayer out of love and respect. Mullá Ḥusayn entreated his companions to show their loyalty and thus expose the unfaithfulness of those who were attacking them.

A third youth, at Mullá Ḥusayn's bidding, attempted to complete the prayer that his two slain companions had left unfinished. He, too, suffered the same fate. As he approached the end of his prayer and with power and vigor called out the words "There is no God but God," he, in his turn, fell dead.

Such ruthless behavior impelled Mullá Ḥusayn to throw open the gates of the caravansary and rise to fend off this unexpected attack. He leaped onto his horse, gave the signal to charge, and, sword in hand, led his companions in demolishing the forces that had been massing at the gates and now filled the caravansary. His adversaries fled before the fury of his onslaught. It was the story of Bárfurúsh repeated: Again the enemy fled in panic, again they pleaded for peace, again they implored for mercy.

This was to be the first in a series of such encounters that would occur over a period of some eleven months. The believers met every attack with a counterattack and humiliated their opponents time after time. They would rally to Mullá Ḥusayn's encouraging cry, which all took up in turn: "Mount your steeds, O heroes of God!"

Mullá Ḥusayn and his companions finally arrived at the small shrine of Shaykh Ṭabarsí, about fourteen miles from Bárfurúsh. Persia is home to thousands of sanctuaries and shrines that commemorate various saints and holy men. The shrine of Shaykh Ṭabarsí was one such shrine, built to honor a famous saint—a Shí'ah Muslim cleric who had transmitted many sayings of the Prophet Muḥammad and the Imáms. Here Mullá Ḥusayn and his companions sought shelter from the continuing onslaught of attacks against them. The shrine sat on a three or four thousand square meter plot of land. In the middle sat the shrine itself, surrounded by a courtyard, the edges of which were bound by a hedge.

The night before Mullá Ḥusayn and his companions arrived at the shrine of Shaykh Ṭabarsí, the keeper of the shrine had had a strange dream. In this dream he saw a holy man with seventy-two warriors and many companions. He dreamed that they came to that place and engaged in the most heroic of battles, triumphing over the forces arrayed against them, and that finally, the Prophet of God Himself arrived one night to speak with them.

When Mullá Ḥusayn appeared the next day, the keeper of the shrine immediately recognized him as the man he had seen in his dream and told him of it.

Mullá Ḥusayn replied, "All that you witnessed will come to pass. Those glorious scenes will again be enacted before your eyes."

The keeper of the shrine eventually threw in his lot with Mullá Ḥusayn and the heroic defenders of what soon came to be known as the fort of Shaykh Ṭabarsí.

Realizing that the protection the shrine afforded was not sufficient to stave off their enemies, Mullá Ḥusayn and his companions set about erecting defenses and fortifications to protect themselves.

Shortly after Mullá Ḥusayn and his companions completed their fortifications, they learned that a distinguished believer by the name of Mírzá Ḥusayn-'Alí from the province of Núr was on his way to visit them. Mírzá Ḥusayn-'Alí inspected the fort and expressed his satisfaction with the work that had been done. The fort was only missing one vital thing, he said: the presence of Quddús. Mírzá Ḥusayn-'Alí told Mullá Ḥusayn to send seven men to Sárí, where Quddús was being held, to demand that he be released to them. He assured Mullá Ḥusayn that "The fear of God and the dread of His punishment" would persuade Quddús's captor to free him without hesitation.

In fact, the messengers Mullá Ḥusayn sent to Sárí were successful in securing his release from the official in whose home he had been held captive.

Inside the fort the followers of the Báb would hold out against assault, starvation, and treachery. They would outwit and outfight the entire army of the king; this God-intoxicated handful would be pitted against a trained army that was well equipped, supported by the masses of the people, blessed by the clergy, headed by a prince of royal blood, backed by the resources of the state, and enthusiastically approved of by the king himself.

When Quddús entered the fort, he asked Mullá Ḥusayn to determine the exact number of the assembled companions. One by one Mullá Ḥusayn counted them off as they came through the gate. There were 312 in all. He was on his way to make his report to Quddús when a young man who had come on foot from Bárfurúsh rushed through the gate and begged to be allowed to join them. Thus the number reported to Quddús was exactly 313.

Quddús said to them, "Whatever the tongue of the Prophet of God has spoken concerning the Promised One must needs be fulfilled. . . ." The companions were reminded of the prophecy given for this day, that "the assembling of three hundred and thirteen chosen supporters" would be yet another proof that would herald the coming of the Promised One on earth.

When the news of Quddús's presence in the fort reached the Sa'ídu'l-'Ulamá of Bárfurúsh, his fury increased. Driven by an unrelenting hatred, he sent a burning appeal to the king, who had only recently ascended to the throne, claiming that the Persian dynasty—and even the monarchy itself—was in grave peril.

He said that Mullá Ḥusayn and his band of companions had raised the "standard of revolt" and that this "wretched band of irresponsible agitators" was striking at the very foundations of the king's authority. Citizens from a number of villages near the fort of Shaykh Ṭabarsí were sympathizing with the Bábís and were pledging their allegiance to their cause. He characterized the fort as a "massive stronghold," claiming that Mullá Ḥusayn and his cohorts were conspiring against the king and planning to proclaim their independent sovereignty. He suggested that if the king were to take some decisive action to extinguish this movement early in his reign, it would win the people's confidence and admiration. By the same token, he claimed that if the king were to vacillate or show any indulgence toward the Bábís, all of Persia would reject his authority and join the Báb's cause.

The king was alarmed and responded by sending an army of twelve thousand men to drive this small band out of the fort of Shaykh Ṭabarsí and to destroy them all. Food and water were cut off from them, and soon the companions within were reduced to grave conditions. The army was installed on a hill overlooking the fort.

As Quddús stood with Mullá Ḥusayn, watching the king's army, he said, "The scarcity of water has distressed our companions. God willing, this very night a downpour of rain will overtake our opponents, followed by a heavy snowfall, which will assist us to repulse their contemplated assault."

That night as the great mass of soldiers prepared to launch an assault on the fort, a torrential rain overtook them. It ruined much of their ammunition. Sufficient rainwater was quickly gathered inside the fort to quench the thirst of the friends for quite a while.

A historical record of that period notes, ". . . A snowfall such as the people of the neighbourhood even in the depth of winter had never experienced, added considerably to the annoyance which the rain had caused." These storms brought hardship and ruin to the camp of the king's soldiers, but they brought refreshment to the fort.

One of the most memorable encounters took place one morning just before dawn, when the gates of the fort were thrown open to meet an attack.

"Mount your steeds, O heroes of God!" came the command from Quddús.

This stirring call rallied all hearts. Following Quddús, they rushed full charge toward the stronghold of the prince, the leader of the king's army. Mullá Ḥusayn thrust his way right into the royal quarters. The prince, sensing that his life was in danger, had already thrown himself from a back window into the moat and had escaped barefooted, leaving the army bewildered and routed by a handful of Mullá Ḥusayn's companions.

Comte de Gobineau writes in his account, "In a few moments his [the prince's] army already in such confusion, was scattered by the three hundred men of Mullá Ḥusayn! Was not this the sword of the Lord and of Gideon?"

In the prince's quarters, the companions found coffers filled with gold and silver. They looked at them, then left them behind, taking only a pot of gunpowder and the prince's abandoned sword, which they gave to Mullá Ḥusayn, whose own sword had been struck by a bullet.

A detachment of soldiers, meanwhile, surrounded Quddús and fired a volley at him, wounding him in the mouth and throat. Mullá Ḥusayn rushed to his aid. He seized Quddús's sword, and, brandishing this blade in one hand and the captured sword of the prince in the other, he attacked the enemy and, aided by 110 of his fellow disciples, put the entire army to flight within half an hour. Quddús recovered from his wound, minimizing its importance.

Each time the enemy was routed, Quddús would remind the companions of their real purpose. "We have repulsed the assailants," he said, "we need not carry further the punishment. Our purpose is to protect ourselves that we may be able to continue our labours for the regeneration of men. We have no intention whatever of causing unnecessary harm to anyone."

Repeatedly, the companions of Mullá Ḥusayn and Quddús tried to persuade their enemies to permit them to go on their way without shedding more blood. Even one of the leaders of the king's army has testified to this. When questioned at a later date by prince Aḥmad Mírzá about Ṭabarsí and Mullá Ḥusayn, 'Abbás-Qulí Khán gave the following account:

". . . one day Mullá Ḥusayn, having on his head a green turban, and over his shoulder a shroud, came forth from the castle, stood forth in the open field, and, leaning on a lance which he held in his hand said: 'O people, why, without enquiry and under the influence of passion and prejudiced misrepresentation, do ye act so cruelly towards us, and strive without cause to shed innocent blood? Be ashamed before the Creator of the universe, and at least give us passage, that we may depart out of this land.' Seeing that the soldiers were moved, I opened fire, and ordered the troops to shout so as to drown his voice. Again I saw him lean on his lance and heard him cry: 'Is there any who will help me?' three times, so that all heard his cry. At that moment all the soldiers were silent, and some began to weep, and many of the horsemen were visibly affected. Fearing that the army might be seduced from their allegiance, I again ordered them to fire and shout. Then I saw Mullá Ḥusayn unsheathe his sword, raise his face towards heaven, and heard him exclaim: 'O God, I have completed the proof to this host, but it availeth not.' Then he began to attack us on the right and on the left. I swear by God that on that day he wielded the sword in such wise as transcends the power of man."

Eventually, the scarcity of water compelled the companions to dig a well inside the fort. Mullá Ḥusayn, who was watching the work, said, "To-day we shall have all the water we require for our bath. Cleansed of all earthly defilements, we shall seek the court of the Almighty and shall hasten to our eternal abode. Whoso is willing to partake of the cup of martyrdom, let him prepare himself and wait for the hour when he can seal with his life-blood his faith in his Cause. This night, ere the hour of dawn, let those who wish to join me be ready to issue forth from behind these walls and, scattering once again the dark forces which have beset our path, ascend untrammelled to the heights of glory."

That afternoon Mullá Ḥusayn washed himself thoroughly, clothed himself with freshly washed garments, and placed the Báb's green turban on his head. An indefinable joy radiated from his face. He spent a long time in conversation with Quddús. He also spent time with his companions that evening, cheering and encouraging them.

Soon after midnight, the morning star appeared in the sky. Mullá Ḥusayn, gazing at it, recognized it as the star that "heralded to him the dawning light of eternal reunion with his Beloved."

He mounted his charger and signaled for the gate of the fort to be thrown open. He rode out at the head of his 313 companions, crying, "O Lord of the Age!" So intense and powerful was this shout in praise of the Báb that forest, fort, and camp vibrated to its resounding echo.

Mullá Ḥusayn charged the barricades from behind which the army was planning to launch its most concentrated offensive. He crushed his way through them one after the other until all seven of the barricades had fallen. His gallantry and courage were never greater, but his days of horsemanship and heroism were now at an end.

With victory complete, Mullá Ḥusayn's horse became entangled in a tent rope. Before Mullá Ḥusayn could free himself, he was struck in the breast by a bullet that had been fired by someone from a neighboring tree. One of the leaders of the enemy, 'Abbás-Qulí Khán, had hidden in the sheltering branches of the tree, lying in wait to ambush his opponents. Taking advantage of the moment, he fired the fatal shot, not knowing who he had wounded.

Mullá Ḥusayn was bleeding profusely. He dismounted, staggered a few steps, then fell to the ground, exhausted and unconscious. Two of his companions bore him back to the fort.

Quddús ordered the companions to grant them privacy and to refuse admittance to anyone else, saying, "Leave me alone with him. There are certain confidential matters which I desire him alone to know."

The two friends retired to another room. One of them stood near the door and heard Quddús speak gently to Mullá Ḥusayn with the greatest love. "You have hastened the hour of your departure and have abandoned me to the mercy of my foes. Please God, I will ere long join you and taste the sweetness of heaven's ineffable delights."

It was early February of 1849. Less than five years had passed since that night in Shíráz when the Báb had spoken to Mullá Ḥusayn, saying, "O thou who art the first to believe in Me! Verily I say, I am the Báb, the Gate of God." On that never-to-be-forgotten night in 1844, the Báb had declared the Message of God that would quicken the souls of men.

Now Mullá Ḥusayn lay dying in the fort of Shaykh Ṭabarsí. His last words, addressed to Quddús, were "May my life be a ransom for you. Are you well pleased with me?"

Some time later Quddús called for the door to be opened and for his companions to come in. "I have bade my last farewell to him," he said. "Things which previously I deemed it unallowable to utter I have now shared with him." They knew then that Mullá Ḥusayn was dead. They entered to say farewell, moved to tears by the faint smile of happiness that still lingered on his face. So peaceful was his expression that he seemed to have fallen asleep.

Quddús attended to the burial, clothing Mullá Ḥusayn in his own shirt and giving instructions about where to bury him. His mortal remains were laid to rest in the little inner room of the shrine of Shaykh Ṭabarsí. As Quddús bid his last farewell to his friend, he said, "Well is it with you to have remained to your last hour faithful to the Covenant of God. I pray God to grant that no division ever be caused between you and me."

Mullá Ḥusayn had distinguished himself in every encounter by his acts of valor, chivalry, skill, and strength. His fine mind and great learning, his high sense of justice, his tenacity of faith, and his unswerving devotion to God marked him as an outstanding figure among those who have borne witness to the power of the Faith of the Báb.

The historian Gobineau wrote of him, "At last, he passed away. The new religion which found in him its first martyr, lost, in the same stroke, a man whose moral strength and ability would have been of great value to it, had he lived longer. The Muḥammadans naturally feel a hatred for the memory of this leader, which is as deep as the love and veneration shown for him by the Bábís."

The Christian clergyman Dr. T. K. Cheyne wrote, "Frail of form, but a gallant soldier and an impassioned lover of God, he combined qualities and characteristics which even in the spiritual aristocracy of Persia are seldom found united in the same person."

The death of Mullá Ḥusayn caused inexpressible sorrow to the Báb, a sorrow that gave rise to eulogies and prayers equivalent to three times the volume of the Qur'án. In one of His writings the Báb declared that the very dust of the ground where the remains of Mullá Ḥusayn lie buried is endowed with such a potency as to bring joy to the disconsolate and healing to the sick.

That great Figure whose coming the Báb unceasingly proclaimed—Him whom God would make manifest—wrote at a later date that were it not for Mullá Ḥusayn, the Cause of God would not have been established.*

Mullá Ḥusayn was thirty-six when he was slain. After his burial Quddús gave instructions to inter the bodies of the thirty-

* See Bahá'u'lláh, *Kitáb-i-Íqán,* p. 223.

six who had fallen with him that night in one and the same grave near the shrine.

"Let the loved ones of God," Quddús said as they were lowered into the earth, "take heed of the example of these martyrs of our Faith. Let them in life be and remain as united as these are now in death."

Quddús was now in sole command of the followers of the Báb in the fort. When their supply of provisions was nearly exhausted, he distributed the last of some rice among them and warned of the hardships that lay ahead.

"Whoever feels himself strong enough to withstand the calamities that are soon to befall us, let him remain with us in this fort. And whoever perceives in himself the least hesitation and fear, let him betake himself away from this place. Let him leave immediately ere the enemy has again assembled his forces and assailed us. The way will soon be barred before our face; we shall very soon encounter the severest hardship and fall a victim to devastating afflictions."

The very night Quddús gave this warning, one fearful soul betrayed his companions. He wrote a letter to 'Abbás-Qulí Khán, the king's general, informing him that Mullá Ḥusayn, "the pillar upon which the strength and security of the fort" depended, was dead. The letter said that the people within the fort were "worn with famine" and were being "grievously treated." The letter was carried by a messenger, who, with his share of the rice given to him by Quddús, stole out of the fort at midnight and delivered the letter to the general.

The welcome news of Mullá Ḥusayn's death gave 'Abbás-Qulí Khán the nerve to attempt a fresh attack. Fearing that the messenger might spread the report of Mullá Ḥusayn's death and thus rob him of some of the glory of victory, he killed him instantly. He massed his soldiers for an advance and, at the head of two detachments, had the fort surrounded.

Quddús understood at once what had happened. "The betrayer has announced the death of Mullá Ḥusayn to 'Abbás-Qulí Khán . . ." he said. "Sally out and, with the aid of eighteen men marching at your side, administer a befitting chastisement upon the aggressor and his host."

Nineteen of the companions plunged headlong into the ranks of the enemy. They were pitted against no less than two regiments of infantry and cavalry. They counterattacked with such fury that 'Abbás-Qulí Khán became terrified and fell from his horse. In his panic and haste, he left one of his boots hanging from the stirrup. He ran away half shod and bewildered. In despair, he fled to the prince and confessed the ignominious reverse he had suffered at the hands of those nineteen companions of Mullá Ḥusayn.

This same 'Abbás-Qulí Khán later wrote of these defenders of Ṭabarsí, ". . . in truth, I know not what had been shown to these people, or what they had seen, that they came forth to battle with such alacrity and joy. . . . the imagination of man cannot conceive the vehemence of their courage and valour."

Gobineau records that the army "built large towers as high as the various levels of the fortress or even higher and, through a continuous plunging fire, they rendered the circulation of the Bábís within their fort extremely dangerous . . . but, in a few days, the Bábí chiefs, taking advantage of the long nights, raised their fortifications so that their height exceeded that of the attacking towers of the enemy."

Exasperated by these evidences of unquenchable fervor, the commanding officer erected a great tower upon which he placed his biggest cannon. This enabled him to direct his fire into the heart of the fort.

When the faithful saw this, they began to dig underground passages and to retreat there. But the ground of Mázindarán where the fort was located lies near the Caspian Sea and is saturated with moisture. This, coupled with the rain that fell continually, forced the Bábís to dwell in mud and water until their garments rotted away with the damp.

Outraged at their failure to conquer this pitiful band of untrained students, the leading officers of the army, under the command of the prince, gathered a huge force and constructed trenches and barricades. They brought up more cannons and cannonballs. They hurled flaming projectiles into the fort and gave orders to begin a heavy bombardment.

Gobineau writes, "In a very short time, the outer defenses of the fortress were dismantled; nothing was left of them but fallen girders, smoked and burning timbers, scattered stones."

While the bombardment was in process, Quddús emerged from his room and walked to the center of the fort. His manner was one of the greatest tranquillity. A cannonball fell suddenly into the fort. It embedded itself in the earth before him, then rolled free. It came to a stop in front of him. Calmly, Quddús placed his foot on it and rolled it back and forth.

"How utterly unaware," he said, "are these boastful aggressors of the power of God's avenging wrath! . . . Seek they to intimidate the heroes of God, in whose sight the pomp of royalty is but an empty shadow, with such contemptible evidences of their cruelty?"

Quddús turned to his friends. ". . . Beware," he said, "lest you allow the encroachments of self and desire to impair so glorious a station. Fear not the threats of the wicked, neither be dismayed by the clamour of the ungodly. Each one of you has his appointed hour, and when that time is come, neither the assaults of your enemy nor the endeavours of your friends will be able either to retard or to advance that hour. If the powers of the earth league themselves against you, they will be powerless, ere that hour strikes, to lessen by one jot or tittle the span of your life. Should you allow your hearts to be agitated for but one moment by the booming of these guns which, with increasing violence, will continue to shower their shot upon this fort, you will have cast yourselves out of the stronghold of Divine protection."

This appeal breathed much-needed confidence into the hearts of those who heard it, for their troubles were mounting. Their food was at last reduced to the flesh of the abandoned horses they had brought away from the enemy's camp. Later they had to content themselves with grass snatched from the ground. Finally, they consumed the leaves and bark of trees and the leather of their saddles, their belts, their scabbards, and their shoes. They even subsisted on the ground bones of the horses fallen in battle. For eighteen days their only sustenance was a mouthful of water each morning.

"God knows," one of the survivors testified, "that we had ceased to hunger for food." Quddús quickened their enthusiasm and brightened their hopes each day at sunrise and again at sunset by telling of the spiritual beauty and greatness of the Báb.

Many lost their lives, yet the dwindling band remained unconquered. Their actions fulfilled prophecies that foretold the coming of God's Promised One in the "last days." Several spoke of the "halting of those who had believed in the Lord about Ṭabarsí, and their martyrdom."

The young king, Náṣiri'd-Din Sháh, at last grew impatient. "We thought that our army would go without hesitation through fire and water, that, fearless, it would fight a lion or a whale, but we have sent it to fight a handful of weak and defenseless men and it has achieved nothing!"

He and his prime minister, Mírzá Taqí Khán, lashed out against their army leaders. In the most bitter terms they accused them of rank incompetency. They threatened to punish them with the same treatment that had been planned for the followers of the Báb. The king, in his anxiety and anger, threatened the lives of every person in the province around the fort of Shaykh Ṭabarsí. "I shall exterminate its inhabitants to the last man!" he said.

The prince and the general, 'Abbás-Qulí Khán, knew that it was useless to try to explain to an angry king that, although the defenders of the fort were not professional soldiers, it was impossible to force their surrender. 'Abbás-Qulí Khán himself expressed this dilemma by admitting in his own words that the companions of Quddús were "scholars and men of learning . . . strangers to the roar of cannon, the rattle of musketry, and the field of battle. . . . Notwithstanding this, it seemed as if in time of battle a new spirit were breathed into their frames . . . the imagination of man cannot conceive the vehemence of their courage and valour. They used to expose their bodies to the bullets and cannon-balls not only fearlessly and courageously, but eagerly and joyously, seeming to regard the battle-field as a banquet, and to be bent on casting away their lives."

The prince was informed of the threats the king had made. He was afraid that any further delay in subduing Quddús and his companions might result in the loss of his prestige, perhaps his own life. Therefore he resorted to treachery. He despaired of conquering honestly, so he conceived a plan of betrayal.

The prince sent a Qur'án to Quddús and swore on that holy book that he would set free all the defenders of the fort and permit them to go their way. They would not even be molested, the prince promised. He vowed that he himself, at his own expense, would arrange for their safe departure with honor to their homes.

Quddús received the book, kissed it reverently, and quoted from it the sacred words "O our Lord, decide between us and between our people with truth; for the best to decide art Thou."*

---

* Qur'án 7:89.

Then he read the pledge and assembled his companions, ordering them to prepare to leave the fort. "By our response to their invitation, we shall enable them to demonstrate the sincerity of their intentions."

At the gate of the fort, they mounted the horses that were to take them to the prince's camp. A dinner was placed before Quddús and his starving friends, but he refused to touch it, knowing that the hour of death was upon him.

The prince repeated his promise. "My oath is irrevocable and sacred," he said.

One of the companions said to Quddús, "I am of the opinion that what his tongue professes, his heart does not believe at all."

Quddús, who shared this view, told his companions to disperse that very night, before it was too late. Wanting to continue enjoying his companionship, they implored him not to send them away from his side.

"Weep not," were his final words to them, "the reunion which will follow this separation will be such as shall eternally endure. We have committed our Cause to the care of God; whatever be His will and pleasure, the same we joyously accept."

This was the final scene of that somber tragedy at the fort of Shaykh Ṭabarsí. The prince violated his sacred pledge. Quddús and his companions were seized, stripped of their meager possessions, and some were sold as slaves. Others were slain outright, killed by the spears and swords of the officers who were hungry for revenge. The fort was bombarded, plundered, and demolished.

One account states, "the whole world marvelled at the manner of their sacrifice," adding, "The mind is bewildered at their deeds, and the soul marvelleth at their fortitude and bodily endurance."*

---

* Bahá'u'lláh, *Kitáb-i-Íqán*, pp. 224–25.

No less than nine of the Báb's first eighteen disciples, known as the Letters of the Living, fell in this disaster.

The historian Nicolas speaks of the futile attempt of the Persian civil and religious authorities to erase every trace of that gallant spot. "All the fortifications constructed by the Bábís," he writes, "were razed to the ground, and even the ground was leveled to remove any evidences of the heroic defense of those who had died for their Faith. They imagined that this would silence history."

Quddús went with the prince to Bárfurúsh, the city of the cowardly Sa'ídu'l-'Ulamá. Bárfurúsh also happened to be Quddús's hometown.

The Sa'ídu'l-'Ulamá was no longer afraid to come out of his home. With all the religious leaders of Bárfurúsh, he went to welcome the prince and to extend his congratulations on his triumphal return. The entire town was hung with flags to celebrate the victory. Bonfires blazed at night. Three days of festivities took place.

The prince gave no indication to the Sa'ídu'l-'Ulamá as to what was to be done with Quddús. The prince himself was extremely reluctant to mistreat his captive. He had captured Quddús by treachery, but now that his own prestige was secure, he did not wish any further shame to be attached to his share in this hateful episode.

The prince intended to take Quddús to Ṭihrán, the capital, and deliver him into the hands of the king. This, he felt, would relieve him of the responsibility of deciding Quddús's fate. What was more important, it would also bring additional honors to him along the route of march. However, the Sa'ídu'l-'Ulamá's unquenchable hostility interfered with his plan. When he perceived that Quddús might slip from his grasp, he appealed to the mob once more in the same way that he had appealed to them on that first day when Mullá Ḥusayn and his companions had appeared on the plain of Bárfurúsh. He encouraged their basest sentiments. He whipped them into a frenzy. The whole of Bárfurúsh was aroused by the persistency and viciousness of his call to action.

"I have vowed to deny myself both food and sleep," the Sa'ídu'l-'Ulamá cried from the pulpit, "until such time as I am able to end the life of [Quddús] with my own hands!"

The crowd rallied around him and became so ugly that the prince feared for his own safety. He summoned all the priests of Bárfurúsh to consult upon measures to quiet and restrain the populace.

Quddús was also summoned into their presence. At that moment, the prince realized that the hatred of the entire city was solidly against him. He spoke words reminiscent of those of Pontius Pilate: "I wash my hands of all responsibility for any harm that may befall this man. You are free to do what you like with him. You will yourselves be answerable to God on the Day of Judgment."

As soon as he had spoken these words, the prince surrendered Quddús into the hands of the Sa'ídu'l-'Ulamá. He mounted his horse and, in a final act of cowardice, fled from the city, turning his back on Quddús.

There was now no restraining the people. They pounced on Quddús with uncontrolled violence. He was stripped of his clothes. He was paraded through the streets barefooted, bareheaded, and loaded down with chains. He was followed each step of the way by a howling mob. They jeered at him, spat upon him, and flung refuse at him.

Amidst his suffering, Quddús asked the pardon of God for his persecutors. "Forgive, O my God, the trespasses of this people. Deal with them in Thy mercy, for they know not what we already have discovered and cherish. I have striven to show them the path that leads to their salvation; behold how they have risen to overwhelm and kill me! Show them, O God, the way of Truth, and turn their ignorance into faith."

One of the traitors who had deserted the fort passed Quddús in his hour of agony. He saw how helpless Quddús now was. Emboldened, he came forward and struck him in the face.

"You claimed that your voice was the voice of God," he scoffed. "If you speak the truth, burst your bonds asunder and free yourself."

Quddús looked into his eyes with determination. "May God requite you for your deed," he said, "inasmuch as you have helped to add to the measure of my afflictions."

When the family of Quddús heard of his agonies, they recalled the prophetic words he had spoken to them years before in that same city.

His stepmother, who had been kind and loving to him, had wanted him to marry. She had longed to witness his wedding but feared that her longing would remain unfulfilled.

Quddús had comforted her, saying, "The day of my wedding is not yet come. That day will be unspeakably glorious. Not within the confines of this house, but out in the open air, under the vault of heaven, . . . before the gaze of the great multitude, I shall celebrate my nuptials and witness the consummation of my hopes."

Now that promise had come true. As Quddús approached the public square, he remembered those tender years and the words he had spoken. He raised his voice. "Would that my mother were with me, and could see with her own eyes the splendour of my nuptials!"

In the middle of the night, a devoted friend gathered what remained of Quddús's burned and mutilated body. He buried it in a place not far from the scene of his martyrdom.

Nabíl in *The Dawn-Breakers* declares that the story of Mullá Ḥusayn, Quddús, and the defense of the fort of Shaykh Ṭabarsí "must ever remain as one of the most moving episodes of modern times."

The words Quddús spoke in the fort of Ṭabarsí now made themselves felt, fulfilling his prediction: "How utterly unaware are these boastful aggressors of the power of God's avenging wrath!"

After the passing of but a short time, the Sa'ídu'l-'Ulamá was struck down by the same fate that had crushed Ḥusayn Khán, Mírzá 'Alí-Aṣg͟har, Muḥammad S͟háh, and Ḥájí Mírzá Áqásí. Thus still another leader in the plot against the Báb and his followers was seized in the grip of destruction.

He became afflicted with a strange disease for which there was no cure. In spite of the furs that he wore, in spite of the fire that burned constantly in his room, he could never become warm. Even as he trembled with the cold, he suffered from a fever so high that nothing could quench his burning thirst.

The Sa'ídu'l-'Ulamá died of his illness, and his beautiful house was abandoned and eventually crumbled into ruins. Little by little the practice grew of dumping refuse on the site where it had once so proudly stood. This made such an impression on the people of Mázindarán that when they quarreled among themselves, the final insult was often, "May thy house meet the same fate as the house of Sa'ídu'l-'Ulamá!"

News of the tragic fate that had overtaken the heroes of S͟hayk͟h Ṭabarsí reached the Báb in C͟hihríq. It brought great sadness to His heart. He penned eulogies in honor of Quddús, Mullá Ḥusayn, and others who had sacrificed their lives at Ṭabarsí. He wrote that He, too, would soon join these twin immortals, each of whom by his life and by his death had shed imperishable luster upon the Faith of God.

He instructed one of His followers to visit Ṭabarsí and Bárfurús͟h.

"Arise," He urged, "and with complete detachment proceed, in the guise of a traveler, to Mázindarán, and there visit, on My behalf, the spot which enshrines the bodies of those who, with their blood, have sealed their faith in My Cause. As you approach the precincts of that hallowed ground, put off your shoes and, bowing your head in reverence to their memory, invoke their names and prayerfully make the circuit of their shrine. Bring back to Me, as a remembrance of your visit, a handful of that holy earth which covers the remains of My beloved ones, Quddús and Mullá Ḥusayn. Strive to be back ere the day of Naw-Rúz,* that you may celebrate with Me that festival, the only one I probably shall ever see again."

---

* *Naw-Rúz,* meaning literally "New Day," refers in this instance to the Iranian and Zoroastrian New Year, which falls on the first day of the spring equinox in the Northern Hemisphere (normally on 21 March, but sometimes on the 20th or the 22nd).

15

A Wonder among Women

A Wonder among Women

One of the most courageous of all the followers of the Báb was a woman. She was among His chosen disciples, whom He called Letters of the Living. She was known as Ṭáhirih, which means "The Pure One." Members of her family ranked high among the religious leaders of Persia. Her father was one of the most famous of all. From childhood, she was regarded by her fellow townsmen as a prodigy. Her knowledge and gifts were so outstanding that her father often was heard to lament, "Would that she had been a boy, for he would have shed illumination upon my household, and would have succeeded me!"

She was renowned for both her intelligence and her beauty. Her brother 'Abdu'l-Vahháb said, "None of us, her brothers or her cousins dared to speak in her presence, her learning so intimidated us, and if we ventured to express some hypothesis upon a disputed point of doctrine, she demonstrated in such a clear, precise and conclusive manner that we were going astray, that we instantly withdrew confused."

A. L. M. Nicolas's historical account tells us that "Her reputation became universal throughout Persia, and the most haughty 'Ulamás [scholars] consented to adopt some of her hypotheses and opinions."

One day while visiting in the home of her cousin, she discovered some books in his library that interested her very much. They were written by Shaykh Aḥmad and his successor, Siyyid Káẓim. Her cousin warned her that her father would be very angry if he found her reading them, as he was vehemently opposed to their thinking.

"For a long time now," Ṭáhirih answered, "I have thirsted after this; I have yearned for these explanations, these inner truths. Give me whatever you have of these books. Never mind if it angers my father."

The cousin was persuaded, and Ṭáhirih took the books home to study. Predictably, her father raised violent objections, had heated discussions with her, and criticized and denounced the writings of Shaykh Aḥmad. She eagerly read all of the works of Shaykh Aḥmad and Siyyid Káẓim that she could find. Shaykh Aḥmad was dead, but Siyyid Káẓim was still living in Karbilá, so Ṭáhirih secretly began corresponding with him. His letters excited in her an ever keener interest in the coming of a promised Messenger of God. She had a great longing to go to Karbilá to study under Siyyid Káẓim.

She knew that her father would never grant his permission. However, with the help of her uncle, she secured permission to make a pilgrimage to the shrines at Karbilá and Najaf. Her family willingly granted permission for this, most likely believing that a pilgrimage might bring her back to her senses and to more orthodox ways. They did not suspect that her true purpose in going was to meet Siyyid Káẓim.

She made the journey in 1843, eager to study under Siyyid Káẓim. During those days she thought only of the approaching appearance of a new spiritual Teacher in the world. Ṭáhirih told her uncle that she wished to be the first woman to serve Him when He appeared.

"Oh, when will the day come," she said, "when new laws will be revealed on the earth! I shall be the first to follow those new Teachings and to give my life for my sisters!"*

---

* Quoted in Martha L. Root, *Ṭáhirih the Pure,* p. 56.

Ṭáhirih's grief was very deep when she reached Karbilá and found that Siyyid Káẓim had died just ten days before her arrival. However, her sorrow softened when she was permitted to stay in his home and was given access to all of his writings, some of which had never been published. She studied them avidly.

One night in a dream a young man appeared before her. He raised his hands toward heaven and in a beautiful voice recited many wonderful verses, one of which she memorized and wrote down. She awakened with a feeling of great joy.

Sometime later, a copy of the Báb's commentary on the Súrih of Joseph in the Qur'án reached her. Within its pages she discovered the same prayer that she had written down from her dream. To her intense delight she realized that the message was true and that its author must be that great spiritual Teacher she awaited.

Ṭáhirih immediately wrote to the Báb and entrusted her sister's husband, Mírzá Muḥammad-'Alí, with the sealed letter. To Mírzá Muḥammad-Alí she said, "Say to Him, from me, 'The effulgence of Thy face flashed forth, and the rays of Thy visage arose on high. Then speak the word, "Am I not your Lord?" and "Thou art, Thou art!" we will all reply.'"

Ṭáhirih's acceptance of the Báb brought immediate and violent protests from her father, her uncle, her husband, and her brothers. In an effort to protect the family's illustrious name, they all tried to quiet her and to curb her desire to tell others of her discovery.

Ṭáhirih was aflame with the message of the Báb. It is said of her early days of teaching in Karbilá that "All who met her in Karbilá were ensnared by her bewitching eloquence and felt the fascination of her words. None could resist her charm; few could escape the contagion of her belief. All testified to the extraordinary traits of her character, marvelled at her amazing personality, and were convinced of the sincerity of her convictions."

When the learned religious leaders of Karbilá discovered that she was an ardent follower of the Báb and was spreading His teachings in the very center of their religious life, they complained bitterly to the government.

They were especially angered when Ṭáhirih wanted to celebrate the birthday of the Báb, which fell within the month of the commemoration of the martyrdom of the Imám Ḥusayn. Defying tradition and custom, she discarded her mourning garb and attired herself in clothes that showed her happiness.

Officials were dispatched at once to arrest her, but they seized a friend of hers by mistake. Ṭáhirih wrote immediately to the governor, saying that she was at his disposal and instructing him not to harm anyone else.

The governor put Ṭáhirih's residence under guard so that no one could go in or out. He wrote to Ba<u>gh</u>dád for instructions. finally, after three months, Ṭahirih announced her intention to proceed to Ba<u>gh</u>dád to await the instructions there. The governor then released her.

Before her departure from Karbilá she unburdened her heart by writing a letter to each of the clerics of that city, condemning their bigotry. These leaders assigned to women a rank little higher than that of animals and even suggested that they lacked souls. Ṭáhirih ably defended her faith in this letter and exposed the clerics' unjust and backward views.

From Karbilá she went to Ba<u>gh</u>dád, accompanied by several followers of the Báb including, among others, Mullá Ḥusayn's mother and sister, in whom she had kindled a great love for the Faith. Sadly, Ṭáhirih was pelted with stones as she left Karbilá.

Ṭáhirih lost no time after her arrival in Ba<u>gh</u>dád before she began teaching the message of the Báb there. She spoke with such power and eloquence that those who had seen and heard her before she became a follower of the Báb were amazed. They said, "This is not the woman we knew before."

Her lectures began to attract very large audiences from among the peoples of all religions. One of her most outstanding characteristics was her ability to arouse a keen desire in her listeners to investigate the truth of the Báb's mission for themselves. Within a short time her extraordinary attraction had won many supporters. A large number had followed her from Karbilá to Baghdád in order to attend her classes.

The clerics of Baghdád became aroused as her words began to woo away their own followers. She was emptying their classes. Many rose up against her, so she challenged them publicly. Through the governor she invited them all to meet her in a great public discussion of the truth or falsehood of the Báb's teachings. They refused, made excuses, and instead complained to the government about the revolution she was stirring up.

The following story is told of a Jewish physician, Ḥakím Masih, who, in the company of the king, passed through Baghdád on his way to Karbilá. One day he came upon a large group of people, mostly clergyman, listening to a lecture by a woman who was sitting veiled from their sight behind a curtain. He went in to listen. As soon as the woman finished her lecture, they began arguing with her. Her speech was so logical and convincing that the doctor was very much attracted. The clerics were unable to answer her proofs. He was astonished and soon became convinced that this woman was right. He thought that this magic speaker must be the Promised One of whom everyone was speaking. He attended her lectures and learned of the message of the Báb and began to believe in Him.

One day a delegation of the ablest religious leaders of Baghdád came to see Ṭáhirih. Her popularity had grown so astonishingly that they became alarmed at the effect she might have upon their people. They decided to unite against her. This delegation included representatives from the two leading sects of Islam and from the Jewish and Christian communities as well. Their mission was to convince her of the folly of her actions. Ṭáhirih was able to silence every protest. She astounded the delegation with the force of her argument and the depth of her knowledge. Disillusioned at their complete failure, the delegation withdrew.

So great was the influence that Ṭáhirih exerted on the people and so intense became the excitement caused by her teaching, that she was seized by the authorities and placed in the house of the muftí* of Ba<u>gh</u>dád by order of the governor of Ba<u>gh</u>dád. She was kept there under virtual arrest until the governor could receive instructions about what to do with her from the central Turkish government in Constantinople, as Iraq was still part of the Ottoman empire at that time.

During her imprisonment in Ba<u>gh</u>dád, Ṭáhirih defended her faith and her own character before the muftí with great ability. Before she left his home, he told her sincerely, "O Qurratu'l-'Ayn! I swear by God that I share in thy belief. I am apprehensive, however, of the swords of the family of 'U<u>th</u>mán."†

That same muftí later wrote a book in Arabic in which he spoke of Ṭáhirih's stay in his home. He said that every morning in the early hours of dawn she would arise to pray and meditate. She fasted frequently. He stated that he had never seen a woman more virtuous and more devoted to God, nor had he seen any man more learned or more courageous than she.

One evening the muftí's father came to call on his son. He did not even greet Ṭáhirih. Instead, in her presence, he began

---

* Judge.

† "The family of 'U<u>th</u>mán" refers to the Turkish Empire.

to berate his son for his kindness to her and cursed her as an enemy of religion. The father said with grim satisfaction that a message had just arrived from Constantinople. The sulṭán of Turkey had given Ṭáhirih her life and her freedom, but she was commanded to leave Turkish territory immediately.

"Make preparations to leave Iraq tomorrow," the father told her bluntly.

The muftí was ashamed of his father's behavior. He apologized to Ṭáhirih. After she left his home, he confided to his friends, "I see in her such knowledge, education, politeness and good character as I have not seen in any great man of this century."

The judge himself told Ṭáhirih, "The answer has come from Constantinople. The King has commanded that you be set free, but only on condition that you leave his realms. Go then, tomorrow, make your preparations for the journey, and hasten away from this land."

Ṭáhirih and more than thirty friends crossed the border from Iraq to Persia and entered the province of Kirmán<u>sh</u>áh. The muftí graciously sent ten horsemen under the command of a general to ensure a safe journey.

In the village of Karand Ṭáhirih remained and taught for three days, openly proclaiming the teachings of the Báb. She was successful in awakening an interest among all classes of people. Some twelve hundred persons are reported to have declared their belief in the Báb as a result.

Leaving Karand, Ṭáhirih moved on to the city of Kirmán<u>sh</u>áh, where, according to the *The Dawn Breakers,* she received an enthusiastic welcome. Clergymen, government officials, and others came out to welcome so famous a figure. They were impressed by her eloquence, her fearlessness, her extensive knowledge, and the force of her character. She translated one of the writings of the Báb and had it read publicly. The governor and his family acknowledged the truth of the Cause of the Báb in her presence. They showed their great admiration and love for Ṭáhirih.

A different account of Ṭáhirih's stay in Kirmanshah is found in *Memorials of the Faithful.** According to this account, the people of the city came in a constant stream to learn about the new religion. This soon upset the 'ulamás,† who ordered the expulsion of Ṭáhirih and her traveling companions. As a result, the mayor of the city allowed a mob to sack the houses where they had been staying and to loot their possessions. All of the followers of the Báb were put in a coach, driven out into the desert, and abandoned. The coach was left, but the horses were taken back to the city. Thus the travelers were left without food and had no change of clothing nor any means of transportation other than walking.

Ṭáhirih wrote to the governor of Kirmánshah explaining what had happened and saying, "We were your guests . . . ; do you think it was kind to treat us like this?" A member of the group walked back to the city to deliver the message.

The governor, unaware of what had happened, was dismayed and surprised to learn of the injustice. When he investigated and learned that all had been done at the 'ulamás' instigation, he ordered that all of the stolen property be returned, that Ṭáhirih and her companions be given their horses, and that they be escorted safely to the city of Hamadán. He even invited them to return to Kirmánshah, but Ṭáhirih declined.

Moving east toward her home in Qasvín, Ṭáhirih stopped in the small village of Ṣaḥnih for two days. Her reception there outshone even that of Karand. Upon her departure the inhab-

* See 'Abdu'l-Bahá, *Memorials of the Faithful,* pp. 193–94 (69.15–69.16).

† Literally "learned men," "scholars"; "clerical authorities," "theologians," "divines": the Muslim religious hierarchy.

itants of the village begged to be allowed to gather together the members of their community and come with her. They were prepared to leave everything behind and join her in the spread and promotion of the Faith of the Báb. Ṭáhirih, however, advised them to remain where they were and to teach among their own people.

Ṭáhirih went next to Hamadán, where the religious leaders were divided in their attitudes toward her. Some tried to arouse the people against her while others loudly praised her.

One of the leading clerics of Hamadán deeply resented her fame and wanted to kill her. He would have openly urged the people to attack her, but he was afraid of the government.

Ṭáhirih knew of the cleric's desire, and she wrote him a long letter explaining carefully the teachings of the Báb. She sent it to him by a faithful friend, Mullá Ibráhím. He arrived with this letter just at an hour when several of these unfriendly clergymen were meeting to decide what steps they could take against Ṭáhirih to silence her. They considered the letter impudent. It enraged them. They all fell upon Mullá Ibráhím and beat him until he was unconscious. When he was carried back to Ṭáhirih, still unconscious, she did not weep at the sight of him as those about her had expected her to do. She astonished them all by saying, "Come, get up, Mullá Ibráhím. Happiness and peace be upon you that you have suffered in the path of your Beloved! Rise up, and continue to work for Him!"

When Mullá Ibráhím opened his eyes, Ṭáhirih smiled at him.

"O Mullá Ibráhím," she said, "for one beating you became unconscious; this is the time we are ready to give our lives. Did not the disciples of Christ do it, and the disciples of Muḥammad?"*

---

* Quoted in Martha L. Root, *Ṭáhirih the Pure,* p. 66.

Mullá Ibráhím actually arose from his dizziness, departed from her presence, and began to serve again.

From Hamadán Ṭáhirih planned to go to Ṭihrán, where she hoped to meet the king, Muḥammad Sháh, so that she could tell him about the teachings of the Báb. However, one of the clerics who had refused to meet her in open debate when she was in Kirmánsháh had secretly written to her father in Qazvín. He told him that his daughter was disgracing the reputation of all of the clergy, let alone her family.

Her father at once sent his son with a strong party of relatives to Hamadán to welcome Ṭáhirih and to urge her to come home. Sometime before they arrived from Qazvín, Ṭáhirih intuitively realized this and said to her companions, "They are coming for us, so we shall start back to Qazvín before they reach here." She gave up her plans to visit Ṭihrán and returned to her home with her escort.

That first night when Ṭáhirih arrived in Qazvín, there was a family council. Her father and her uncle strongly reproached her for her behavior.

"Though you regard your excellence and learning of such small account in comparison with the virtues of the Shírází lad,* still, had you been my son (instead of my daughter) and had you put forward this claim (of being the Báb), I would have accepted it."

Her uncle Taqí cursed the Báb and struck Ṭáhirih in anger with several violent blows. With her quick intuition of the avenging hand of God, Ṭáhirih uttered fatal words of foresight.

"O Uncle," she cried, "I see your mouth fill with blood!"

These words so infuriated him that he threatened to have her branded with hot irons. The family council broke up in

* A reference to the Báb, who came from Shíráz.

anger. The next day the family tried to persuade her to return to her husband, hoping this would keep her under restraint.

"He, in that he rejects God's religion, is unclean; between us there can be naught in common," she replied.

Her husband, who considered himself to be one of the great religious leaders of Persia, sent a message to Ṭáhirih attempting to persuade her to transfer her residence to his house. She replied, "Say to my presumptuous and arrogant kinsman, 'If your desire had really been to be a faithful mate and companion to me, you would have hastened to meet me in Karbilá and would on foot have guided my howdah* all the way to Qazvín. I would, while journeying with you, have aroused you from you sleep of heedlessness and would have shown you the way of truth. But this was not to be. Three years have elapsed since our separation. Neither in this world nor in the next can I ever be associated with you. I have cast you out of my life for ever."

Her husband, in a burst of fury, pronounced her a heretic and strove to undermine her position and sully her fame. In anger he divorced her a few weeks later.

Ṭáhirih's uncle, Mullá Taqí, was murdered one Friday in the mosque. He was stabbed in the back of the neck and in the mouth. Although the killer, who was not a follower of the Báb, eventually confessed to the crime, still Ṭáhirih was accused of instigating the slaying. Her ex-husband and the rest of the family recalled the prophetic words she had spoken on the night of her return: "O Uncle, I see your mouth fill with blood!"

The entire city was aroused. The officers of the government were commanded to arrest all prominent followers of the Báb. The houses of all who were known to be related to Bábís were plundered.

---

* A litter carried by a camel, mule, horse, or elephant for carrying a single passenger.

Ṭáhirih herself was placed in strict confinement. The authorities imprisoned her in the cellar of her father's home, and the women who were assigned to watch her were told never to let her out of their sight. She must not escape.

A member of Ṭáhirih's family, one day years later while showing visitors the cellar in which she had been confined, explained that Ṭáhirih's father truly loved his gifted daughter, even though he clashed violently with her in matters of religious belief. He imprisoned her in his home in an effort to protect her from the savagery of those who were ready to brand her with irons because she believed in the Báb, but even he could not save her.

In a spirit of revenge, although well aware of her innocence, Ṭáhirih's ex-husband persuaded the governor to put her on trial for the murder of her uncle Taqí. Her father refused to let her leave his house, but the officials came and took her from him by force. She was carried away to the government house and put in prison. They also arrested her servant, Káfiyih, and other women.

The women were interrogated, but their response was "This deed has been perpetrated without our knowledge."

Ṭáhirih's ex-husband, seething with hatred, fearful she would go free, urged the governor to inflict some harsh punishment upon Ṭáhirih and her companions.

Acting on this suggestion, the governor gave the executioner orders to bring in the irons for branding.

To terrorize Ṭáhirih and perhaps secure a false confession by torture, they placed Káfiyih's hands under a sliding door, intending to brand them from the other side.

Ṭáhirih knew that she was helpless. Her only refuge was Almighty God. She uncovered her face, turning toward the prison of the Báb at Máh-Kú, and began to pray. The hot irons were brought forward, and Káfiyih's hands were prepared for the branding. At that terrifying moment, a voice could be heard shouting in the street outside, "The murderer is found!"

The murderer had confessed. He had come alone and of his own accord to the government house to save the innocent people from suffering. Ṭáhirih and Káfiyih were freed. Ṭáhirih was returned to her father's house, still a prisoner. Her husband made another unsuccessful attempt on her life by trying to poison her. In spite of all this opposition Ṭáhirih continued to teach many people.

She profoundly affected the city of Qazvín. Although the city took pride in the fact that no fewer than a hundred of the highest religious leaders of Shí'ah Islam dwelt within its gates, and although she was a prisoner for much of her stay, Ṭáhirih won many victories in Qazvín.

The *Journal Asiatique* in a study of this period frankly asks the question, "How could it be that a woman, in Persia where woman is considered so weak a creature, and above all in a city like Qazvín, where the clergy possessed so great an influence, where the 'Ulamás, by their number and importance attracted the attention of the government and of the people,—how could it be that *there,* precisely under such untoward circumstances, a woman could have organized so strong a group of heretics? There lies a question which puzzles even the Persian historian, Sipihr, for such an occurrence was without precedent!"

Ṭáhirih sent a message to her former husband, now the chief cleric of Qazvín. She dared him to take her life, saying, "If my Cause be the Cause of Truth, if the Lord whom I worship be none other than the one true God, He will, ere nine days have elapsed, deliver me from the yoke of your tyranny. Should He fail to achieve my deliverance, you are free to act as you desire. You will have irrevocably established the falsity of my belief."

From that moment on, Ṭáhirih was watched more closely than ever, but in spite of all efforts, she escaped quietly in the night before the ninth day. Her sudden and mysterious removal filled her foes with fear and her friends with concern. The authorities immediately entered the houses and searched all night for her. They were both angered and baffled by her disappearance and by the fulfillment of her prediction.

Meanwhile, Ṭáhirih escaped to Ṭihrán. She spent a week there, then traveled east to the province of Khurásán to take part in a conference of believers who were meeting at the tiny village of Badasht. Ṭáhirih left at once to join the group. Her enemies were still on the watch for her everywhere along the road, but she escaped from Ṭihrán and journeyed to Badasht. It was early in the summer of 1848.

Eighty-one of the leading followers of the Báb gathered at that village to meet in consultation. Quddús was among those present, since this was before the days of the fort of Shaykh Ṭabarsí. The purposes of the gathering were twofold. first, it would decide upon the steps to be taken so that the Faith of the Báb would no longer be looked upon as a sect of Islam, but rather as a new, independent religion with its own Prophet and holy writings. Second, it would consider the means of freeing the Báb from His cruel imprisonment in Chihríq. The gathering succeeded in its first goal but failed in the second.

The followers of the Báb were at first divided as to whether to make a complete break from the religious laws, institutions, traditions, and rituals of the past. Ṭáhirih herself was an instrument of that separation. She became its outward symbol when one day she appeared without her veil. She had cast aside this emblem of women's inferior station.

The effect was electric. Even her fellow believers were shocked. They stood aghast at this unexpected and unprecedented sight. A few condemned so radical a change, while others supported her. Happiness and triumph shone from Ṭáhirih's face. Dignified and confident that a new day had dawned, Ṭáhirih arose from her seat. She was completely indifferent to the tumult that her unveiled appearance had caused. It was considered indecent in nineteenth-century Persian society for men to look upon a woman's uncovered face.

Ṭáhirih's vision was universal. She knew that the Báb's teachings had eliminated the need for such traditions of the past. The injustice and slavery practiced against both men and women were now to be ended. She stood before her fellow believers radiating both an inward and an outward beauty.

"The Trumpet is sounding! The great Trump is blown! The universal Advent is now proclaimed!" she cried out. "I am the blast of the trumpet, I am the call of the bugle. Like Gabriel, I would awaken sleeping souls."

Gone were the days of dread and subjection for any of the creatures of God. Exultant with joy, she delivered a fervent and eloquent appeal to that assembly. Some on that day recalled the words of the prophecy that foretold the day of the Promised One, when Fáṭimih, the daughter of Muḥammad, would appear unveiled before them. Others probably remembered the sound of the "Bugle" and the "stunning trumpet-blast" promised in the Qur'án for the "last days."*

Ṭáhirih finished her appeal by inviting all who were present to celebrate this great occasion befittingly.

"This day is the day of festivity and universal rejoicing," she said, "the day on which the fetters of the past are burst asunder. Let those who have shared in this great achievement arise and embrace each other."

The conference ended after several days. Ṭáhirih was on her way back from Badasht when she was captured and sent under escort to the capital, Ṭihrán. When she was brought into the presence of the king, he commented, upon seeing her, "I like her looks: leave her, and let her be."

She was then taken as a prisoner to the home of the mayor of Ṭihrán, Maḥmúd Khán. The king sent a letter to Ṭáhirih at the mayor's house. He urged her to deny the Báb and again become a true Muslim. He promised her that if she would do

* See Qur'án 39:68, 74:8, 8:30.

this, he would give her an exalted position as guardian of the women of his household and would even make her his bride.

Ṭáhirih replied on the back of the king's letter in verse, saying in essence that the kingdom, wealth, and ruling were for him, but wandering and calamity were for her. The king, reading the reply, was deeply moved. He spoke of her spirit and courage. He said, "So far, history has not shown such a woman to us."

Ṭáhirih was given considerable freedom during her imprisonment in the mayor's house, and she was able to continue her teaching. She was still aglow with the fire and fervor of Badasht. It was during this period in Ṭihrán that she reached the height of her popularity and fame. She openly denounced the restraints that had so unjustly shackled her sex for so many centuries in the East. She aroused the women by giving brilliant discourses on the matchless tenets of her religion.

Sir Francis Younghusband, who wrote of Ṭáhirih's life, says, "So strong in her faith did she become that although she was both rich and noble she gave up wealth, child, name and position for her Master's service and set herself to proclaim and establish his doctrine. . . ." He adds elsewhere, "The beauty of her speech was such as to draw guests away from a marriage feast rather than listen to music provided by the host."

Comte de Gobineau writes of her, "Many who have known her and heard her at different times have stated that, for a person so learned and so well read, the outstanding characteristic of her discourse was an amazing simplicity and still, when she spoke, her audience was deeply stirred and filled with admiration, often in tears."

Ṭáhirih stirred up the entire capital city to such an extent that finally the authorities took action against her. The government sent a special delegation to question her about her faith. They held seven conferences with her in which she offered proofs demonstrating that the Báb was the expected Messenger of God.

She quoted from the Qur'án to convince them. During the last of these conferences, Ṭáhirih became exasperated with their obstinate refusal to accept anything but the most literal interpretation of sacred scripture, particularly certain prophecies.

"Your reasoning is that of an ignorant and stupid child; how long will you cling to these follies and lies? When will you lift your eyes toward the Sun of Truth?" she exclaimed.

Her attitude shocked the delegation. They returned to their homes and wrote out a formal denunciation saying that Ṭáhirih refused to give up her faith. Upon the recommendation of this delegation, Ṭáhirih was sentenced to death.

Ṭáhirih was now placed in strict confinement in a single room in the house of the mayor of Ṭihrán, Maḥmúd Khán. The wife of the mayor, while not a follower of the Báb, became very attached to her. Before Ṭáhirih was taken away to be slain, this woman had become a devoted friend. She is reported to have related the following:

"One night, whilst Ṭáhirih was staying in my home, I was summoned to her presence and found her fully adorned, dressed in a gown of snow-white silk. Her room was redolent with the choicest perfume. I expressed to her my surprise at so unusual a sight.

"'I am preparing to meet my Beloved,' she said, 'and wish to free you from the cares and anxieties of my imprisonment.'

"I was much startled at first, and wept at the thought of separation from her.

"'Weep not,' she sought to reassure me. 'The time of your lamentation is not yet come. I wish to share with you my last wishes, for the hour when I shall be arrested and condemned to suffer martyrdom is fast approaching. I would request you to allow your son to accompany me to the scene of my death and to ensure that the guards and executioner into whose hands I shall be delivered will not compel me to divest myself of this attire. It is also my wish that my body be thrown into a pit, and that that pit be filled with earth and stones. . . .

"'My last request is that you permit no one henceforth to enter my chamber. From now until the time when I shall be summoned to leave this house, let no one be allowed to disturb my devotions. This day I intend to fast—a fast which I shall not break until I am brought face to face with my Beloved.'

"She bade me, with these words, lock the door of her chamber and not open it until the hour of her departure should strike. . . .

"I locked the door of her chamber and retired to my own, in a state of uncontrollable sorrow. I lay sleepless and disconsolate upon my bed. The thought of her approaching martyrdom lacerated my soul. . . . That day and night, I several times, unable to contain myself, arose and stole away to the threshold of that room. . . . I was enchanted by the melody of that voice which intoned the praise of her Beloved."

The mayor's wife recalled that she heard a knocking at the door four hours after sunset. She hastened to her son and told him of Ṭáhirih's last wishes. Her son pledged his word that he would fulfill every instruction, then he opened the door.

The attendants of the man who was to execute Ṭáhirih were standing at the gate, demanding that she be delivered into their hands.

The mayor's wife related, ". . . I was struck with terror by the news, and, as I tottered to her door and with trembling hands unlocked it, found her veiled and prepared to leave her apartment. . . . As soon as she saw me, she approached and kissed me. She placed in my hand the key to her chest, in which she said she had left for me a few trivial things as a remembrance of her stay in my house.

"'Whenever you open this chest,' she said, 'and behold the things it contains, you will, I hope, remember me and rejoice in my gladness.'

"With these words she bade me her last farewell, and, accompanied by my son, disappeared from before my eyes.... What pangs of anguish I felt that moment, as I beheld her beauteous form gradually fade away in the distance! She mounted the steed... sent for her, and, escorted by my son and a number of attendants, who marched on each side of her, rode out to the garden that was to be the scene of her martyrdom."

They led Ṭáhirih to a garden outside of the gates of Ṭihrán. The executioner and his lieutenants were in the midst of a drunken brawl when they arrived. flushed with wine and roaring with laughter, they were unaware of Ṭáhirih's approach.

Ṭáhirih dismounted and turned to the mayor's son, who had accompanied her as a friend. She asked him to act as an intermediary.

"They apparently wish to strangle me," she said. "I set aside, long ago, a silken kerchief which I hoped would be used for this purpose. I deliver it into your hands and wish you to induce that dissolate drunkard to use it as a means whereby he can take my life."

The mayor's son approached the executioner. As the young man came up to him, he waved him aside.

"Interrupt not the gaiety of our festival!" he shouted. Then he laughed uproariously and turned back to his party. "Let that miserable wretch be strangled," he mouthed to his attendants, "and her body be thrown into a pit!"

The boy gave the attendants the kerchief. This young man has, himself, given an eyewitness account of that fateful moment.

"... They consented to grant her request," he reported. "That same kerchief was wound round her neck and was made the instrument of her martyrdom. I hastened immediately afterwards to the gardener and asked him whether he could suggest a place where I could conceal the body. He directed me... to a well that had been dug recently and left unfinished. With the help of a few others, I lowered her into her grave and filled the well with earth and stones in the manner she herself had wished. Those who saw her in her last moments were profoundly affected. . . ."

Dr. Jakob Polak, Austrian physician to the king, in a book written in 1856, states that he was an eyewitness of Ṭáhirih's last hours. She endured her death with "super-human fortitude," he said.

Thus ended the life of Ṭáhirih. She was one of the greatest of the Letters of the Living, the Báb's chosen disciples. She was the first martyr for women's suffrage as well. As the hour of her death approached, she turned to the one into whose custody she had been placed and declared boldly, "You can kill me as soon as you like, but you cannot stop the emancipation of women!"

Her career was dazzling, brief, tragic, and eventful. Her fame spread with remarkable swiftness.

Lord Curzon in his book on Persia states bluntly, "Of no small account, then, must be the tenets of a creed that can awaken in its followers so rare and beautiful a spirit of self-sacrifice."

Sarah Bernhart, the famous actress, requested the playwright Catulle Mendes to write a dramatized version of Ṭáhirih's life. The playwright himself called her the "Persian Joan of Arc."

The British orientalist Professor E. G. Browne said that if the Faith of the Báb had no other claim to greatness than that it had produced a heroine like Ṭáhirih, it would be sufficient. "The appearance of such a woman, . . ." he writes, "is, in any country and any age, a rare phenomenon, but in such a country as Persia it is a prodigy—nay, almost a miracle."

The French diplomat Comte de Gobineau writes, "She was held with every justification to be a prodigy."

"No memory," writes Sir Valentine Chirol, "is more deeply venerated or kindles greater enthusiasm than hers, and the influence she wielded in her lifetime still inures to her sex."

The famous Turkish poet Sulaymán Nazím Bey exclaims, "O Ṭáhirih! You are worth a thousand Náṣiri'd-Dín Sháhs!"

Marianna Hainisch, the mother of one of Austria's presidents, says, "The greatest ideal of womanhood has been Ṭáhirih."

"This noble woman," writes Dr. T. K. Cheyne, a renowned English clergyman, ". . . has the credit of opening the catalogue of social reforms in Persia." And in what is probably his most penetrating comment about Ṭáhirih Dr. Cheyne writes, "Looking back on the short career [of Ṭáhirih] one is chiefly struck by her fiery enthusiasm and by her absolute unworldliness. This world was, in fact, to her . . . a mere handful of dust."

Ṭáhirih was faithful to the Cause of the Báb from the first moment of her acceptance until the last hour of her death. Not for an instant did she swerve from that confident belief expressed in her message sent to Him in those beginning days in Shíráz: "Then speak the word, 'Am I not your Lord?' and: '. . . Thou art!' we will all reply."

Ṭáhirih lived and died by the words she had spoken so boldly to another great disciple of the Báb one evening in Ṭihrán so long ago. She had been listening to a brilliant and eloquent discourse on the Faith of the Báb, given by Vaḥíd himself. He spoke of the signs and proofs of the coming of the Báb. Ṭáhirih listened patiently for some time, then suddenly she interrupted.

"O Yaḥya! Let deeds, not words, testify to thy faith," she cried out, "if thou art a man of true learning. Cease idly repeating the traditions of the past, for the day of service, of steadfast action, is come. Now is the time to show forth the true signs of God, to rend asunder the veils of idle fancy, to promote the Word of God, and to sacrifice ourselves in His path. Let deeds, not words, be our adorning!"

Ṭáhirih had now justified those words by her death in a garden in the shadow of Persia's greatest city.

She was at the height of her beauty and power when she was slain in August 1852 at the age of thirty-six. Siyyid Káẓim had called her Qurratu'l-'Ayn—"Solace of the Eyes." But the name by which she lives forever in the hearts of her people is Ṭáhirih—"The Pure One."

16

The Death of the Wisest Persian

The Death of the Wisest Persian

Vaḥíd, who had been sent by the king as his personal representative to investigate the truth of the Báb's mission, was the next to fall in this nationwide wave of persecutions.

In the early days of the siege at the fort of Shaykh Ṭabarsí, Vaḥíd had hurried to Ṭihrán to make the necessary preparations for joining Mullá Ḥusayn and Quddús inside the fort. He was about to leave Ṭihrán when he learned that it was too late, that his friends had already been captured or slain.

During this visit to Ṭihrán, Vaḥíd met a companion who wrote down his recollection of that meeting: "I observed in his [Vaḥíd's] august countenance the signs of a glory and power which I had not noticed during my first journey with him to the capital, nor on other occasions of meeting, and I knew that these signs portended the near approach of his departure from the world. Subsequently he said several times in the course of conversation: 'This is my last journey, and hereafter you will see me no more' . . . Sometimes when we were together, and the conversation took an appropriate turn, he would remark: '. . . I swear, by that loved One in the grasp of whose power my soul lies, that I know and could tell where and how I shall be slain, and who it is that shall slay me. And how glorious and blessed a thing it is that my blood should be shed for the uplifting of the Word of Truth!'"

After this last visit to Ṭihrán, Vaḥíd journeyed to Ṭáhirih's native town of Qazvín, and from there went to Qum, Káshán, Iṣfahán, Ardistán, and Ardikán. In each of these cities he met his fellow believers and was able to stimulate their enthusiasm and reinforce their efforts.

In every city he would explain the fundamental teachings of the Báb with zest and fearlessness. He succeeded in winning a considerable number of the most able and notable citizens to His Cause. Thus Vaḥíd became an important target for the prime minister and all other enemies of the Báb.

The story of Vaḥíd's investigation of the Báb, undertaken on behalf of the former king and prime minister, was well known to the people. That these two had agreed to abide by Vaḥíd's findings was also well known, as was the fact that they had broken their pledge when they heard that Vaḥíd had become a follower of the Báb.

Vaḥíd was a man of great influence, a man of wealth and fame. In addition to his beautiful house in Yazd where his wife and four sons lived, he also had a home in Dáráb, and still another in Nayríz. These homes were noted for their elegance and their superb furnishings.

Vaḥíd visited his home in the city of Yazd in the heart of Persia on the feast of the new year. It coincided with the anniversary of the Báb's declaration of His mission. The most important religious leaders and notables came out to meet him. The Navváb-i-Raḍaví, who was the most bitter of Vaḥíd's enemies, was also present. He resented the splendor of Vaḥíd's reception and hinted maliciously that it was not really the national festival of the new year that Vaḥíd was celebrating.

"The Sháh's imperial banquet," he said, "can scarcely hope to rival the sumptuous repast you have spread before us. I suspect that in addition to this national festival which to-day we are celebrating, you commemorate another one besides it."

Vaḥíd made a bold and sarcastic retort that made those who were present laugh. They all applauded his stinging rebuke because they were aware of the Navváb's stinginess and wickedness. This ridicule enraged the Navváb. He promised himself that if it lay in his power, Vaḥíd would die violently because of it.

Vaḥíd took this occasion to proclaim without reservation the principles of the Báb's faith. Some people were irresistibly attracted. Others, unable to challenge successfully the defense that Vaḥíd made for his new faith, denounced it inwardly, swearing to do whatever they could to extinguish it. They joined forces with the Navváb and made plans to overthrow Vaḥíd without delay.

Nicolas, in his history of those days, writes, "'To love and to conceal one's secret is impossible,' says the poet; so . . . [Vaḥíd] began to preach openly in the Mosques, in the streets, in the bazaars, on the public squares, in a word, wherever he could find listeners. Such an enthusiasm brought forth fruit and the conversions were numerous and sincere. The Mullás, deeply troubled, violently denounced the sacrilege to the governor of the city."

The priests were agreed on one vital point: Vaḥíd must be destroyed. They spread the report of that new year's day banquet, saying, "Though his listeners ranked among the most illustrious of the mujtahids [doctors of Islamic law] of the city, no one could be found in that assemblage to venture a protest against his vehement assertions of the claims of his creed. The silence kept by those who heard him has been responsible for the wave of enthusiasm which has swept over the city in his favour, and has brought no less than half of its inhabitants to his feet, while the remainder are being fast attracted."

This report raced like a grass fire through the surrounding district. It engendered hatred, but, at the same time, it brought crowds of interested people from distant towns and villages. They flocked to Vaḥíd's home to hear about the Báb, and a great many embraced the new religion.

"What are we to do?" they asked Vaḥíd. "In what manner do you advise us to show forth the sincerity of our faith and the intensity of our devotion?"

Each day from early morning until late at night, Vaḥíd was absorbed in teaching them, answering their questions, and inspiring them to return home to teach in their own villages.

For forty days this feverish teaching activity continued. Vaḥíd's home became a rallying point for both men and women. The Navváb finally convinced the governor of Yazd that if Vaḥíd were not restrained, the city would soon revolt against the king's government, and that he, the governor, would be to blame. The governor was new, young, and inexperienced and thus easily manipulated. The Navváb entreated him to send a force of armed men to surround Vaḥíd's home and put an end to this teaching. The governor succumbed to the Navváb's entreaties and ordered out a detachment of soldiers.

The Navváb quickly sent his personal instructions to a mob of townspeople to rush to Vaḥíd's home and do all they could to add to his humiliation. He implied that Vaḥíd's death would be a welcome thing in the eyes of God.

Even after his house was completely surrounded by a regiment of soldiers and the infuriated mob, Vaḥíd continued speaking to a large gathering of friends and followers in the yard below from an upper window.

The people gathered below were alarmed at the sight of the soldiers and the great mob of townspeople. They turned to Vaḥíd in their distress, asking for instructions. His servant, Ḥasan, quickly saddled Vaḥíd's horse and brought it into the courtyard below his window so that he might flee for safety. Vaḥíd called upon his friends to be calm.

"This very steed," Vaḥíd said as his eyes fell upon the horse his servant had saddled and brought for him, "the late Muḥammad Sháh gave me, that with it I might undertake the mission with which he entrusted me, of conducting an impartial investigation into the nature of the Faith proclaimed by the . . . Báb. He asked me to report personally to him the results of my enquiry, inasmuch as I was the only one among the ecclesiastical leaders of Ṭihrán in whom he could repose implicit confidence. . . .

"When I came into His presence, however, and heard His words, the opposite of that which I had imagined took place. In the course of my first audience with Him, I was utterly abashed and confounded; by the end of the second, I felt as helpless and ignorant as a child; the third found me as lowly as the dust beneath His feet. He had indeed ceased to be the contemptible siyyid I had previously imagined. To me, He was the manifestation of God Himself, the living embodiment of the Divine Spirit. Ever since that day, I have yearned to lay down my life for His sake. I rejoice that the day I have longed to witness is fast approaching."

Vaḥíd's friends became frightened. They feared that he was speaking of that very day and hour, for the soldiers and the mob were preparing to assault them. Seeing the agitation that had seized them, Vaḥíd again urged them to be calm and patient. He told them to rest assured that God, the omnipotent Avenger, would soon crush with defeat the forces arrayed against the faithful.

Shortly after Vaḥíd had uttered these words, the news came that a great number of friendly companions were approaching his home to save him. This rescue party flung themselves upon the attackers, crying, "O Lord of the Age!" Their valor and utter fearlessness alarmed and scattered the entire detachment of soldiers, who abandoned their arms and fled for shelter.

Later that night Vaḥíd met the leader of the rescue party, who had plans to attack and conquer the enemy. Vaḥíd attempted to discourage him from carrying out this plan, which was not in keeping with the teachings of the Báb and would only incite further violent clashes with the local authorities. Vaḥíd urged this friend to leave Yazd immediately and to leave him and the other companions in Yazd to the care and protection of God.

"Not until our appointed time arrives," Vaḥíd said, "will the enemy be able to inflict upon us the slightest injury."

However, the friend chose to remain and positioned himself and his band of men outside the military fort to which the soldiers had retreated, forcing these who were in and around it to seek refuge inside the fort, adding to the humiliation of their earlier defeat.

Meanwhile the Navváb was attempting to stir up enough animosity among the townspeople to motivate them to attack Vaḥíd's house.

Vaḥíd sent a messenger through the streets of Yazd with the warning that he would not attack anyone but that he would defend himself and his home. This warning succeeded in preventing the Navváb from finding any support among the townspeople for attacking Vaḥíd.

The Navváb now turned his attention to the group of Bábís who were positioned outside the military fort. A mob rushed forth to attack them, and the soldiers in the fort began firing on them. The leader of the group of Bábís was struck by a bullet and injured, and a number of his supporters were hurt. The leader's brother quickly moved him to a place of safety, then carried him, at the leader's request, to Vaḥíd's house with the enemy in hot pursuit. After another skirmish in which the enemy was again routed, Vaḥíd directed his companions to disperse to safety. He knew that the hour for his own departure from Yazd had come. He advised his wife to take the children and all of their belongings and go to her father's house for safety. He instructed her to leave all of his personal possessions behind.

"This palatial residence," he told her, "I have built with the sole intention that it should be eventually demolished in the path of the Cause, and the stately furnishings with which I have adorned it have been purchased in the hope that one day I shall be able to sacrifice them for the sake of my Beloved." Vaḥíd continued, saying, "Then will friend and foe alike realise that he who owned this was endowed with so great and priceless a heritage that an earthly mansion, however sumptuously adorned and magnificently equipped, had no worth in his eyes; that it had sunk, in his estimation, to the state of a heap of bones to which only the dogs of the earth could feel attracted." He hoped that this evidence of his willingness to make material sacrifices for the sake of his beliefs would help to open others' eyes and inspire them to follow in his footsteps.

Vaḥíd said farewell to his dear wife and bade a tender goodbye to two of his sons. The other two sons would leave Yazd with him.

In the middle of the night he collected the writings of the Báb that were in his possession and gave them to his servant, Ḥasan, with the order to take them and await his arrival outside the city gate. He told Ḥasan exactly which route to take, warning that if he were to disregard the instructions he would never be able to meet him again.

Ḥasan mounted his horse and prepared to leave. He heard the cries of the patrolling sentinels who were keeping a night watch over the city. Afraid that they might capture him and seize the manuscripts, he took what he thought to be a safer route to the gates of the city. As he was passing through one section of town, he was recognized by the sentinels. They opened fire on him, downing his horse and capturing Ḥasan alive.

Meanwhile, Vaḥíd, accompanied by his two sons, followed the route he had told Ḥasan to take and was soon safely outside the city. The moment Vaḥíd left Yazd, his enemies, under the leadership of the Navváb, rushed to his house to plunder his possessions. They carried away all of the furnishings, then demolished the house completely.

Vaḥíd set out at once for his home in Nayríz. That first night he walked over twenty miles until he at last approached the village where his brother lived. Vaḥíd did not enter his brother's house; instead, he encamped in the recesses of a nearby mountain. His brother, hearing of his presence there, secretly sent out horses and provisions Vaḥíd needed for his journey to Nayríz.

A body of the governor's mounted troops was sent from Yazd in pursuit of Vaḥíd. They followed his trail to his brother's village, thinking they would find him there. They searched the house where they suspected he was concealed. Unable to find him, they appeased their anger and disappointment by seizing as much of his brother's property as they could carry away, then returned to Yazd.

The Navváb still was not satisfied. Vaḥíd's teaching in Yazd had stopped, but Vaḥíd had escaped. He would not pursue Vaḥíd himself. He left that to the governor. Instead, in concert with the leading priests of Yazd, he took a far more gratifying step.

Nicolas reports that after the Navváb confirmed Vaḥíd's departure, "he gave a sigh of relief. Besides, he felt that to pursue the fugitives would involve some peril and that, therefore, it would be infinitely more practical, more beneficial, more profitable and less dangerous to torture the Bábís, or those presumed to be Bábís—provided that they were wealthy—who had remained in the city. He sought out the most prosperous, ordered their execution, and confiscated their possessions, avenging thus his outraged religion, a matter of perhaps little concern to him, and filling his coffers, which pleased him immensely."

Having failed in their plans to capture and slay Vaḥíd, the authorities had to content themselves with the torture of his servant, Ḥasan. They led him out to a loaded cannon. They thought they might frighten Ḥasan into pleading for mercy and thus force him to renounce his newfound beliefs. After all, he was only a servant. Vaḥíd was a man of great nobility and wisdom, and he might be expected to know what he was doing, but this ignorant servant would certainly save his own life now that his master was gone. If they could make him cry for mercy, they could publicize his recantation. This at least would be one way to humiliate Vaḥíd. The officer gave the command that was calculated to bring Ḥasan to his knees.

He ordered the attendants to bind Ḥasan with his back to the mouth of the cannon.

Ḥasan entreated them not to do that. "Bind me, I pray you," he pleaded, "with my face towards the gun, that I may see it fired."

The gunners and onlookers were astonished at Ḥasan's composure and cheerfulness. Anyone who can be cheerful in such a plight must have great faith and fortitude.

All along the road to Nayríz Vaḥíd continued his teaching. Wherever he made camp, his first action was to go immediately to the neighboring village or town. He would gather all the people together, then he would announce to them the glad tidings of the Báb's appearance. In the mountain village of Bavánát, the leading clergyman of the village, Ḥájí Siyyid Ismá'íl, accepted the Faith.

Vaḥíd was utterly indifferent to fatigue. In whatever place he succeeded in attracting souls to the faith of the Báb, he would stay the night so that he could deepen their understanding and prepare them to continue the work of teaching after his departure. If none arose to accept or to inquire further, he would leave that village at once.

"Through whichever village I pass," he often said, "and fail to inhale from its inhabitants the fragrance of belief, its food and its drink are both distasteful to me."

When news of Vaḥíd's approach to Nayríz spread, there was an exodus from the city to greet him. The governor forbade it, sending a messenger to warn the people that those who persisted would lose their lives, their wives, and their possessions.

Not one of the people who had set out heeded this warning. They continued on their way. The governor was dismayed when his messenger reported their disdainful neglect of his warning. He began to fear that those who defied his orders might eventually rise against him. He decided he must take some strong action to protect his position and maintain his prestige.

The very first thing Vaḥíd did upon reaching Nayríz, even before going to his own home, was to enter the place of worship and address the congregation that had gathered there. He called upon them to embrace the faith of the Báb. The Promised One of God has appeared, he told them. Still dusty from his journey, Vaḥíd ascended the pulpit and spoke with such convincing eloquence that the whole audience was electrified by his appeal. When the first flush of excitement subsided, Vaḥíd continued speaking.

"My sole purpose in coming to Nayríz," he explained, "is to proclaim the Cause of God. I thank and glorify Him for having enabled me to touch your hearts with His Message."

No less than a thousand persons from his own area and five hundred from other sections of Nayríz spontaneously responded to his appeal and accepted the new faith.

"No need for me to tarry any longer in your midst," Vaḥíd told the crowd. He had to leave the city because if he remained any longer the governor might harm those who had embraced the new faith.

The people assured Vaḥíd of their belief, saying, "We are ready and resigned to the Will of God. God grant us His grace to withstand the calamities that may yet befall us. We cannot, however, reconcile ourselves to so abrupt and hasty a separation from you."

Vaḥíd submitted to their wishes and agreed to stay a few days longer in Nayríz. At this news a crowd of men and women gathered around him and, with cheers and praise, escorted him to the entrance of his house.

The governor was terrified to hear that Vaḥíd had won such an avalanche of victories in such an astonishingly short time. The finest citizens from all fields were accepting the faith of the Báb. This number included the governor's own nephew.

The governor felt that he must destroy this influence before it undermined his own position with the king and the prime minister. He recruited a thousand soldiers, both cavalry and infantry. He supplied them with ammunition and ordered them to make a sudden attack on Vaḥíd and bring him back as a prisoner.

Vaḥíd was informed of the plans for this secret attack. He and his companions followed the pattern of their fellow believers at Shaykh Ṭabarsí and sought refuge. The prince who was the governor of Shíráz joined forces against Vaḥíd and his companions. He gave the same instructions that had been given at Shaykh Ṭabarsí—to exterminate all of the Bábís. Vaḥíd and his friends had taken refuge in the fort of Khájih, where they were besieged in the same manner in which Quddús and Mullá Ḥusayn had been besieged at Ṭabarsí. They were deprived of water and food. Finally, by the same treachery used at Ṭabarsí, they were betrayed into coming out from their sheltered protection.

The governor of Nayríz, failing time after time to win by force, eventually resorted to deceit, contrary to the pure spirit of Muḥammad's teachings. A Qur'án was sent to Vaḥíd with the following solemn promise:

"This Qur'án, to which we affix our seals, is the witness of the integrity of our purpose. Let that holy Book decide whether the claim you advance is true or false. The malediction of God and His Prophet rest upon us if we should attempt to deceive you."

Vaḥíd received the book with great reverence. "Our appointed hour has struck," he said. ". . . Though I am well aware of their designs, I feel it my duty to accept their call and take the opportunity to attempt once again to unfold the verities of my beloved Faith."

With five companions, Vaḥíd left the fort and entered the governor's camp. For three days and three nights he spoke to them of the Báb. Though outwardly they appeared to listen and treat him with respect, inwardly they were secretly plotting how they could get the rest of his friends out of the fort so that they could all be destroyed.

A plot to persuade Vaḥíd's friends to leave their fort to join Vaḥíd at the camp of the soldiers was conceived and proved successful. This was the beginning of the slaughter. Vaḥíd's companions were seized and arrested the moment they set foot outside the fort. When the news of their capture reached the governor and his staff, they immediately began to take their revenge upon Vaḥíd. They consulted about what would be the best way to evade fulfilling the oath that they had sent with the Qur'án into the fort.

Their scheme was simple. A man notorious for his ruthlessness and cruelty volunteered to kill Vaḥíd because he had not taken the oath. He was ready to do what the others felt unable to carry out.

"I can arrest at any time," he boasted indignantly, "and put to death whomever I deem guilty of having violated the laws of the land."

He summoned all the relatives of those people who had perished in the long struggle to conquer the fort in which Vaḥíd and his friends had been sheltered. He called upon them to carry out the death sentence against Vaḥíd, thus relieving, in his own mind, both the governor and himself of any responsibility for their deaths. He offered to three men in particular the privilege and pleasure of being the first to strike Vaḥíd before turning him over to the mob. He knew these three men would be without mercy.

Nayríz echoed to the sound of drums and cymbals as Vaḥíd was brought before the people. The eager crowd was held back while the three men took their turns. The first, Mullá Riḍá, snatched Vaḥíd's turban from his head, uncoiled it, then wound it about his neck and dragged him to the ground. Vaḥíd was then tied to a horse. The horse was whipped so that it would drag Vaḥíd through the streets of the city. The second man, Ṣafar, as well as the third man, Áqá Khán, struck and beat Vaḥíd at will and with such ferocity that the onlookers began to worry that there might be no sport left for them.

In the midst of his agony Vaḥíd called out, "Thou knowest, O my Beloved, that I have abandoned the world for Thy sake, and have placed my trust in Thee alone. I am impatient to hasten to Thee. . . ."

The mob fell upon Vaḥíd in a great wave. Their fists and weapons pounded him into insensibility and tore his flesh. Horsemen scattered the crowd so that they could have their turn. Women danced around the corpse, rejoicing to the beat of the drums and cymbals.

A. L. M. Nicolas in his history writes that the multitude, "aroused by the scene, stoned and beat to death the unfortunate man. They then severed the head, tore off the skin, stuffed it with straw and sent that trophy to Shíráz!"

The frenzied crowd did the same to the heads of Vaḥíd's companions and sent them as a gift to the prince in Shíráz who had called for the extermination of Vaḥíd and his friends. These were to be proof to him of the thorough execution of his commands.

The prince was feasting when the caravan bearing these awful trophies arrived.

It was a festival day in Shíráz. Nicolas recalls, "The bazaars were adorned with flags—joy was general. Suddenly there was absolute silence. They saw coming thirty-two camels, each carrying an unfortunate prisoner, a woman or a child, bound and thrown crosswise over the saddle like a bundle. All around them were soldiers carrying long lances and upon each lance was impaled the head of a Bábí who had been slain at Nayríz. The hideousness of the sight deeply affected the holiday population of Shíráz and they returned, saddened, to their dwellings.

"The horrible caravan passed through the bazaars and continued to the palace of the governor. This personage was in his garden where he had gathered . . . the rich, the eminent citizens of Shíráz. The music ceased, the dancing stopped. . . ."

Mihr-'Alí Khán stepped toward the prince, bearing his trophies. He told the prince of his own brave deeds in the assault on Vaḥíd and his companions. Mihr-'Alí Khán then named all the prisoners who had been brought, men, women, and children. He received congratulations from the prince for his great victory. Special favors were bestowed upon him and his fellow leaders for this gift of severed heads.

These events literally fulfilled a well-known Islamic tradition about the coming of the Promised One, which prophesies, "In Him [shall be] the perfection of Moses, the preciousness of Jesus, and the patience of Job; His saints shall be abased in His time, and their heads shall be exchanged as presents, . . . they shall be slain and burned, and shall be afraid, fearful, and dismayed; the earth shall be dyed with their blood, and lamentation and wailing shall prevail amongst their women; these are my saints indeed."

The governor of Nayríz still was not satisfied. He hungered for even greater revenge against those who had survived his betrayal. He planned for their annihilation so that none would live to tell the tale of his treachery.

Nicolas writes that the governor's "hatred knew no bounds and it was to last as long as he lived. It was actually the very poor that had been sent to Shíráz, the rich had been kept back. . . . [The governor] had entrusted them to a guard who was ordered to walk them through the city beating them as they went. The people of Nayríz were greatly entertained that time."

The end of Vaḥíd's noble life was the signal for the outbreak of a fierce wave of violence in Nayríz that lasted long beyond that day of betrayal. The fort in which Vaḥíd and his friends had sought refuge was burned to the ground. Their property was seized, their houses were destroyed, and many were thrown into dungeons before being subjected to a final fiendish torture. The greedy officials made certain that the prisoners had nothing of value left before they were slain. During that black period, many were crucified.

The fate that befell the betrayers of Ṭabarsí struck almost at once against one of the most treacherous leaders of the Nayríz upheaval. Mihr-'Alí Khán, who had escorted those trophies of severed heads to the prince at Shíráz, whose lips had sung the praises of his own valor, was suddenly struck dumb. He was no longer able to boast of his victorious march with his gruesome prize to the palace of the prince. Mihr-'Alí Khán fell ill shortly after that march. His lips could form words, but no sound would come out. He remained mute and speechless until the very day of his death. On that last day, as he was about to expire, those who stood around him saw from the movement of his lips that he was whispering something. They leaned down to catch his last words and heard the only sound that had issued from his lips since he had been stricken. Three times he whispered faintly the words, "Bábí! Bábí! Bábí!" Then he fell back dead.

It is reported that all of those who were chiefly responsible for these cruelties came to a tragic end and died overwhelmed with calamity.

Another great figure among the followers of the Báb had fallen, a man who would later be described by Him whom God would make manifest as "that unique and peerless figure of his age." The illustrious Vaḥíd, who was known as the most learned, most eloquent, and most influential of the king's subjects, had surrendered all that men hold dear for the privilege of laying down his life in the path of God. The day of Vaḥíd's martyrdom was but ten days before that of his Beloved One, the Báb.

17

The Seven Heroes of Ṭihrán

The Seven Heroes of Ṭihrán

The death of Vaḥíd came as an added blow to the heart of the Báb. He was already in great sorrow because of the suffering at Ṭabarsí when He learned of the betrayal that had occurred at Nayríz. Yet even these tragedies were not the only troubles that had beclouded the remaining days of His fast-ebbing life. The Báb's beloved uncle, Ḥájí Mírzá Siyyid 'Alí, who had reared Him from childhood and who had so faithfully served His Cause, had, several months earlier, been engulfed in this same wave of persecution.

The Báb's uncle had earlier visited Him in the castle of Chihríq, fulfilling a prediction the Báb had made some two years earlier. At the time, He had been preparing to leave Shíráz to go to Iṣfahán. He told His uncle as He said good-bye, "I will again meet you amid the mountains of Ádhírbáyján, from whence I will send you forth to obtain the crown of martyrdom. I Myself will follow you, together with one of My loyal disciples, and will join you in the realm of eternity."

When the Báb's uncle entered Ṭihrán, his friends warned him of the grave danger of his presence there.

"Why fear for my safety?" he confidently replied. "Would that I, too, could share in the banquet which the hand of Providence is spreading for His chosen ones!"

Shortly after this a traitor who pretended to be interested in the Báb's teachings attended classes and thus secured the names and addresses of about fifty followers of the Báb. He turned over this list to Maḥmúd Khán, the mayor of Ṭihrán. The mayor immediately ordered that all fifty be arrested. Fourteen were seized and brought before the authorities. One of these fourteen was the Báb's uncle, Ḥájí Mírzá Siyyid 'Alí. All fourteen were placed in confinement in the home of the mayor. It was on the upper floor of this same house that Ṭáhirih was also held prisoner.

Every kind of ill-treatment was inflicted on these fourteen captives to induce them to reveal the names and addresses of the other believers in the city. The prime minister, Mírzá Taqí Khán, was informed of their capture. According to historical record, this archenemy of the Báb was the son of a former prime minister's head cook. He had risen in a few short years from the kitchen to become chief advisor to the king through a policy of self-advancement and ruthlessness. He immediately issued an order threatening with execution whoever among the fourteen was unwilling to deny his faith.

Seven individuals were unable to withstand the pressure he exerted and were released at once. The other seven, who remained steadfast, became known as the "Seven Martyrs of Ṭihrán." The Báb's uncle was one of these seven.

His friends urged him to escape the trouble that loomed ahead and save his life. A considerable number of wealthy merchants even offered to pay a ransom to free him, but the Báb's uncle rejected their offer. Finally, he was brought before the prime minister.

The prime minister explained that he was reluctant to inflict any harm on the Báb's uncle because he was a descendant of the Prophet Muḥammad. Furthermore, he said, "Eminent merchants of Shíráz and Ṭihrán are willing, nay eager, to pay your ransom. . . . A word of recantation from you is sufficient to set you free and ensure your return, with honours, to your native city. I pledge my word that, should you be willing to acquiesce, the remaining days of your life will be spent with honour and dignity under the sheltering shadow of your sovereign."

The Báb's uncle boldly replied, "Your Excellency . . . My repudiation of the truths enshrined in this Revelation would be tantamount to a rejection of all the Revelations that have preceded it. To refuse to acknowledge the Mission of the Siyyid-i-Báb, would be to apostatise from the Faith of my forefathers and to deny the Divine character of the Message which Muḥammad, Jesus, Moses, and all the Prophets of the past have revealed."

The prime minister grew impatient.

The Báb's uncle continued, "God knows that whatever I have heard and read concerning the sayings and doings of those Messengers, I have been privileged to witness the same from this Youth, this beloved Kinsman of mine, from His earliest boyhood to this, the thirtieth year of His life. . . . I only request of you that you allow me to be the first to lay down my life in the path of my beloved Kinsman."

The prime minister was stupefied by this answer. Without uttering a word, he motioned that the Báb's uncle should be taken out and beheaded.

As he was being conducted to his death, Ḥájí Mírzá Siyyid 'Alí called out to the crowd that swarmed around him.

"For over a thousand years, you have prayed and prayed again that the promised Qá'im* be made manifest. . . . And now that He is come, you have driven Him to a hopeless exile in a remote and sequestered corner of Á<u>dh</u>irbáyján and have risen to exterminate His companions. . . . With my last breath, I pray that the Almighty may wipe away the stain of your guilt and enable you to awaken from the sleep of heedlessness."

The executioner was shaken by those words. Pretending that the sword he had been holding in readiness needed to be sharpened, he hurried away and never returned. He told the story of that moving event many times, expressing his repentance for the act he had been compelled to perpetrate. Whenever he spoke

* "He Who Shall Arise," a title designating the Promised One of Islam.

of the Báb's uncle, he could not repress his tears, which bore witness to the depths to which his heart had been stirred.

The second person to fall beneath the headman's axe at this time in Ṭihrán was Mírzá Qurbán-'Alí. He was a native of Bárfurúsh, but his reputation was such that he was admired and respected by many of the notables in the provinces of Mázindarán and Khurásán as well as in Ṭihrán, the capital. So greatly was he esteemed that when he visited Karbilá, a vast concourse of people lined the road all along his route in order to pay tribute to him. In fact, wherever he went, he was greeted with acclaim. Even the king's mother was a great admirer of Qurbán-'Alí. Because of her close friendship and admiration for him, she told the king that Qurbán-'Alí was being branded with lies.

"He is no Bábí," she insisted, "but has been falsely accused."

So they sent for Qurbán-'Alí. The prime minister brought him to the palace under guard. His arrest had already caused a commotion such as Ṭihrán rarely experienced. Huge crowds followed Qurbán-'Alí as he was led through the streets. Some cried out encouragement to him. Others wondered what he could have done to deserve such treatment. The people packed the approaches to the government headquarters, anxious to hear some word about his fate.

At first Qurbán-'Alí was treated with great respect. The authorities assured him of their confidence in his innocence and expressed concern that so grave an injustice should have been done to him. They believed a false charge had been made against him.

Qurbán-'Alí replied that although he didn't know whether the Báb accepted him, he had accepted the Báb and considered himself one of His followers and servants.

The authorities tried to persuade him to give up this foolishness. He was far too intelligent to be anyone's servant, far too important to lower himself in the eyes of his fellow men. They promised Qurbán-'Alí a permanent salary and a generous pension if he would deny this misguided sect and recant his faith.

Qurbán-'Alí spoke with quiet conviction. "This life and these drops of blood of mine are of but small account; were the empire of the world mine, and had I a thousand lives, I would freely cast them all at the feet of His friends. . . ."

The prime minister himself tried to show Qurbán-'Alí the foolishness of his stubborn attitude.

"Since last night," he said, "I have been besieged by all classes of State officials who have vigorously interceded in your behalf. From what I learn of the position you occupy and the influence your words exercise, you are not much inferior to the . . . Báb Himself. Had you claimed for yourself the position of leadership, better would it have been than to declare your allegiance to one who is certainly inferior to you in knowledge."

Qurbán-'Alí shook his head. "The knowledge which I have acquired," he boldly retorted, "has led me to bow down in allegiance before Him whom I have recognised to be my Lord and Leader. Ever since I attained the age of manhood, I have regarded justice and fairness as the ruling motives of my life. I have judged Him fairly, and have reached the conclusion that should this Youth, to whose transcendent power friend and foe alike testify, be false, every Prophet of God, from time immemorial down to the present day, should be denounced as the very embodiment of falsehood!"

The king and his mother each in turn tried to sway Qurbán-'Alí from his belief, but neither the sweetness of bribes nor the threat of death had any effect. The treasure that the Báb offered him, he said, was matchless. Seeing their astonishment at his refusal to accept honors and riches in place of death, he tried to explain.

"I am assured of the unquestioning devotion of over a thousand admirers, and yet I am powerless to change the heart of the least among them. This Youth, however, has proved Himself capable of transmuting, through the elixir of His love, the souls of the most degraded among His fellow men. Upon a thousand like me He has, unaided and alone, exerted such influence that, without even attaining His presence, they have flung aside their own desires and have clung passionately to His will."

The prime minister hesitated. He was reluctant to pronounce the sentence of death against one of Qurbán-'Alí's exalted station.

"Why hesitate?" burst forth the impatient victim. "Are you not aware that all names descend from Heaven? He whose name is 'Alí,* in whose path I am laying down my life, has from time immemorial inscribed my name, Qurbán-'Alí,† in the scroll of His chosen martyrs. This is indeed . . . the day on which I shall seal with my life-blood my faith in His Cause. . . . rest assured that I shall never blame you for your act. The sooner you strike off my head, the greater will be my gratitude to you."

The prime minister became angry. "Take him away from this place!" he cried. "Another moment, and this dervish will have cast his spell over me!"

Qurbán-'Alí replied, "You are proof against that magic that can captivate only the pure in heart. You and your like can never be made to realise the entrancing power of that Divine elixir which, swift as the twinkling of an eye, transmutes the souls of men."

---

* A reference to the Báb.

† *Qurbán* means "Sacrifice," and *'Alí* can be taken as an allusion to the Báb, whose given name was 'Alí-Muḥammad; hence *Qurbán-'Alí* can be taken to mean "Sacrifice for the Báb."

Infuriated, the prime minister arose from his seat, shaking with anger. "Nothing but the edge of the sword can silence the voice of this deluded people," he shouted. "No need," he told the executioner, "to bring any more members of this hateful people before me. Words are powerless to overcome their unswerving obstinacy. Whomever you are able to induce to recant his faith, release him; as for the rest, strike off their heads!"

As Qurbán-'Alí was led to the scene of his death, he spoke with exultation. "Hasten to slay me," he cried with joy, "for through this death you will have offered me the chalice of everlasting life. Though my withered breath you now extinguish, with a myriad lives will my Beloved reward me; lives such as no mortal heart can conceive!"

A great crowd pressed in about him. He said that the Promised One had arisen in Shíráz in the person of the Báb. But the people were deaf to his call.

Qurbán-'Alí cried, "Oh, the perversity of this generation! . . . Though my soul brims over with ecstasy, I can, alas, find no heart to share with me its charm, nor mind to apprehend its glory."

He approached the spot where the Báb's uncle had been slain. When Qurbán-'Alí saw that broken body, he gathered it into his arms. He looked out over that sea of hatred, then summoned the executioner.

"Approach," he told him, "and strike your blow, for my faithful comrade is unwilling to release himself from my embrace, and calls me to hasten together with him to the court of the Well-Beloved."

The blow was struck. Sounds of distress and sorrow stirred even through that hostile crowd as the two martyrs were united for all time.

The next of the seven martyrs was Ḥájí Mullá Ismá'íl.

Like Qurbán-'Alí, Ḥájí Mullá Ismá'íl had planned to go to the fort of Shaykh Ṭabarsí to join Mullá Ḥusayn and Quddús, but he had been stricken with illness. When he recovered he learned that the siege was over and his friends had been massacred. He began to teach the Faith with renewed energy in an effort to make up for the tragic losses the Cause of the Báb had suffered at Ṭabarsí.

Mullá Ismá'íl was arrested in Ṭihrán with the others. He was told that if he would give up the Báb's Faith and denounce its Author, he would be released, otherwise he would suffer death. He refused. As he passed through the crowd, they cursed him and threw stones at him.

Even at the headsman's block a few personal friends broke through the crowd and tried to persuade Mullá Ismá'íl to deny the Báb. They pleaded with him. Mullá Ismá'íl looked away from them and looked toward those two martyrs who had preceded him. They were still entwined in each other's embrace.

"Well done, beloved companions!" he cried, fixing his gaze on their gory heads. "You have turned Ṭihrán into a paradise!" Drawing from his pocket a coin, which he handed to his executioner, Mullá Ismá'íl begged him to purchase for him something with which he could sweeten his mouth. This the executioner did. Mullá Ismá'íl took some of it and gave the rest to the executioner, saying, "I have forgiven you your act; approach and deal your blow. For thirty years I have yearned to witness this blessed day, and was fearful lest I should carry this wish with me unfulfilled to the grave. Accept me, O my God," he cried, turning his eyes toward heaven, "unworthy though I be, and deign to inscribe my name upon the scroll of those immortals who have laid down their lives on the altar of sacrifice."

Mullá Ismá'íl was still offering his devotions when the executioner, at his request, suddenly cut short his prayer.

The deaths of the other four martyrs of Ṭihrán followed in swift succession.

For three days and three nights the bodies of these heroic men remained abandoned in the public square adjoining the imperial palace. Thousands gathered around their corpses, kicked them with their feet, and spat on their faces. They were pelted with stones, cursed, and mocked by the angry multitude. Heaps of refuse were flung upon the remains. Not one hand was raised to halt the atrocities.

The religious authorities refused to permit the bodies to be buried. They were cast into a pit outside the city, where, in a common grave, they remained as united in body as they had been in spirit when they kneeled at the headsman's feet.

One of the most significant things about these seven martyrs of Ṭihrán is that they were men representing all of the most important classes of Persian society—divines, dervishes, merchants, shopkeepers, and government officials. They were men who had enjoyed the respect and consideration of all; furthermore, they died fearlessly, willingly, almost eagerly.

The eventful day on which they were executed brought to the Báb more secret followers than many sermons could have done. The testimony of their actions and the fervor of their devotion to the Báb's Cause left a deep and lasting impression on all who were present.

Thus closes the tragic story of the lives of all but one or two of the chief disciples of the Báb. A relentless foe had struck down in swift succession Mullá Ḥusayn, Quddús, Vaḥíd, and the Báb's uncle. This same wave of hatred had also swept to destruction Ṭáhirih, Qurbán-'Alí, and Mullá Ismá'íl. The wind of death now changed direction and blew toward the Báb's prison-castle in Chihríq.

18

The Dawn and the Sun

The Dawn and the Sun

The prime minister, Mírzá Taqí Khán, dispatched orders to the governor of Ádhirbáyján for the Báb to be brought from the prison at Chihríq to Tabríz. He vowed to himself that this would be the last journey the Báb ever made on this earth. The governor, not suspecting the prime minister's intentions, sent one of his most trusted officers with a mounted escort to carry out the task.

Forty days before the arrival of that officer and his soldiers at Chihríq, the Báb collected all the documents and writings in His possession. He placed them in a chest along with His pen case, His seals, and His rings. He entrusted the box to Mullá Báqir, one of the Letters of the Living. The Báb also wrote a letter to Mírzá Aḥmad, who for a long time had served faithfully as His secretary. He put the key to the box in Mírzá Aḥmad's letter and instructed Mullá Báqir to take the utmost care of the chest and the letter. He emphasized the sacred character of this trust and told Mullá Báqir to conceal its contents from everyone except Mírzá Aḥmad.

Mullá Báqir went to Mírzá Aḥmad in Qum, where he delivered the letter and the chest to him. Mírzá Aḥmad read the letter and was deeply moved. He told his friends that he must leave at once for Ṭihrán to deliver the trust. They all feared that the end of the Báb's earthly life was nearing, and they were eager to know what was in that treasured chest. They overwhelmed Mírzá Aḥmad with entreaties until he agreed to disclose a little something of what it contained. Nabíl, the historian, was present on that occasion and witnessed the opening of that beautiful chest.

"We marvelled when we beheld, among the things which that coffer contained," he writes, "a scroll of blue paper, of the most delicate texture, on which the Báb, in His own exquisite handwriting, . . . had penned, in the form of a pentacle, what numbered about five hundred verses, all consisting of derivatives from the word *'Bahá.'**

"We were overcome with admiration as we gazed upon a masterpiece which no calligraphist, we believed, could rival. That scroll was replaced in the coffer and handed back to Mírzá Aḥmad, who, on the very day he received it, proceeded to Ṭihrán." Before Mírzá Aḥmad departed, he informed his friends that all he could divulge of that letter was the injunction that the trust was to be delivered into the hands of Mírzá Ḥusayn 'Alí in Ṭihrán.

The sight of this beautiful document caused great excitement among the followers of the Báb. They knew how often the Báb had told them to expect someone far greater than Himself soon after His passing. Was the praise of this name *"Bahá"* yet another indication of the direction they must turn?

Now that the shadow of death was hovering over Him, the Báb knew He must make clear once and for all the link that bound Him to His Successor. As disaster struck on all sides, He sought to keep alive the fading hopes of those whom He would soon leave behind.

From that very first night when He had disclosed His mission to Mullá Ḥusayn, the Báb constantly referred to the One who would come after Him. He alluded to this great event in nearly all of His writings. The Báb frequently told His followers that He, Himself, was merely the channel of grace from some great Person as yet unknown.

The Báb warned His followers against the mistake the Jews had made in refusing to accept Christ because of their under-

* Glory.

standing of the Old Testament, the mistake the Christians had made in refusing to accept Muḥammad because of their understanding of the New Testament, and the mistake the Muslims were now making in denying the Báb because of their understanding of the Qur'án. ". . . Beware, beware," He cautioned them, "that the words sent down in the Bayán [the Báb's Book] shut thee not out as by a veil from Him."*

He wrote, "I Myself am, verily, but a ring upon the hand of Him Whom God shall make manifest. . . ." "Were He to appear at this very moment, I would be the first to adore Him, and the first to bow down before Him."†

"The Bayán deriveth all its glory from 'Him Whom God shall make manifest,'" the Báb declared. "The Bayán and such as are believers therein yearn more ardently after Him than the yearning of any lover after his beloved. . . ."‡

Although this great Figure was still hidden from their eyes, the Báb promised His followers that His own Revelation was like a seed in comparison to the Revelation of the One who was to come, which would be like a mighty tree that would shelter all humanity. "The germ that holds within itself the potentialities of the Revelation that is to come," He said, "is endowed with a potency superior to the combined forces of all those who follow Me."§

Now, on a special scroll, written in His own hand, the Báb had paid a final tribute of great love and respect for the One whose name was *"Bahá."* It was no longer a vague reference or a concealed intimation, but a clear hint at the very person who

---

* The Báb, quoted in Bahá'u'lláh, *Epistle to the Son of the Wolf,* p. 153.

† The Báb, *Selections from the Writings of the Báb,* p. 168; the Báb, quoted in Bahá'u'lláh, *Epistle to the Son of the Wolf,* p. 171.

‡ The Báb, quoted in Shoghi Effendi, *The World Order of Bahá'u'lláh,* pp. 100–01.

§ Shoghi Effendi, *The World Order of Bahá'u'lláh,* p. 100.

was destined to redeem all mankind. The Báb knew that His own hour of death was drawing near.

The first meeting of the followers of the Báb at the conference of Badasht provided an intimation of the identity of *"Bahá."* Mírzá Ḥusayn 'Alí was the moving figure behind that conference at which so many of the most outstanding of the Báb's followers were present.

Nabíl, the historian, relates, "It was then the beginning of summer. Upon His arrival, [Mírzá Ḥusayn 'Alí] rented three gardens, one of which He assigned exclusively to the use of Quddús, another He set apart for Ṭáhirih and her attendant, and reserved the third for Himself. Those who had gathered in Badasht were . . . from the time of their arrival to the day of their dispersion . . . the guests of [Mírzá Ḥusayn 'Alí]. . . . Upon each He bestowed a new name. He Himself was henceforth designated by the name of Bahá; upon the last Letter of the Living was conferred the appellation of Quddús, and to Qurratu'l-'Ayn was given the title of Ṭáhirih."

The close relationship of spirit between the Báb and Bahá'u'lláh, as Mírzá Ḥusayn 'Alí would henceforth be known, is nowhere better demonstrated than at Badasht. None of those companions knew the source of the bold, defiant, and far-reaching changes in the old laws and traditions that took place there, and no one suspected that it was Bahá'u'lláh's hand that steadily and unerringly steered the course of that conference.

"To each of those who had convened at Badasht," Nabíl continues, "a special Tablet was subsequently revealed by the Báb, each of whom He addressed by the name recently conferred upon him." From that time on, they were known only by those names.

Ṭáhirih, in a daring act of liberation, removed her veil at the conference, asserting the advances in the station of women brought about by the Báb. When some of the followers later complained about Ṭáhirih's boldness, saying that she had been indiscreet to cast aside her veil, the Báb replied in these stirring words: "What am I to say regarding her whom the Tongue of Power and Glory [Bahá'u'lláh], has named Ṭáhirih [the Pure One]?"

At that same conference, Ṭáhirih concluded one of her eloquent addresses by glancing toward Bahá'u'lláh and quoting a prophetic verse from the Qur'án: "Verily, amid gardens and rivers shall the pious dwell in the seat of truth, in the presence of the potent King."*

Then Ṭáhirih declared that she was the blast of the bugle that annulled the past ages. Dr. T. K. Cheyne writes, "It is said, too, that this short speech of the brave woman was followed by the recitation by Bahá'u'lláh of the Súrih of Resurrection . . . The inner meaning of this was that mankind was about to pass into a new cosmic cycle, for which a new set of laws and customs would be indispensable."

Bahá'u'lláh arranged for the departure of the friends from Badasht, just as He had arranged for their arrival. On the way home, Ṭáhirih composed an ode each day and shared it with her companions. These verses told of the obsolete conventions, rituals, and traditions that had chained the consciences of men and women in the past, and how these fetters had at last been boldly challenged and fearlessly swept away by the meeting held at Badasht. The companions memorized the odes and chanted them in unison as they walked along together. Mountain and valley echoed with the shouts of that enthusiastic band as they hailed the extinction of the old and the birth of the new Day.

The following pages are written to show the Báb's deep awareness of the coming of "Him Whom God shall make manifest." They show how the Báb carefully prepared certain souls to

---

* Qur'án 54:54–55.

know, recognize, love, and accept Bahá'u'lláh after His own martyrdom so that the Faith of God might go on to fulfill its destiny.

During those earliest days when students of scripture in America, Europe, Asia, and Africa were expecting the advent of the Promised One, Shaykh Aḥmad and Siyyid Káẓim both repeatedly told their followers that the hour of His coming was now at hand. There would be twin Messengers in this day, they said. They would both appear in Persia. They would follow each other in rapid succession, exactly as foretold in the holy scriptures. They would be the two successive "trumpet blasts" mentioned in the Qur'án for the "last days"; the return of Elijah followed by the Lord of Hosts foretold in the Old Testament; the "second woe" and the "third woe" that would follow quickly, as promised in the Book of Revelation for the day when the Lord would come "quickly into His temple." The Báb Himself emphasized the brief time that would separate His own mission from that of the One to come after Him: "Glorified art Thou, O My God! Bear Thou witness that, through this Book, I have covenanted with all created things concerning the Mission of Him Whom Thou shalt make manifest, ere the covenant concerning Mine own Mission had been established. . . ."*

Shaykh Aḥmad and Siyyid Káẓim had promised their followers that some of them would live to see both of these Messengers of God. After the Dawn—that is, the Báb's Revelation—they were told, they would see the promised Sun—meaning the Revelation of Bahá'u'lláh.

Shaykh Aḥmad had been in Ṭihrán when Bahá'u'lláh was born in 1817. The following historical account of his visit has been preserved:

---

* The Báb, quoted in Bahá'u'lláh, *Epistle to the Son of the Wolf,* p. 160.

"Shaykh Aḥmad, who recognized in its full measure the meaning of this auspicious event [the birth of Bahá'u'lláh], yearned to spend the remaining days of his life within the precincts of the court of this Divine, this new-born King. But this was not to be. . . . His yearning unsatisfied, he felt compelled to submit to God's irrevocable decree," and turned his face away from the city.

"Ere his departure from that city, he breathed a prayer that this hidden Treasure of God, now born amongst his countrymen, might be preserved and cherished by them, that they might recognise the full measure of His blessedness and glory, and might be enabled to proclaim His excellence to all nations and peoples."

Shaykh Aḥmad considered the moment of Bahá'u'lláh's birth to be the hour foretold in the prophecy "Ere long shall ye behold the countenance of your Lord resplendent as the moon in its full glory. And yet, ye shall fail to unite in acknowledging His truth and embracing His Faith."

Shaykh Aḥmad also believed this to be the hour of fulfillment for those prophetic words, "One of the most mighty signs that shall signalise the advent of the promised Hour is this: 'A woman shall give birth to One who shall be her Lord.'"

Similar words appear in the Book of Isaiah referring to the time of the end when the promised Savior would appear: "For thy Maker is thine husband; the Lord of Hosts is His name; the God of the whole earth shall He be called."*

Shaykh Aḥmad repeatedly impressed upon his followers the certainty of the appearance of twin Messengers of God. Mírzá Maḥmúd, a follower of Shaykh Aḥmad, recalls in this eyewitness account some of the excitement of those days of expectancy:

* Isa. 54:5.

"One morning, at the hour of dawn," he said, "I found him [Shaykh Aḥmad] fallen upon his face, . . . in rapt devotion. . . . To my great surprise he turned to me and said: 'That which I have been announcing to you is now revealed. At this very hour the light of the promised One has broken and is shedding illumination upon the world. O Maḥmúd, verily I say, you shall live to behold that Day of days.'"

Sometime afterwards, while conversing with the followers of the Báb, Mírzá Maḥmúd was informed of the date of the Báb's birthday, which is October 20, 1819. He realized that the day to which Shaykh Aḥmad had referred did not correspond with this date, as there was actually a difference of two years. This puzzled him greatly.

Long afterwards, Mírzá Maḥmúd met a friend who told him of Bahá'u'lláh and shared with him some of Bahá'u'lláh's writings. He was moved to the depths of his soul.

"I asked him the date of the birth of Bahá'u'lláh," Mírzá Maḥmúd said.

His friend replied that Bahá'u'lláh had been born at dawn on the 12th of November in 1817.

"It was the very day and hour!" Mírzá Maḥmud reported. "Instinctively I fell prostrate upon the ground and exclaimed: 'Glorified art Thou, O my God, for having enabled me to attain unto this promised Day.'"

The hour of Bahá'u'lláh's birth marked the fulfillment of still another prophecy that spoke of the twin Messengers who would appear at the time of the end. It was foretold that the Herald in that day would say of Him Who was yet to come, "I am two years younger than my Lord."

Siyyid Káẓim, who succeeded Shaykh Aḥmad, continued to prepare his followers for that same approaching day. "Verily I say," he told them, "after the Qá'im [the Báb], the Qayyúm [Bahá'u'lláh] will be made manifest. For when the star of the

Former [the Báb] has set, the sun of the beauty of Ḥusayn [Bahá'u'lláh] will rise and illuminate the whole world."

There is yet another proof of the unique oneness that linked the mission of the Báb with that of Bahá'u'lláh. According to the Gregorian calendar of the West, the Báb was born on October 20, 1819, and Bahá'u'lláh was born on November 12, 1817. However, according to the Muslim calendar of the East (in Persia, the land of Their birth), Their birthdays fall on consecutive days—the first and second days of the month. These twin successive holy days are celebrated as one great, joyous festival.

Siyyid Káẓim told his followers, "What stress he [Shaykh Aḥmad] laid upon their significance as foreshadowing the advent of those twin Revelations which are to follow each other in rapid succession, and each of which is destined to suffuse the world with all its glory! How many times did he exclaim: 'Well is it with him who will recognise their significance and behold their splendour!'

"How often, addressing me," Siyyid Káẓim concluded, "did he remark: 'Neither of us shall live to gaze upon their . . . glory. But many of the faithful among your disciples shall witness the Day which we, alas, can never hope to behold!'"

When the Báb was on His way to Ṭihrán to meet the king, the prime minister gave word that He was to be turned back and sent to prison in Máh-Kú. Thus, within sight of a great victory, only thirty miles from the capital, the Báb was denied the opportunity to meet the king. In that hour of keen disappointment, a letter was delivered to the Báb at the village of Kulayn. The letter came from Bahá'u'lláh.

Nabíl, the historian, records that a man named Mullá Muḥammad had been commissioned by Bahá'u'lláh to present to the Báb a sealed letter together with certain gifts, which as soon as they were delivered into His hands, provoked in His soul sentiments of unusual delight. The Báb's face glowed with joy as He overwhelmed the bearer with indications of His gratitude and favor.

"That message," Nabíl writes, "received at an hour of uncertainty and suspense, imparted solace and strength to the Báb. It dispelled the gloom that had settled upon His heart, and imbued His soul with the certainty of victory. . . . The cry, 'Beloved, My Well-Beloved,' which in His bitter grief and loneliness He was wont to utter, gave way to expressions of thanksgiving and praise, of hope and triumph. The exultation which glowed upon His face never forsook Him until the day when the news of the great disaster which befell the heroes of Shaykh Ṭabarsí again beclouded the radiance of His countenance. . . ."

'Abdu'l-Karím, a devoted follower of the Báb, gives the following eyewitness account of an incident that took place one night during the Báb's stay at Kulayn in the time following the delivery of Bahá'u'lláh's letter:

"My companions and I were fast asleep in the vicinity of the tent of the Báb when the trampling of horsemen suddenly awakened us. We were informed that the tent of the Báb was vacant and that those who had gone out in search of Him had failed to find Him.

"We heard Muḥammad Big [the captain of the Báb's escort] remonstrate with the guards. 'Why feel disturbed?' he pleaded. 'Are not His magnanimity and nobleness of soul sufficiently established in your eyes to convince you that He will never, for the sake of His own safety, consent to involve others in embarrassment? He, no doubt, must have retired, in the silence of this moonlit night, to a place where He can seek undisturbed communion with God. He will unquestionably return to His tent. He will never desert us.'

"In his eagerness to reassure his colleagues, Muḥammad Big set out on foot along the road leading to Ṭihrán. I, too, with my companions, followed him. Shortly after, the rest of the guards were seen, each on horseback, marching behind us.

"We had covered about a maydán* when, by the dim light of the early dawn, we discerned in the distance the lonely figure of the Báb. He was coming towards us from the direction of Ṭihrán.

"'Did you believe Me to have escaped?' were His words to Muḥammad Big as He approached him.

"'Far be it from me,' was the instant reply as he flung himself at the feet of the Báb, 'to entertain such thoughts,' Muḥammad Big assured Him.

"Muḥammad Big bowed down at the feet of the Báb. He was too awed by the serene majesty which that radiant face revealed that morning to utter another word.

"A look of confidence had settled upon His countenance, His words were invested with such transcendent power, that a feeling of profound reverence wrapped our very souls. No one dared to question Him as to the cause of so remarkable a change in His speech and demeanour. Nor did He Himself choose to allay our curiosity and wonder."

Nabíl records in *The Dawn-Breakers* another time when Bahá'u'lláh wrote to the Báb. The letter was sent from Ṭihrán to the Báb while He was in prison at Chihríq. "Shortly after," Nabíl states, "a reply, penned in the Báb's own handwriting, . . . was received."

The Báb made specific promises to certain of His followers that they would meet the One whose coming He had foretold. Some of them He carefully prepared for that meeting. Mullá

* A unit of measurement, a *maydán* is a subdivision of a *farsakh*, the length of which varied in different parts of Persia according to the terrain. The local interpretation of the term was the distance that a laden mule would walk in an hour, which ranged from three to four miles.

Báqir received a letter from the Báb in which He prophesied that Mullá Báqir would meet the Promised One face to face. To Sayyáḥ, another disciple, He made the same verbal promise. To 'Aẓím the Báb wrote a special tablet in which He gave the name and foretold the approaching advent of this One whom they were all awaiting. All of the Báb's promises were fulfilled.

Shaykh Sulṭán was also one of the followers who received such a promise. He journeyed to Shíráz with a friend by the name of Shaykh Ḥasan. They were both eager to meet the Báb, but Shaykh Sulṭán fell ill before his wish was fulfilled. One night he received a message saying that the Báb had heard of his illness and would visit him after dark. Shaykh Sulṭán describes that visit in his own words:

"The Báb, who had bidden me extinguish the lamp in my room ere He arrived, came straight to my bedside. In the midst of the darkness . . . , I was holding fast to the hem of His garment and was imploring Him: '. . . allow me to sacrifice myself for Thee; for no one else except Thee is able to confer upon me this favour.'

"'O Shaykh!' the Báb replied, '. . . It behoves us both to cling to the garment of the Best-Beloved and to seek from Him the joy and glory of martyrdom in His path. Rest assured I will, in your behalf, supplicate the Almighty to enable you to attain His presence. Remember Me on that Day, a Day such as the world has never seen before.'

"The allusion of the Báb that night to His 'Best-Beloved' excited my wonder and curiosity. . . . I was sorely perplexed and knew not how to unravel this mystery. When I reached Karbilá and attained the presence of Bahá'u'lláh, I became firmly convinced that He alone could claim such affection from the Báb, that He, and only He, could be worthy of such adoration."

Shaykh Sulṭán's companion on that trip to Shíráz, Shaykh Ḥasan, was given the same promise by the Báb. He has testified to that promise in the following account:

"Addressing me one day, He said: '. . . You should proceed to Karbilá and should abide in that holy city, inasmuch as you are destined to behold, with your own eyes, the beauteous countenance of the Promised Ḥusayn. As you gaze upon that radiant face, do also remember Me. Convey to Him the expression of My loving devotion.' He again emphatically added these words: 'Verily, I say, I have entrusted you with a great mission. Beware lest your heart grow faint, lest you forget the glory with which I have invested you.'

"Soon after, I journeyed to Karbilá and lived, as bidden, in that holy city. . . . What afflictions befell me at the hands of the Shaykhís, those who professed to be the followers of Shaykh Aḥmad and yet failed to recognise the Báb! . . . I patiently submitted to the indignities inflicted upon me. For two years I lived in that city. . . .

". . . while I was passing by the gate of the inner courtyard of the shrine of the Imám Ḥusayn,* my eyes, for the first time, fell upon Bahá'u'lláh. What shall I recount regarding the countenance which I beheld? The beauty of that face, those exquisite features which no pen or brush dare describe, His penetrating glance, His kindly face, the majesty of His bearing, the sweetness of His smile, the luxuriance of His jet-black flowing locks, all left an indelible impression upon my soul. . . .

"How lovingly He advanced towards me! He took me by the hand and, in a tone which at once betrayed power and beauty, addressed me. . . . He walked with me all along the market-street, and in the end He said: 'Praise be to God that

* In Shí'ah Islam, the Third Imám, son of 'Alí and Fáṭimih, grandson of the Prophet Muḥammad.

you have remained in Karbilá, and have beheld with your own eyes the countenance of the Promised Ḥusayn.'

"I recalled instantly the promise which had been given me by the Báb. His words, which I had regarded as referring to a remote future, I had not shared with anyone. These words of Bahá'u'lláh moved me to the depths of my being. I felt impelled to proclaim to a heedless people, at that very moment and with all my soul and power, the advent of the promised Ḥusayn.

"He bade me, however, repress my feelings and conceal my emotions. 'Not yet,' He breathed into my ears; 'the appointed Hour is approaching. It has not yet struck. Rest assured and be patient.'

"From that moment all my sorrows vanished. My soul was flooded with joy. In those days I was so poor that most of the time I hungered for food. I felt so rich, however, that all the treasures of the earth melted away into nothingness when compared with that which I already possessed. . . ."

From that day, October 5, 1851, Shaykh Ḥasan became magnetized by the charm of his newly found Master, and, but for Bahá'u'lláh's restraint, would have proclaimed to all that the One promised by the Báb had already appeared.

In the city of Baghdád, only a short distance from Karbilá, Bahá'u'lláh was soon to make the same public declaration to His followers that the Báb had made to His disciples in Shíráz. This was the meaning hidden in that prophecy quoted to Mullá Ḥusayn by the Báb Himself on the roof of the prison-castle of Máh-Kú: "Shíráz will be thrown into a tumult; a Youth of sugar-tongue will appear. I fear lest the breath of His mouth should agitate and upset Baghdád."

There was a constant link between the Báb and Bahá'u'lláh through the Báb's disciples, especially those whose tragic story has been told in the preceding chapters. Bahá'u'lláh played a vital and moving part in the tale of Shaykh Ṭabarsí, Nayríz, Ṭihrán, and the conference of Badasht, as well as in the lives of Mullá Ḥusayn, Quddús, Vaḥíd, and Ṭáhirih.

When the Báb bade Mullá Ḥusayn farewell in Shíráz before leaving for Mecca to announce His mission, He spoke the following words to him:

". . . Follow the course of your journey towards the north, and visit on your way Iṣfahán, Káshán, Qum, and Ṭihrán. Beseech almighty Providence that He may graciously enable you to attain, in that capital, the seat of true sovereignty, and to enter the mansion of the Beloved. A secret lies hidden in that city. When made manifest, it shall turn the earth into paradise. My hope is that you may partake of its grace and recognise its splendour. . . ."

To soften the blow of disappointment for Mullá Ḥusayn at being left behind, the Báb once again emphasized the importance of Ṭihrán and of Mullá Ḥusayn's visit there. "Grieve not that you have not been chosen to accompany Me. . . . I shall, instead, direct your steps to that city which enshrines a Mystery of such transcendent holiness as neither Ḥijáz nor Shíráz can hope to rival."*

Mullá Ḥusayn reached Ṭihrán. He spent the daylight hours teaching the message of the Báb, but from sunset to dawn he remained alone in his room, most likely in prayer and meditation, beseeching God to disclose to him this holy mystery of which the Báb had spoken and to lead him to the "Mansion" of the Promised One yet to come.

---

* *Ḥijáz* refers to western Arabia, which is associated with the life of the Prophet Muḥammad and is home to the holy cities of Mecca and Medina. Mecca is the site of the Ka'bih, the holiest spot in Islam, which was constructed by Abraham. Shíráz is the birthplace of the Báb.

Mullá Ḥusayn met Mullá Muḥammad of Núr at this time. Mullá Ḥusayn asked him if he knew of anyone from the family of the late Mírzá Buzurg of Núr—a man renowned for his character, his charm, and his artistic and intellectual attainments—who was particularly distinguished above others.

"Yea, among his sons now living, one has distinguished Himself by the very traits which characterized His father," Mullá Muḥammad told him. "By His virtuous life, His high attainments, His loving-kindness and liberality, He has proved Himself a noble descendant of a noble father."

"What is His occupation?" Mullá Ḥusayn asked.

"He cheers the disconsolate and feeds the hungry."

"What of His rank and position?"

"He has none apart from befriending the poor and the stranger."

"What is His name?" Mullá Ḥusayn asked.

"Ḥusayn-'Alí."

"What is His age?"

"Eight and twenty."

The eagerness with which Mullá Ḥusayn questioned Mullá Muḥammad and the sense of delight with which he welcomed every detail given to him greatly surprised Mullá Muḥammad.

Beaming with satisfaction and joy, Mullá Ḥusayn once more inquired, "I presume you often meet him?"

"I frequently visit His home."

"Will you deliver into His hands a trust from me?"

Mullá Ḥusayn then gave Mullá Muḥammad a scroll of the Báb's writings.

"Should He deign to answer me," Mullá Ḥusayn added, "will you be kind enough to acquaint me with His reply?"

Mullá Muḥammad took the scroll the next morning at dawn to Bahá'u'lláh. Bahá'u'lláh—still known as Mírzá Ḥusayn 'Ali at this time—accepted it and bade Mullá Muḥammad be seated.

He unfolded the scroll, glanced at its contents, and began reading parts of it aloud to those who were present. He stopped reading and turned to His friends.

"Verily," He said, "I say, whoso believes in the Qur'án and recognises its Divine origin, and yet hesitates, though it be for a moment, to admit that these soul-stirring words are endowed with the same regenerating power, has most assuredly erred in his judgment and strayed far from the path of justice."

Bahá'u'lláh gave a gift to Mullá Muḥammad to bring to Mullá Ḥusayn. It was a small gift of Russian sugar and tea. He asked that His appreciation and love be conveyed to Mullá Ḥusayn along with the gift.

Mullá Ḥusayn received the gifts with great joy and exultation. Mullá Muḥammad reported, "Words fail me to describe the intensity of his emotion. He started to his feet, received with bowed head the gift from my hand, and fervently kissed it."

Mullá Ḥusayn embraced Mullá Muḥammad and kissed his eyes, which had so recently gazed upon Bahá'u'lláh.

"My dearly beloved friend!" he exclaimed. "I pray that even as you have rejoiced my heart, God may grant you eternal felicity and fill your heart with imperishable gladness."

Mullá Muḥammad was puzzled. He wondered what kind of bond united these two souls. What could have kindled such a fellowship between strangers? And why should Mullá Ḥusayn, who considered riches and fame as the merest trifles, have shown such gladness at the sight of this tiny gift from the hands of Bahá'u'lláh? He could not fathom this mystery.

A few days later Mullá Ḥusayn left for Khurásán. As he said farewell to Mullá Muḥammad he warned him, "Breathe not to anyone what you have heard and witnessed. Let this be a secret hidden within your breast. Divulge not His name, for they who envy His position will arise to harm Him. . . . Pray that the Almighty may protect Him, that, through Him, He may exalt the downtrodden, enrich the poor, and redeem the fallen. The secret of this thing is concealed from our eyes. Ours is the duty to raise the call of the New Day and to proclaim this Divine Message unto all people.

"Many a soul," Mullá Ḥusayn concluded, "will, in this city, shed his blood in this path. That blood will water the Tree of God, will cause it to flourish, and to overshadow all mankind."

With these parting words, Mullá Ḥusayn left Ṭihrán. He wrote a report to the Báb, telling Him of his teaching work and describing to Him his experience with Bahá'u'lláh in Ṭihrán. Quddús and the Báb's uncle were both with the Báb when that letter from Mullá Ḥusayn arrived. The Báb's uncle has left an account of that moment:

"That night," he said, "I saw such evidences of joy and gladness on the faces of the Báb and of Quddús as I am unable to describe. I often heard the Báb, in those days, exultingly repeat the words, 'How marvellous, how exceedingly marvellous, is that which has occurred between the months of Jamádí and Rajab!'*

"As He was reading the communication addressed to Him by Mullá Ḥusayn, He turned to Quddús and, showing him certain passages of that letter, explained the reason for His joyous expressions of surprise."

The Báb's uncle told his fellow companions what he had witnessed that night. He also mentioned the Báb's reference to the wonder of the days between Jamádí and Rajab. This impressed Mírzá Aḥmad, who waited until Mullá Ḥusayn returned to Shíráz to ask him what had happened at that particular time.

Mullá Ḥusayn smiled and said he remembered well that between the months of Jamádí and Rajab he happened to be in Ṭihrán.

---

* Months of the Muslim lunar calendar.

He would give no further explanation. "This was sufficient, however," he said, "to convince me that in the city of Ṭihrán there lay hidden a Mystery which, when revealed to the world, would bring unspeakable joy to the hearts of both the Báb and Quddús."

Mullá Ḥusayn met Bahá'u'lláh a second time just before he began his journey on foot to the Báb's prison in Máh-Kú. He was ushered with secrecy into the presence of Bahá'u'lláh, and shortly after this interview, Mullá Ḥusayn set out for his last visit with the Báb. From Máh-Kú he returned yet another time to the presence of Bahá'u'lláh. Their last meeting was inside the fort of Shaykh Ṭabarsí.

Quddús also knew the joy of meeting Bahá'u'lláh. When the Báb and Quddús returned from Medina to Búshihr, the Báb sent Quddús to Shíráz. He said to him in parting, ". . . In the streets of Shíráz, indignities will be heaped upon you, and the severest injuries will afflict your body. You will survive the ignominious behavior of your foes, and will attain the presence of Him who is the one object of our adoration and love. In His presence you will forget all the harm and disgrace that shall have befallen you. . . ."

Quddús suffered greatly in Shíráz. From there he went to Ṭihrán, where he was admitted into the presence of Bahá'u'lláh, and all of the Báb's promises came true.

Quddús and Bahá'u'lláh met again at the conference of Badasht. When Bahá'u'lláh was informed of Quddús's arrival at a town near Badasht, He set out on horseback to meet him. They returned to Badasht together the next morning at sunrise.

Shortly after this conference, when Quddús and a party of the followers of the Báb were being ruthlessly attacked, Bahá'u'lláh came to their rescue. He immediately gave His protection to Quddús. He clothed Quddús in His own garments to disguise him so that he would not be recognized, then sent him to a place of safety.

When Quddús was imprisoned in Sárí by Muḥammad Taqí, it was Bahá'u'lláh who was responsible for securing his release so that Quddús might join Mullá Ḥusayn at the fort of Shaykh Ṭabarsí. Bahá'u'lláh Himself then visited them there.

The night before Mullá Ḥusayn and his group arrived at Shaykh Ṭabarsí, the guardian of the shrine dreamed that a holy man, accompanied by seventy-two warriors and a large company of his friends, came and fought valiantly and triumphantly. He dreamed that the Prophet of God, Himself, came one night and visited that blessed company.

Soon after this Bahá'u'lláh arrived at a nearby village. He sent word to Mullá Ḥusayn that he and all his companions were to be His guests that night, and that He would join them at the fort of Shaykh Ṭabarsí that very afternoon. The following is an eyewitness account of that meeting:

"The tidings . . . imparted an indefinable joy to the heart of Mullá Ḥusayn. He hastened immediately to his companions and bade them bestir themselves for the reception of Bahá'u'lláh. He himself joined them in sweeping and sprinkling with water the dusty approaches to the shrine, and attended . . . to whatever was necessary for the arrival of the beloved Visitor. As soon as he saw Him approaching . . . , he rushed forward, tenderly embraced Him, and conducted Him to the place of honour. . . . We were too blind in those days to recognise the glory of Him whom our leader had introduced with such reverence and love into our midst. What Mullá Ḥusayn had perceived, our dull vision was yet unable to recognise. With what solicitude he received Him in his arms! What feelings of rapturous delight filled his heart on seeing Him! He was so lost in admiration that he was utterly oblivious of us all. His soul was so wrapt in contemplation of that countenance that we who were awaiting his permission to be seated were kept standing a long time beside him. It was Bahá'u'lláh Himself who finally bade us be seated. We, too, were soon made to feel . . . the charm of His utterance. . . ."

Bahá'u'lláh examined the fort, then assisted the companions with suggestions on how to strengthen their defenses to help protect their lives. He dispelled their fears and raised their determination to sacrifice all for God.

Bahá'u'lláh said, "The one thing this fort and company require is the presence of Quddús. His association with this company would render it complete and perfect." He instructed Mullá Ḥusayn to send seven friends to Sárí to demand that Muḥammad-Taqí deliver Quddús into their hands. Mullá Ḥusayn and his companions were surprised, knowing that Quddús was being held prisoner. Bahá'u'lláh assured them, "The fear of God and the dread of His punishment will prompt him to surrender unhesitatingly his captive."

Before Bahá'u'lláh left Ṭabarsí, He told the friends to be patient and resigned to the Will of God. "If it be His will, We shall once again visit you at this same spot, and shall lend you Our assistance. . . ."

Mullá Ḥusayn sent seven of his companions to Sárí with Bahá'u'lláh's message. Muḥammad-Taqí released Quddús at once, to the astonishment of all.

Mullá Ḥusayn's companions were deeply moved by the effect of Bahá'u'lláh's presence upon them all. One of them has left this memory of Mullá Ḥusayn's reaction to that visit:

". . . I can still remember him [Mullá Ḥusayn] as he advanced towards me, in the stillness of those dark and lonely hours which I devoted to meditation and prayer, whispering in my ears these words: 'Banish from your mind . . . ,' he told me, 'these perplexing subtleties . . . arise and seek with me to quaff the cup of martyrdom. Then you will be able to comprehend, as the year '80* dawns upon the world, the secret of the things which now lie hidden from you.'"

Bahá'u'lláh's guiding hand constantly reached out to assist the companions of the Báb. Ṭáhirih, perhaps more than any other disciple, was indebted to Him for His protection and kindness.

When she was imprisoned in Qazvín and threatened with hot irons, she boldly declared to her captor, "If my Cause be the Cause of Truth, if the Lord whom I worship be none other than the one true God, He will, ere nine days have elapsed, deliver me from the yoke of your tyranny."

It was Bahá'u'lláh who rescued Ṭáhirih from her prison in Qazvín. When He heard of her captivity, He sent a woman disguised as a beggar to the home where Ṭáhirih was confined. He instructed that she deliver a letter to Ṭáhirih, who would then of her own will, unmolested by her captors, walk out free from that prison-house. The woman disguised as a beggar was instructed to await Ṭáhirih's appearance at the entrance.

"As soon as Ṭáhirih has joined you," Bahá'u'lláh informed this messenger, "start immediately for Ṭihrán. This very night, I shall despatch to the neighborhood of the gate of Qazvín an attendant, with three horses, that you will take with you and station at a place that you will appoint outside the walls of Qazvín. You will conduct Ṭáhirih to that spot, will mount the horses, and will, by an unfrequented route, endeavour to reach at daybreak the outskirts of the capital. As soon as the gates are opened, you must enter the city and proceed immediately to My house. You should exercise the utmost caution lest her identity be disclosed."

---

* Refers to the year 1280 A.H., or A.D. 1863–64, in which Bahá'u'lláh declared His mission in Baghdád.

Bahá'u'lláh reassured the worried messenger, who felt that such a delivery would require a miracle, "The Almighty will assuredly guide your steps and will surround you with His unfailing protection."

Nabíl writes, "The hour which Ṭáhirih had fixed for her deliverance found her already securely established under the sheltering shadow of Bahá'u'lláh. She knew full well into whose presence she had been admitted; she was profoundly aware of the sacredness of the hospitality she had been so graciously accorded." She perceived through her own intuitive knowledge the future glory of Bahá'u'lláh.

"I have myself been shown in Ṭihrán," Nabíl affirms, ". . . the verses which she, in her own handwriting, had penned, every letter of which bore eloquent testimony to her faith in the exalted Missions of both the Báb and Bahá'u'lláh."

Bahá'u'lláh rescued Ṭáhirih another time immediately after the conference of Badas͟ht. On the way to their homes, the party had stopped in the village of Níyálá. They were camped at the foot of a mountain when suddenly at the hour of dawn, they were awakened by a shower of stones. The people of the village were hurling rocks at them from the top of the mountain. The attack was unexpected and fierce. The cries of the mob, the sound of the rolling rocks and showering stones alarmed the friends, and they fled for safety.

Bahá'u'lláh found Ṭáhirih in grave danger. She and one believer from S͟hípráz had been unable to escape. The enemy had demolished the camp and was plundering the property. The follower from S͟híráz was already badly wounded but was risking his life to defend what remained of the companions' possessions.

Bahá'u'lláh walked into the crowd of attackers armed only with the sword of His tongue. He convinced them of the cruelty and shamefulness of their behavior and induced them to restore the property that they had not yet carried off. He rescued Ṭáhirih from their hands and escorted her to a place of safety.

Nabíl writes of these frequent victories that Bahá'u'lláh won by His word alone: "All classes of men marvelled at His miraculous success in emerging unscathed from the most perilous encounters. Nothing short of Divine protection, they thought, could have ensured His safety on such occasions."

Bahá'u'lláh also lent His strength and assistance to Vaḥíd. The following is a historical account of their friendship:

"[Vaḥíd] hastened to the capital and undertook the necessary preparations for his journey to the fort of Ṭabarsí. He was preparing to leave, when Bahá'u'lláh arrived from Mázindarán and informed him of the impossibility of joining his brethren. He was greatly saddened at the news, and his only consolation in those days was to visit Bahá'u'lláh frequently, and to obtain the benefit of His wise and priceless counsels."

It was following these visits with Bahá'u'lláh that one of Vaḥíd's friends wrote, ". . . I observed in his [Vaḥíd's] august countenance the signs of a glory and power which I had not noticed during my first journey with him to the capital, nor on other occasions of meeting. . . ."

The companion, Sayyáḥ, whom the Báb commissioned to go to Ṭabarsí and Bárfurúsh on His behalf, and to bring back some of the holy earth that covered the remains of Mullá Ḥusayn and Quddús, visited Bahá'u'lláh before returning to the Báb's prison of Chihríq. Vaḥíd was an honored guest of Bahá'u'lláh at the time of Sayyáḥ's coming.

Sayyáḥ appeared at Bahá'u'lláh's door in the bitter cold of winter. He was barefooted, poorly clad, and disheveled. Vaḥíd was told of Sayyáḥ's arrival from Ṭabarsí. Completely oblivious of the dignity and honor to which a man of his position and fame was accustomed, Vaḥíd rushed forward to meet him and threw himself at Sayyáḥ's feet. He embraced his legs, which were covered to the knees with mud from the earth of Ṭabarsí.

It was to this same Sayyáḥ that Bahá'u'lláh gave a letter to take to the Báb at Chihríq. Shortly afterward a reply came from the prison in the Báb's own handwriting.

Bahá'u'lláh overwhelmed Sayyáḥ with His kindness during this visit and showered the same love upon Vaḥíd. The brother of Bahá'u'lláh has said, "I was amazed that day at the many evidences of loving solicitude which Bahá'u'lláh evinced towards Vaḥíd. He showed him such favors as I had never seen Him extend to anyone. The manner of His conversation left no doubt in me that this same Vaḥíd would ere long distinguish himself by deeds no less remarkable than those which had immortalised the defenders of the fort of Ṭabarsí."

Following this final visit to Bahá'u'lláh's home, Vaḥíd set out on his last journey to Yazd and Nayríz, where he eventually laid down his life for his faith.

The same love and encouragement that Bahá'u'lláh gave to Vaḥíd was bestowed on Ḥujjat of the city of Zanján in the north. Ḥujjat was the hero of the most violent upheaval of all. In the village of Zanján, nearly two thousand followers of the Báb, including Ḥujjat, gave up their lives. When the Báb had passed through Zanján on His way to prison, He foretold this disaster, saying, "This town will be thrown into a great tumult, and its streets will run with blood."

The Báb's prediction came true, and the much-loved Ḥujjat, along with many of his companions, was besieged by a host of soldiers in Zanján. The governor of Zanján sent a crier through the streets saying that all who threw in their lot with Ḥujjat would be endangering their own lives, forfeiting their property, and exposing their wives and children to misery and shame.

This warning divided the city into two camps—those who believed in the Báb and those who did not. There were pathetic sights of families being separated by their belief or lack of belief in the Báb. Fathers turned away from their sons, wives from their husbands, children from their mothers. Every tie of worldly affection seemed to be dissolved on that day. Zanján became a city of panic. Men ran frantically to and fro, trying to collect their wives and children and to persuade them to stand with them. Families divided their belongings and their children. Many wept over what they had to abandon. Whole houses were deserted. When a man, a woman, or a child would tear himself or herself from family and friends and rush to the support of Ḥujjat, a cry of joy would go up from one camp, and a moan of despair from the other.

It was such a day as foretold by Christ regarding the days of the end, when "brother shall deliver up the brother to death, and the father the child: and the children shall rise up against their parents, and cause them to be put to death."*

This was the day similarly prophesied by Muḥammad, the day on which "man shall fly from his brother, and his mother and his father, and his wife and his children."†

One night during the struggle at Zanján, the followers of the Báb carried out His instructions to repeat the following praises of the Almighty:

"God the Great!"

"God the Most Great!"

"God the Most Beauteous!"

"God the Most Glorious!"

"God the Most Pure!"

In unison they repeated these phrases over and over.

"So loud and compelling was that cry," a historical account states, "that the enemy was rudely awakened from sleep, aban-

---

* Matt. 10:21.

† Qur'án 80:34.

doned the camp in horror, and, hurrying to the environs of the governor's residence, sought shelter in the neighbouring houses. A few were so shocked with terror that they instantly dropped dead."

Part of the soldiers' camp was in the midst of noisy revelry. Their boisterous party was suddenly interrupted by the shouts of those voices raised in praise of God. Officers who were holding their wine glasses in their hands dropped them instantly. Men and women rushed headlong from the building as if stunned by the outcry. Gambling tables were overturned in the disorder that followed. Half dressed, a number ran out into the wilderness. Others fled to the homes of the religious leaders.

As soon as the camp discovered that it was not a dreadful attack being launched against them, but words of praise being raised to the glory of God, they returned to their posts and pleasures, reassured, though greatly humiliated by this experience.

Ḥujjat had boldly testified in the presence of the king, the prime minister, and the assembled priests and other religious leaders that the Báb was the Promised One.

"It is my firm and unalterable conviction," he told them, "that this Siyyid of Shíráz [the Báb] is the very One whose advent you yourself, with all the peoples of the world, are eagerly awaiting. He is our Lord, our promised Deliverer." Furthermore, he said, "God knows that if this same Siyyid were to entrust me with the meanest service in His household, I would deem it an honour such as the highest favours of my sovereign could never hope to surpass."

Ḥujjat returned to his home urging everyone to accept the Báb. "The goal for which the world has been striving is now here . . ." he told them. "The sun of Truth has risen. . . . Fix your eyes upon the Báb, not upon me, the least of His slaves.

My wisdom compared to His is as an unlighted candle to the sun at midday. . . ."

Shortly before his death, Ḥujjat was grievously wounded by a stray bullet. His wife and child were slain before his eyes. Though filled with the greatest grief, he refused to yield to complete sorrow. He would not permit himself to become one who begs for this world's favors. He cried out in his pain, "The day whereon I found Thy beloved One, O my God, . . . I foresaw the woes that I should suffer for Thee. Great as have been until now my sorrows, they can never compare with the agonies that I would willingly suffer in Thy name.

"How can this miserable life of mine, the loss of my wife and of my child, and the sacrifice of the band of my kindred and companions, compare with the blessings which the recognition of Thy Manifestation has bestowed on me! Would that a myriad lives were mine, would that I possessed the riches of the whole earth and its glory, that I might resign them all freely and joyously in Thy path."

Gobineau writes, "I have seen at Zanján the ruins of that fierce encounter; whole sections of the city have not yet been rebuilt and probably never will be."

Nicolas testifies that the entire affair was settled by the same treachery resorted to at Shaykh Ṭabarsí and Nayríz. He summarizes the attitude of Ḥujjat's enemies: "Why not resort to deceit? Why not make the most sacred promises, even though it might later become necessary to massacre those gullibles who had put their trust in them?"

No wonder that the Báb named Zanján "The Exalted Spot."

When, at Chihríq in the summer of 1848, the Báb revealed the "Sermon of Wrath," which foretold the downfall of the prime minister Ḥájí Mírzá Áqásí, it was given to Ḥujjat to deliver. The Báb instructed Ḥujjat to place it personally in the hands of that official.

Immediately after delivering the letter to Ḥájí Mírzá Áqásí, Ḥujjat went to the home of Bahá'u'lláh. Having memorized the entire contents of the document, Ḥujjat recounted the circumstances of its delivery to the prime minister and recited it for Bahá'u'lláh and a few other believers. Ḥujjat's sole comfort in those days was his close association with Bahá'u'lláh, from whom he received the sustaining power that was to enable him to distinguish himself by remarkable deeds in the days to come.

From Bahá'u'lláh's home, Ḥujjat went to Zanján, where he—like his illustrious companions Vaḥíd, Ṭáhirih, Mullá Ḥusayn, and Quddús—laid down his life for the sake of his beliefs.

From the very first moment when the Báb had revealed the commentary for Mullá Ḥusayn on the eve of May 23, 1844, He linked His own Mission with that of Bahá'u'lláh. Nabíl states in his history, "Did not the Báb, in the earliest days of His Mission, allude, in the opening passages of . . . His commentary on the Súrih of Joseph, to the glory and significance of the Revelation of Bahá'u'lláh? Was it not His purpose, by dwelling upon the ingratitude and malice which characterised the treatment of Joseph by his brethren, to predict what Bahá'u'lláh was destined to suffer at the hands of His brother and kindred?"

In His farewell address to the Letters of the Living, the Báb stated clearly that He was but the forerunner of a greater One yet to come.

"I am preparing you for the advent of a mighty Day . . . ," He told them in that parting message. "Scatter throughout the length and breadth of this land, and, with steadfast feet and sanctified hearts, prepare the way for His coming."

Dr. T. K. Cheyne points out how plainly the lives of the Báb and Bahá'u'lláh were woven together during those days for anyone who had eyes to see.

"The end of the Báb's earthly Manifestation is now close upon us," Dr. Cheyne writes. "He knew it himself before the event, and was not displeased at the presentiment. He had already 'set his house in order,' as regards the spiritual affairs of the Bábí community, which he had, if I mistake not, confided to the intuitive wisdom of Bahá'u'lláh. . . ."

The Báb also instructed His disciples to record the names of every individual who accepted the new Faith. "Of all these believers I shall make mention in the Tablet of God," He told them, "so that upon each one of them the Beloved of our hearts may, in the Day when He shall have ascended the throne of glory, confer His inestimable blessings. . . ."

It was from the names of these believers that the first followers of Bahá'u'lláh came, and upon whom He conferred His special blessings and love.

The Báb did everything in His power to assist His followers so that they would know where to turn after His own death. He clearly announced that He was the Promised One, but that He stood in relation to a succeeding and greater One as did John the Baptist in relation to Jesus Christ. He was the Forerunner of One yet more mighty than Himself. Just as John the Baptist had been the Herald, or Gate, of the Christ, so was the Báb the Herald, or Gate, of Bahá'u'lláh.

"Consecrate Thou, O My God, the whole of this Tree unto Him . . . ," He wrote of Bahá'u'lláh. "I have not wished that this Tree should ever bear any branch, leaf, or fruit that would fail to bow down before Him, on the day of His Revelation. . . . And shouldst Thou behold, O my God, any branch, leaf, or fruit upon Me that hath failed to bow down before Him, on the day of His Revelation, cut it off, O My God, from that Tree, for it is not of Me. . . ."

"Ere nine [years] will have elapsed from the inception of this Cause," the Báb wrote in another place, even pointing out the exact year of Bahá'u'lláh's coming, "the realities of the created things will not be made manifest. . . . Be patient, until thou beholdest a new creation." "In the year nine ye will attain unto all good." "In the year nine ye will attain unto the presence of God."

Before nine years had elapsed, in fact during the course of the ninth year (1853), Bahá'u'lláh's mission began, thus fulfilling not only the promise of the Báb and that of Shaykh Aḥmad and Siyyid Káẓim, but also the Islamic tradition that said, "In the year . . . [1844] the earth shall be illumined by His light. . . . If thou livest until the year . . . [1853], thou shalt witness how the nations, the rulers, the peoples, and the Faith of God shall have been renewed."

The Báb's challenging words written at Máh-Kú seal forever the bond that unites Him with Bahá'u'lláh: "Well is it with him who fixeth his gaze upon the Order of Bahá'u'lláh, and rendereth thanks unto his Lord. For He will assuredly be made manifest."*

"I, verily, am a believer in Him," the Báb declares to the world, "and in His Faith, and in His Book, and in His Testimonies, and in His Ways, and in all that proceedeth from Him concerning them."†

Bahá'u'lláh, on His part, had such a love for the Báb that He would not let Him suffer any pain, indignity, or humiliation in which He, Bahá'u'lláh, did not share.

The Báb was first confined in the house of the chief constable of Shíráz. Shortly after this Bahá'u'lláh was confined in the house of one of the religious leaders of Ṭihrán. The Báb's second imprisonment was in the castle of Máh-Kú; that of Bahá'u'lláh followed when He was imprisoned in the residence of the governor of Ámul. The Báb was scourged in the prayer-house of the high priest in Tabríz. The very same punishment

---

* The Báb, quoted in Bahá'u'lláh, *The Kitáb-i-Aqdas*, n189.

† The Báb, quoted in Bahá'u'lláh, *Epistle to the Son of the Wolf*, p. 154.

was inflicted shortly after this upon Bahá'u'lláh in the prayer-house of a religious leader in Ámul. The Báb's third imprisonment was in the castle of Chihríq; that of Bahá'u'lláh followed in the "Black Pit" dungeon of Ṭihrán. The Báb was struck in the face with missiles in the streets of Tabríz. Bahá'u'lláh was pelted with stones and struck in the face with a rock on His way to prison in Ṭihrán. The Báb was slain in the public square of Tabríz. Bahá'u'lláh underwent nearly half a century of living martyrdom. He was exiled and imprisoned for forty years. He was set upon by assassins in Baghdád. He was poisoned in Adrianople. To His grave Bahá'u'lláh carried the scars of the enormous prison chains that had torn the flesh from His shoulders.

Nabíl recounts in his history, "The Báb, whose trials and sufferings had preceded, in almost every case, those of Bahá'u'lláh, had offered Himself to ransom His Beloved from the perils that beset that precious Life; whilst Bahá'u'lláh, on His part, unwilling that He who so greatly loved Him should be the sole Sufferer, shared at every turn the cup that had touched His [the Báb's] lips.

"Such love no eye has ever beheld, nor has mortal heart conceived such mutual devotion. If the branches of every tree were turned into pens, and all the seas into ink, and earth and heaven rolled into one parchment, the immensity of that love would still remain unexplored, and the depths of that devotion unfathomed."

Their missions were bound together for eternity.

Thus it was that the Báb was able to leave the prison of Chihríq in peace and with eagerness to begin what He knew would be His last journey on this earth. He had fulfilled His task. He was the Dawn, and He had faithfully prepared His followers for the coming of the Sun itself.

"I, verily, have not fallen short of My duty to admonish that people, and to devise means whereby they may turn towards

God . . . ," He said. "If, on the day of His Revelation, all that are on earth bear Him allegiance, Mine inmost being will rejoice, inasmuch as all will have attained the summit of their existence, and will have been brought face to face with their Beloved . . . I truly have nurtured all things for this purpose. How, then, can anyone be veiled from Him?" "I have educated all men, that they may recognize this Revelation. . . ."*

The Báb's heart was turned toward Ṭihrán and Bahá'u'lláh when He wrote the following words, which foreshadow the hours that were fast sweeping down upon Him: "I have sacrificed Myself wholly for Thee: I have accepted curses for Thy sake, and have yearned for naught but martyrdom in the path of Thy love."†

The soldiers bearing the prime minister's fatal edict calling for His execution were already at the gates of the prison-castle of Chihríq. The Báb, confident that He had expended every effort in the path of God, had already sent His writings, His pen-case, His seals, and His ring to Bahá'u'lláh, along with a beautiful scroll praising and glorifying His name.

Now He calmly awaited His escort of death.

---

* The Báb, quoted in Bahá'u'lláh, *Epistle to the Son of the Wolf,* pp. 156, 157.

† The Báb, quoted in Shoghi Effendi, *The World Order of Bahá'u'lláh,* p. 101.

19

The Martyrdom of the Báb

The Martyrdom of the Báb

A wave of violence unprecedented in its cruelty, its persistence, and its breadth swept the face of the entire land. From the province of Khurásán on the eastern border of Persia to the city of Tabríz on the west, from the northern cities of Zanján and Ṭihrán stretching as far south as Nayríz, the country was enveloped in darkness. These events brought validity to the prophecy of Shaykh Aḥmad, who had spoken so glowingly of the twin Revelations that were at hand. He had warned his followers to expect these days of suffering. He is reported to have said, "Pray that you may not be present at the beginning of the Manifestation and of the Return, as there will be many civil wars." He added, "If any one of you should still be living at that time, he shall see strange things between the years sixty [1844] and sixty-seven [1851]. . . ."

Nicolas in his account of those days writes, ". . . the Mullás, deeply concerned, feeling that their wavering flock was ready to escape their control, multiplied their slanders and defamation; the grossest lies, the most cruel fictions were circulated among the bewildered masses, divided between terror and admiration."

When news of the death of His beloved uncle reached the Báb and He heard the moving account of the tragic fate of the seven followers who had been martyred in Ṭihrán, His heart was plunged into deep sorrow.

He wrote a special tribute in their honor, testifying to the exalted position they occupied in His eyes. The Báb said that these seven heroes were the "Seven Goats," spoken of in the traditions of Islam, who on the Day of Judgment would "walk in front of" the Promised One.

It was at this moment that the prime minister, Mírzá Taqí Khán, issued the command that brought the Báb out of His prison cell in Chihríq. The prime minister had at last decided to strike at the very head of the religion. The king's army and the members of the clergy were suffering humiliating defeats all across the land. Remove the Báb, the prime minister thought, and order could be restored. He called his counselors together and unfolded to them a plan.

This was a drastic change from the prime minister's original plan. Until now, Mírzá Táqí Khán had felt that the most effective way to destroy the Báb's influence would be to ruin Him morally. Now he planned to bring the Báb out of Chihríq, where, despite His imprisonment and suffering, His holiness and eloquence made him radiate like a sun. Mírzá Táqí Khán intended to show Him to the people, exposing Him as a charlatan and a weak dreamer who did not have the courage to conceive, let alone direct or take part in, the daring enterprises that had occurred at Shaykh Ṭabarsí, Nayríz, and Zanján.

However, the Báb's conduct while He was in prison gave no evidence that He was such a person as the prime minister suggested. He bore all hardships without complaint. He prayed and worked incessantly. Those who came near Him felt the power of His personality. Did they not have the alarming example of what had happened with the two wardens of Máh-Kú and Chihríq? Both men had been bitter enemies of the Báb initially, but through His mere presence among them, they had become enraptured friends.

Had not the authorities sent the greatest religious leader of them all, Vaḥíd, to investigate and discredit the Báb? He, too, upon meeting the Báb had forsaken the king, his own fame, and eventually his very life for this prisoner. Was there any comfort to be found in this? What about the conversion of Manúchihr Khán, the governor of Iṣfahán?

What about the reports from the prison of Chihríq? It was said that the Báb spoke often of His death during these days, that He referred to His death as something He not only expected but also looked forward to. Suppose He should display an undaunted courage if exhibited in chains throughout the country? Suppose the Báb confused and bewildered the subtle doctors they chose to debate against Him? Suppose they bowed down in belief before Him just as the wisest of all, Vaḥíd, had done? Suppose He became more of a hero and martyr than ever to the people as a result of this treatment? What then? Everyone who came near Him felt the fascinating influence of His personality, His manner, and His speech. Even His guards had not been free from that weakness.

The risk was too great. After weighing the matter with care, the prime minister's counselors decided against this plan. They dared not take the chance.

Now the prime minister insisted on more drastic action against the Báb. Mírzá Taqí Khán cursed the laxity with which his predecessor, Ḥájí Mírzá Áqásí, had allowed so great a peril to grow. He was determined that this weak policy must cease at once. To allow the Báb to continue to gain in glory and prestige was unthinkable.

"Nothing," he told them, "short of his public execution can, to my mind, enable this distracted country to recover its tranquillity and peace."

Seeing his wrath, not a single voice dared to speak against his plan, except the minister of war who was later to succeed Mírzá Taqí Khán. He suggested that putting a banished descendant of Muḥammad to death and holding him accountable for the deeds of a band of irresponsible agitators would be cruel. He proposed a less violent course of action.

The prime minister was very displeased. He dismissed this suggestion at once.

"Nothing short of the remedy I advocate can uproot this evil and bring us the peace for which we long," he said.

Disregarding the advice of any who disagreed with him, the prime minister, careful not to divulge his true purpose, dispatched an order to the governor of Ádhirbáyján, commanding that the Báb be brought from Chihríq to Tabríz. The order requested that the Báb be conducted to this city, where He would be held and told later of His fate. The prime minister was afraid to bring the Báb to Ṭihrán for execution lest His presence there set in motion forces that the prime minister would be powerless to control. Therefore, the Báb was to be done to death in Tabríz, in the north.

Three days after the Báb arrived in Tabríz, the governor received a second order. This order instructed him to execute the Báb.

"The task I am called upon to perform is a task that only ignoble people would accept," the governor said. He wanted nothing to do with slaying a descendant of the Prophet Muḥammad. He refused to carry out the order.

The Báb was descended from the family of Baní-Háshim, which was the family of Muḥammad, who, through Ishmael, was descended from Abraham.

Surely the governor was familiar with the Islamic prophecy that said, "should a Youth from Baní-Háshim be made manifest and summon the people to a new Book and to new laws, all should hasten to Him and embrace His Cause."

Determined that nothing should stop this execution, the prime minister then ordered his own brother, Mírzá Ḥasan Khán, to carry out his orders. The brother tried to inform the governor of these new instructions, but the governor refused to meet with him, pretending to be ill. Mírzá Ḥasan Khán then personally took over the plans for the execution.

He ordered the immediate transfer of the Báb to a cell in the city barracks. He had the Báb's turban and sash, both emblems of His noble lineage, removed. He ordered Sám Khán, the head of the execution regiment, to post ten special guards outside the door of the Báb's cell.

As the Báb was being led through the courtyard to His cell in the barracks, a young man from Tabríz rushed forward from the crowd. He was but a youth. His face was haggard, his feet were bare, his hair disheveled. He forced his way through the mob, ignoring the peril to his own life that such an action involved. He flung himself at the Báb's feet.

"Send me not from Thee, O Master," he implored. "Wherever Thou goest, suffer me to follow Thee."

The Báb smiled down upon him and spoke gently. "Muḥammad-'Alí, arise," He told the young man, "and rest assured that you will be with Me. To-morrow you shall witness what God has decreed."

Dr. T. K. Cheyne writes, "It is no doubt a singular coincidence that both [the Báb] and Jesus Christ are reported to have addressed these words to a disciple: 'To-day thou shalt be with Me in Paradise.'"

Mírzá Muḥammad-'Alí was arrested and cast into the same cell with the Báb and condemned to die with Him. Soon the story of this young man became known to everyone. He had learned of the Faith of the Báb when the Báb had first passed through Tabríz on His way to prison at Máh-Kú. At once he became an ardent believer. He longed to visit the Báb in His prison and offer his life for the new religion. The youth's stepfather was a notable citizen of Tabríz. He refused to let his son leave the city. He feared that the boy would shame the family by publicly admitting that he believed in the Báb, so he confined him to his room and put a strict watch over him. The young man began to sicken in this confinement until eventually the stepfather became worried.

Shaykh Ḥasan, who was related to the stepfather, had just been sent to Tabríz by the Báb with a number of manuscripts. He gives the following eyewitness account of his meeting with that young man.

"Every day I visited him," Shaykh Ḥasan recalls, "I witnessed the tears that continually rained from his eyes. After the Báb had departed from Tabríz, one day as I went to see him, I was surprised to note the joy and gladness which had illumined his countenance. His handsome face was wreathed in smiles as he stepped forward to receive me. 'The eyes of my Beloved' he said, as he embraced me, 'have beheld this face, and these eyes have gazed upon His countenance.' 'Let me,' he added, 'tell you the secret of my happiness. After the Báb had been taken back to Chihríq, one day, as I lay confined in my cell, I turned my heart to Him and besought Him in these words: 'Thou beholdest, O my Best-Beloved, my captivity and helplessness, and knowest how eagerly I yearn to look upon Thy face. Dispel the gloom that oppresses my heart, with the light of Thy countenance.' . . . I was so overcome with emotion that I seemed to have lost consciousness. Suddenly I heard the voice of the Báb, and, lo! He was calling me. He bade me arise. I beheld the majesty of His countenance as He appeared before me. He smiled as He looked into my eyes. I rushed forward and flung myself at His feet. 'Rejoice,' He said; 'the hour is approaching when, in this very city, I shall be suspended before the eyes of the multitude and shall fall a victim to the fire of the enemy. I shall choose no one except you to share with Me the cup of martyrdom. Rest assured that this promise which I give you shall be fulfilled.' I was entranced by the beauty of that vision. When I recovered, I found myself immersed in an ocean of joy, a joy the radiance of which all the sorrows of the world could never obscure. That voice keeps ringing in my ears. That vision haunts me both in the daytime and in the night-season. The memory of that ineffable smile has dissipated the loneliness of my confinement. I am firmly convinced that the hour at which His pledge is to be fulfilled can no longer be delayed. I exhorted him to be patient and to conceal his emotions. He promised me not to divulge that secret, and undertook to exercise the utmost forbearance towards Siyyid 'Alí [his stepfather]. I hastened to assure the father of his determination, and succeeded in obtaining his release from his confinement. That youth continued until the day of his martyrdom to associate, in a state of complete serenity and joy, with his parents and kinsmen. Such was his behaviour towards his friends and relatives that, on the day he laid down his life for his Beloved, the people of Tabríz all wept and bewailed him."

The young man's confidence in his vision never diminished, and the day came at last when he saw the Báb with his own eyes in the barracks courtyard. He flung himself at His feet and heard the Báb fulfill His promise with the words "Arise, and rest assured that you will be with Me."

On that last night in His barracks cell, the face of the Báb was aglow with a joy such as had never shone from His face before. Dr. T. K. Cheyne in his account of the Báb writes, "We learn that, at great points in his career . . . such radiance of might and majesty streamed from his countenance that none could bear to look upon the effulgence of his glory and beauty. Nor was it an uncommon occurrence for unbelievers involuntarily to bow down in lowly obeisance on beholding His Holiness. . . ."

Siyyid Ḥusayn has left the following eyewitness account of the Báb's last night on earth:

"Indifferent to the storm that raged about Him, He conversed with us with gaiety and cheerfulness. The sorrows that had weighed so heavily upon Him seemed to have completely vanished.

"'Tomorrow,' He said to us, 'will be the day of My martyrdom. Would that one of you might now arise and, with his own hands, end My life. I prefer to be slain by the hand of a friend rather than by that of the enemy.'

". . . We shrank, however, at the thought of taking away with our own hands so precious a life. We refused, and remained silent. Mírzá Muḥammad-'Alí suddenly sprang to his feet and announced himself ready to obey whatever the Báb might desire. 'This same youth, who has risen to comply with My wish,' the Báb declared . . . , 'will, together with Me, suffer martyrdom. Him will I choose to share with Me its crown.'"

Early the next morning, the chief attendant came to the barracks to conduct the Báb into the presence of the leading doctors of law in Tabríz. They were to authorize His execution by signing a death warrant, thus relieving the prime minister of the entire responsibility.

The Báb was engaged in a confidential conversation with Siyyid Ḥusayn, one of His closest followers, who had been serving as His secretary. Siyyid Ḥusayn had been with the Báb throughout His imprisonment. The Báb was giving him last-minute instructions.

"Confess not your Faith," the Báb advised Siyyid Ḥusayn. "Thereby you will be enabled, when the hour comes, to convey to those who are destined to hear you, the things of which you alone are aware."

The Báb was thus engaged when the chief attendant arrived and interrupted. He insisted on Siyyid Ḥusayn's immediate departure. The Báb turned and addressed the chief attendant.

"Not until I have said to him all those things that I wish to say," the Báb warned, "can any earthly power silence Me. Though all the world be armed against Me, yet shall they be powerless to deter Me from fulfilling, to the last word, My intention."

The chief attendant was amazed at such a bold speech on the part of a prisoner. However, he still insisted that Siyyid Ḥusayn accompany him without further delay. Siyyid Ḥusayn's conversation with the Báb was left unfinished.

The Báb and the youth who was to die with Him were to be led, one by one, into the presence of each of three doctors of law. The guards made certain that the irons about their necks and wrists were secure. To the iron collar about each one's neck they tied a long cord, which was held by another attendant. Then, so that everyone could see them in this humiliating state, they walked them about the town. They led the Báb and Muḥammad-'Alí through the streets and the bazaars, overwhelming them with blows and insults. The Báb was paraded publicly, as Christ had been, an object of derision.

To the people of Tabríz it must have appeared that the Báb was no longer triumphant. He was to die. He was being humbled and degraded just as the prime minister had planned. The crowds packed the streets along which He and Muḥammad-'Alí were led. The people climbed on each other's shoulders to get a better better view of this personage who was talked about so much. What a pity He was so powerless, they must have thought. Quite obviously this could not be a man of God, and certainly not the Promised One.

Followers of the Báb who were in the crowd scattered in all directions. They were trying to arouse among the onlookers a feeling of pity or sympathy that might help them save their Master.

Jesus had entered Jerusalem hailed on all sides, with palm leaves strewn in His path, only to be mocked and reviled in that same city within a week. In like manner the glory that had attended the Báb's first triumphant entry into Tabríz was now forgotten. This time the crowd, restless and excitable, flung insults at Him. Perhaps they wanted to be entertained with miracles and signs of wonder, and the Báb was failing them. They pursued Him as He was led through the streets. They broke through the guards and struck Him in the face. When some missile hurled from the crowd would reach its mark, the guards and the crowd would burst into laughter.

The Báb was then brought before the clergyman who had previously incited his colleagues to scourge Him. As soon as he saw the Báb approaching, he seized the death warrant and thrust it at the attendant.

"No need to bring the Siyyid-i-Báb into my presence," he cried. "This death-warrant I penned the very day I met him. . . . He surely is the same man whom I saw on that occasion, and has not, in the meantime, surrendered any of his claims."

The other priests in turn also refused to meet the Báb face to face.

The chief attendant, having secured the necessary death warrants, delivered the Báb and Muḥammad-'Alí into the hands of Sám Khán, the leader of the regiment that was to carry out the execution.

Sám Khán found himself increasingly affected by the behavior of his captive. He had placed a guard of ten soldiers about the Báb's cell door and had carefully supervised it himself. He was in great fear that his action in taking such a holy life might bring upon him the wrath of God. Finally, unable to bear this worry any longer, he approached the Báb and spoke to Him privately.

"I profess the Christian Faith," he said, "and entertain no ill will against you. If your Cause be the Cause of Truth, enable me to free myself from the obligation to shed your blood."

The Báb reassured him, saying, "Follow your instructions, and if your intention be sincere, the Almighty is surely able to relieve you from your perplexity."

The hour for the execution could not be put off any longer. The crowds had become immense. About ten thousand people were gathered on the roof of the barracks and the tops of the adjoining houses.

Sám Khán ordered his men to drive a nail into the pillar between the doors of the barracks. To the nail they tied the ropes by which the Báb and His young companion were to be separately suspended. Thus was fulfilled before the eyes of the people gazing upon the scene the words of the prophecy in their own sacred writings that foretold that when the Promised One was slain, He would be suspended like unto Christ before the gaze of the public. Muḥammad-'Alí begged Sám Khán to allow him to be positioned so that his own body would shield that of the Báb. He was eventually suspended so that his head rested upon the Báb's breast.

An account of that event in the *Journal Asiatique* states, "The Báb remained silent. His pale handsome face framed by a black beard and a small mustache, his appearance and his refined manners, his white and delicate hands, his simple but very neat garments—everything about him awakened sympathy and compassion."

The enormous crowd was eager to witness the spectacle. Yet each person was willing to change from an enemy into a friend at the least sign of power from the Báb. They were still hungry for drama, and He was disappointing them. Just as the crowd had stood on Golgotha, reviling Jesus, wagging their heads and saying, ". . . Save thyself. If thou be the Son of God, come down from the cross,"* so, too, did the people of Tabríz mock the Báb and jeer at His seeming impotence.

As soon as the Báb and His companion were fastened to the pillar, the regiment of soldiers arranged itself in three files, each file having two hundred and fifty men.

* Matt. 27:40.

The leader of the regiment, Sám Khán, could delay the command no longer. The Báb had told him to do his duty; therefore it was apparently the will of God that his regiment should take the life of the Báb. This must have been a source of great sorrow to him.

Reluctantly, he gave the command to fire.

In turn, each of the files opened fire upon the Báb and His companion until the entire regiment had discharged its volley of bullets.

Over ten thousand eyewitnesses saw the electrifying spectacle that followed. One of the historical accounts of that staggering moment states, "The smoke of the firing of the seven hundred and fifty rifles was such as to turn the light of the noonday sun into darkness.

"As soon as the cloud of smoke had cleared away, an astounded multitude were looking upon a scene which their eyes could scarcely believe. There, standing before them alive and unhurt, was the companion of the Báb, whilst He Himself had vanished uninjured from their sight. Though the cords with which they were suspended had been rent in pieces by the bullets, yet their bodies had miraculously escaped the volleys."

Cries of astonishment, confusion, and fear rang out from the bewildered multitude.

"The Siyyid-i-Báb has gone from our sight!"

An intense clamor arose on all sides. The crowd was already dangerous. The public square became a bedlam as a frantic search for the Báb began.

M. C. Huart, a French author who wrote of this episode, says, "The soldiers in order to quiet the excitement of the crowd which, being extremely agitated, was ready to believe the claims of a religion which thus demonstrated its truth, showed the cords broken by the bullets, implying that no miracle had really taken place."

"Look!" their actions implied. "The seven hundred and fifty musket-balls have shattered the ropes into fragments. This is what freed them. It is nothing more than this. It is no miracle."

Uproars and shouts continued on all sides. The people still were not certain themselves what really had happened.

M. C. Huart, giving his view of that astonishing event, states, "Amazing to believe, the bullets had not struck the condemned but, on the contrary, had broken his bonds and he was delivered. It was a real miracle. . . ."

A. L. M. Nicolas also wrote of this episode, saying, "An extraordinary thing happened, unique in the annals of the history of humanity: the bullets cut the cords that held the Báb and he fell on his feet without a scratch."

The frenzied search for the Báb came to an end just a few feet from the execution post. They found Him back in His cell in the barracks, in the same room He had occupied the night before. He was completing His conversation with His secretary, Siyyid Ḥusayn, giving to him the final instructions that had been interrupted that morning. An expression of unruffled calm was on His face. His body had obviously emerged unscathed from the shower of 750 bullets that had been directed against Him.

The Báb addressed the chief attendant. "I have finished My conversation . . ." He said. "Now you may proceed to fulfil your intention."

The chief attendant was far too disturbed to resume his duties. He must have recalled vividly the words with which the Báb had warned him when he had interrupted that conversation: "Though all the world be armed against Me, yet shall they be powerless to deter Me from fulfilling, to the last word, My intention."

The chief attendant refused to continue with any part of the execution. He left the scene of that barracks cell severely shaken, never to return to his post.

The head of the Christian regiment, Sám Khán, was likewise stunned by what had taken place. He, too, must have remembered clearly the words that the Báb had spoken to him: "If your intention be sincere, the Almighty is surely able to relieve you from your perplexity." Sám Khán had given the order to fire, yet the Báb had been freed. Surely the Lord had delivered him from the need to shed the blood of this holy man. He would not go on with the execution. Sám Khán ordered his regiment to leave the barracks square immediately. He swore before leaving that he would sooner lose his life than finish what he had started.

After Sám Khán and his regiment departed, a colonel of the bodyguard volunteered to carry out the execution.

On that same wall and to that same nail, the Báb and His companion were lashed a second time. The new firing squad formed in line. As the regiment prepared to fire the final volley, the Báb spoke His last words to the gazing multitude.

"Had you believed in Me, O wayward generation," He said, "every one of you would have followed the example of this youth, who stood in rank above most of you, and willingly would have sacrificed himself in My path. The day will come when you will have recognized Me; that day I shall have ceased to be with you."

The rifles were raised, the command given, and the shots thundered. The bodies of the Báb and His youthful companion were shattered by the blast.

As Jesus had expired on the cross so that men might be called back to God, so did the Báb breathe His last against a barracks wall in the city of Tabríz, Persia.

The historian Nicolas in his account of those hours writes, "Christians believe that if Jesus Christ had wished to come down from the cross he could have done so easily; he died of his own free will because it was written that he should and in order that the prophecies might be fulfilled. The same is true of the Báb, so the Bábís say. . . . He likewise died voluntarily because his death was to be the salvation of humanity. Who will ever tell us the words that the Báb uttered in the midst of the unprecedented turmoil which broke out as he ascended? Who will ever know the memories which stirred his noble soul?"

Christ in His agony in the garden of Gethsemane cried out, "O my Father, if it be possible, let this cup pass from me: nevertheless not as I will, but as thou wilt."* The Báb in the frozen winter of Máh-Kú had likewise called out to mankind that it was God's will and not His own that impelled Him to throw himself into the ocean of superstition and hatred that was fatally to engulf him. Both Christ and the Báb uttered the same words of warning, "O wayward generation!"

The martyrdom of the Báb took place at noon on Sunday, July 9, 1850. He was thirty years old.

A historical account of that second and final volley states, "This time the execution was effective. . . . But the crowd, vividly impressed by the spectacle they had witnessed, dispersed slowly, hardly convinced that the Báb was a criminal."

On the evening after His martyrdom, the mangled bodies of the Báb and Muḥammad-'Alí were removed from the courtyard of the barracks. They were left at the edge of a moat outside the gate of the city. Four companies of ten sentinels each were posted to keep watch in turn over the remains so that none of His followers might claim them.

On the morning following the martyrdom, the Russian consul in Tabríz, accompanied by an artist, went to the moat and ordered that a sketch be made of the remains. Nabíl, in *The Dawn-Breakers*, quotes an eyewitness who said, "It was such a faithful portrait of the Báb that I looked upon! No bullet had

---

* Matt. 26:39.

struck His forehead, His cheeks, or His lips. I gazed upon a smile which seemed to be still lingering upon His countenance."

On the afternoon of the second day, Sulaymán K͟hán, a follower of the Báb, arrived from Ṭihrán. He had heard of the threat to the life of the Báb and had left Ṭihrán to try to rescue Him. To his dismay, he arrived too late. He resolved to rescue the bodies of the Báb and His companion in spite of the sentinels, even if it meant risking his own life.

In the middle of that same night, with the help of a friend, he succeeded in bearing away the bodies. While the guards slept, Sulaymán K͟hán and his friend stole the sacred remains and carried them from the edge of the moat to a silk factory owned by another believer. The remains were placed the next day in a casket and were hidden in a safe place.

The sentinels awakened and, finding their trust had been spirited away, sought to justify themselves by pretending that while they slept wild beasts had carried away the bodies. Their superiors also concealed the truth and did not report it to the authorities for fear of compromising their own honor. This allowed the followers of the Báb time to carefully hide His sacred remains and thus protect themselves from further investigation.

Meanwhile, from the pulpits of Tabríz, the religious leaders joyfully proclaimed that the Báb's remains had been devoured by wild animals. They saw this as proof that they were right and the Báb was false, because it was their belief, according to Islamic prophecy, that the body of the Promised One would be preserved from beasts of prey and all manner of creeping things.

Nicolas in his history writes, "The most reliable testimony of the actual witnesses of the drama or of its actors do [*sic*] not leave me any doubt that the body of Siyyid 'Alí-Muḥammad [the Báb] was carried away by pious hands and, at last . . . received a burial worthy of him."

Sulaymán Khán reported the rescue of the remains of the Báb to Bahá'u'lláh in Ṭihrán. Bahá'u'lláh immediately sent a special messenger to Tabríz to arrange for the bodies to be transferred to the capital.

"This decision," Nabíl writes, "was prompted by the wish the Báb Himself had expressed."

In His own handwriting, the Báb had expressed the desire to be buried near Bahá'u'lláh, Him whom God will make manifest. In a letter written in the neighborhood of a shrine near Ṭihrán, Nabíl says that the Báb addressed the saint buried there in the following words: "Well is it with you to have found your resting place . . . under the shadow of My Beloved. Would that I might be entombed within the precincts of that holy ground!"

Bahá'u'lláh respected that wish by having the remains of the Báb transferred to that very spot, but the place would remain secret for more than ten years.

Misfortune and adversity began almost at once to strike down those primarily responsible for the martyrdom of the Báb. The same lack of mercy that had been shown to those who had injured Him throughout His life was now visited upon the last of His persecutors.

Ḥusayn Khán, the governor of Fárs, who had been the first to imprison the Báb, was hurled from power and abandoned by friend and foe alike. Mírzá 'Alí Aṣghar, the religious judge who had scourged Him, was stricken with paralysis and died an agonizing death. The king, Muḥammad Sháh, who had refused to meet the Báb, was struck down by illness and succumbed to a complication of maladies far before his time. His prime minister, Ḥájí Mírzá Áqásí, who had twice banished the Báb to prison, was toppled from power and died in abject poverty and exile.

The mayor of Ṭihrán, Maḥmúd Khán, who held prisoner Ṭáhirih and the seven martyrs of Ṭihrán and assisted in their deaths, was dragged feet first through the city's streets by a rope, then hanged from the gallows.

The new ruler, Náṣiri'd-Dín Sháh, who permitted the slaying of the Báb, was eventually assassinated in a dreadful and dramatic way.

His prime minister, Mírzá Taqí Khán, who had ordered the Báb's execution and who encouraged the wholesale slaughter of so many of His followers, was seized in the grip of this same relentless, punishing retribution. His greatest crime was taking the life of the Báb, but his greatest massacre was that which took place in Zanján after the martyrdom of the Báb. Eighteen hundred followers of the Báb were slain in Zanján alone. Just as at Bárfurúsh the soldiers had promised on their honor to spare the followers of Ḥujjat who willingly came out of their shelters, and, just as at Bárfurúsh, they were betrayed and massacred to the accompaniment of drums and trumpets. Then the victorious army forced those of high standing who were left to march on foot before their horses all the way to Ṭihrán with chains about their necks and shackles on their feet. When they appeared before the prime minister, Mírzá Taqí Khán, he ordered that the veins of three leaders be slashed open. He wished to make an example of them as he had made one of the Báb.

The victims did not betray the least fear or emotion. They told the prime minister that the lack of good faith of which the authorities, the army, and he had been guilty was a crime that Almighty God would not be satisfied to punish in an ordinary way. God would demand, they told him, a more impressive and striking retribution for the slayer of a Prophet and the persecutor of His people. They suggested that the prime minister himself would soon suffer the very same death that he, in his hatred, was now inflicting upon them.

It happened precisely as those victims had foretold. Mírzá Taqí Khán fell from the king's favor. Court intrigue and greed combined to complete his downfall. He was stripped of all the honors he had enjoyed and forced to flee in disgrace from the capital and the king's jealousy. Finally, the hand of revenge caught up with him. The former prime minister's veins were slashed open. His blood stained the wall of the bath in the Palace of Fín for years afterward, bearing witness to the atrocities his own hand had wrought.

The wave of retributive justice was still not at an end. Mírzá Ḥasan Khán, the prime minister's brother, who had carried out the Báb's execution, was subjected to a dreadful punishment from which he died.

The commander of the regiment that volunteered to replace that of Sám Khán lost his life during a bombardment by the British. The regiment itself came to a dreadful end. In spite of the unaccountable failure of Sám Khán and his soldiers to take the life of the Báb, this regiment was willing to renew the attempt and did eventually riddle His body with bullets. Two hundred and fifty of its members, with their officers, were crushed that same year in a terrible earthquake. They were resting on a hot summer's day between Tabríz and Ardabíl, under the shadow of a wall. The structure suddenly collapsed and fell on them, leaving not one survivor.

The remaining five hundred members of the regiment suffered an even more dramatic fate. They were executed by a firing squad. Thus they met the same fate that they had inflicted upon the Báb. Three years after His martyrdom, that regiment mutinied. The authorities ordered that all of its members should be shot. Significantly, there was not only one volley, but, as in the case of the Báb, a second volley was fired to make sure that none survived. Then their bodies were pierced with spears and lances. Their remains were left exposed to the public's gaze.

This event caused much concern and whispering in Tabríz.

"Could it be, by any chance, the vengeance of God that has brought the whole regiment to so dishonourable and tragic an end?" they wondered.

When the leading doctors of law overheard these misgivings and doubts, they were alarmed. They issued a warning stating that all who expressed such thoughts would be severely punished. To demonstrate their seriousness they made an example of a few of the people. Some were fined and some were beaten. All were warned under threat of further punishment to cease such talk at once.

History records that from the very hour that the volley of bullets was fired at the Báb, "a gale of exceptional severity arose and swept over the whole city. A whirlwind of dust of incredible density obscured the light of the sun and blinded the eyes of the people." The city of Tabríz remained wrapped in that fearful darkness from noon until night.

Is it not possible that this was the hour promised in the Book of Amos, who said, "And it shall come to pass in that day, saith the Lord God, that I will cause the sun to go down at noon, and I will darken the earth in the clear day. . . ."*

The "Lamb" had been slain just as promised in the Revelation of St. John. The events that soon took place in the city of the Báb's birth were also foreshadowed in that Book: "And the same hour there was a great earthquake, and the tenth part of the city fell, and in the earthquake were slain of men seven thousand. . . ."†

A written account of the period following the execution of the Báb states, "This earthquake occurred in Shíráz after the martyrdom of the Báb. The city was in a turmoil, and many people were destroyed. Great agitation also took place through diseases, cholera, dearth, scarcity, famine and afflictions, the like of which had never been known."§

The prophecies and promises of Christ were fulfilled with the coming of the Báb, although the religious leaders turned a

---

* Amos 8:9.

† Rev. 5:6, 11:13

§ 'Abdu'l-Bahá, *Some Answered Questions,* p. 55.

blind eye and a deaf ear. These religious authorities, as testified to in the introduction to *The Dawn-Breakers,* the most authentic history of the Báb, "confidently expected that the promised Advent would not substitute a new and richer revelation for the old, but would endorse and fortify the system of which they were the functionaries. It would enhance incalculably their personal prestige, would extend their authority far and wide among the nations, and would win for them the reluctant but abject homage of mankind. When the Báb . . . proclaimed a new code of religious law, and by precept and example instituted a profound moral and spiritual reform, the priests immediately scented mortal danger. They saw their monopoly undermined, their ambitions threatened, their own lives and conduct put to shame. They rose against Him in sanctimonious indignation. . . ."

"The cause of the rejection and persecution of the Báb," this historical analysis continues, "was in its essence the same as that of the rejection and persecution of the Christ. If Jesus had not brought a New Book, if He had not only reiterated the spiritual principles taught by Moses but had continued Moses' rules and regulations too, He might as a merely moral reformer have escaped the vengeance of the Scribes and Pharisees. But to claim that any part of the Mosaic law, even such material ordinances as those that dealt with divorce and the keeping of the Sabbath, could be altered—and altered by an unordained preacher from the village of Nazareth—this was to threaten the interests of the Scribes and Pharisees themselves, and since they were the representatives of Moses and of God, it was blasphemy against the Most High. As soon as the position of Jesus was understood, His persecution began. As He refused to desist, He was put to death.

"For reasons exactly parallel, the Báb was from the beginning opposed by the vested interests of the dominant Church as an uprooter of the Faith."

The most striking parallel in all recorded history to the brief, turbulent ministry of the Báb is undoubtedly the passion of Jesus Christ. There is a remarkable similarity in the distinguishing features of Their careers. Their youthfulness and meekness; the dramatic swiftness with which each ministry moved toward its climax; the boldness with which They challenged the time-honored conventions, laws, and rites of the religions into which They had been born; the role that the religious leaders played as chief instigators of the outrages They were made to suffer; the indignities heaped upon Them; the suddenness of Their arrest; the interrogations to which They were subjected; the scourgings inflicted upon Them; Their passing first in triumph, then in suffering through the streets of the city where They were to be slain; Their public parade through the streets on the way to the place of martyrdom; Their words of hope and promise to a companion who was also to die with Them; the darkness that enveloped the land in the hour of Their martyrdom; and finally Their ignominious suspension before the gaze of a hostile multitude.

The momentous events associated with the martyrdom of the Báb could hardly fail to arouse widespread and keen interest even beyond the confines of the land in which it had occurred.

One particularly moving document about the Báb points out, "This illustrious Soul arose with such power that He shook the supports of the religion, of the morals, the conditions, the habits and the customs of Persia, and instituted new rules, new laws and a new religion. Though the great personages of the State, nearly all the clergy, and the public men arose to destroy and annihilate Him, He alone withstood them and moved the whole of Persia."*

---

* 'Abdu'l-Bahá, *Some Answered Questions,* p. 25.

"Many persons from all parts of the world," one writer states, "set out for Persia, and began to seek with their whole hearts."

A noted French publicist testified that "All Europe was stirred to pity and indignation . . . Among the littérateurs of my generation, in the Paris of 1890," he said, "the martyrdom of the Báb was still as fresh a topic as had been the first news of His death. We wrote poems about Him. Sarah Bernhardt entreated Catulle Mendès for a play on the theme of this historic tragedy."*

A drama titled "The Báb" was published in 1903 and played in one of the leading theaters of St. Petersburg, Russia. The drama was publicized in London and was translated into French in Paris and into German by the poet Fiedler.

M. J. Balteau, in a lecture on the Faith of the Báb, quotes M. Vambery's words spoken in the French Academy, words that testify to the depth and power of the Báb's teachings. The Báb, he states, "has expressed doctrines worthy of the greatest thinkers."

The Cambridge scholar Edward Granville Browne wrote, "Who can fail to be attracted by the gentle spirit of Mírzá 'Alí-Muḥammad? His sorrowful and persecuted life; his purity of conduct, and youth; his courage and uncomplaining patience under misfortune; . . . but most of all his tragic death, all serve to enlist our sympathies on behalf of the young Prophet of Shíráz."

"That Jesus of the age . . . a prophet, and more than a prophet," is the judgment passed by the distinguished English clergyman Dr. T. K. Cheyne. "His combination of mildness and power is so rare," he states, "that we have to place him in a line with super-normal men. . . ."

* Quoted in Shoghi Effendi, *God Passes By*, p. 56.

Sir Francis Younghusband writes in his book *The Gleam,* "The story of the Báb . . . was the story of spiritual heroism unsurpassed. . . . The Báb's passionate sincerity could not be doubted, for he had given his life for his faith. And that there must be something in his message that appealed to men and satisfied their souls was witnessed to by the fact that thousands gave their lives in his cause and millions now follow him. . . . his life must be one of those events in the last hundred years which is really worth study."

The French historian A. L. M. Nicolas writes, "His life is one of the most magnificent examples of courage which it has been the privilege of mankind to behold. . . . He sacrificed himself for humanity, for it he gave his body and his soul, for it he endured privations, insults, torture and martyrdom. He sealed, with his very lifeblood, the covenant of universal brotherhood. Like Jesus he paid with his life for the proclamation of a reign of concord, equity and brotherly love. More than anyone he knew what dreadful dangers he was heaping upon himself . . . but all these considerations could not weaken his resolve. Fear had no hold upon his soul and, perfectly calm, never looking back, in full possession of all his powers, he walked into the furnace."

At last the clergy and the state could pride themselves on having crushed the life from the Cause they had battled so long. The Báb was no more. His chief disciples were destroyed. The mass of His followers throughout the land had been beaten, exhausted, and silenced.

The king and the prime minister must have rejoiced in the thought that they would never hear of the Báb again. His faith, it seemed, was swiftly receding into oblivion, and the wings of death appeared to be hovering over it. The combined forces that had engulfed it on every side had all but put out the light that the young Prince of Glory had kindled in His land.

Yet, at that very moment in a suburb of the capital, Bahá'u'lláh was receiving a visitor, a friend who was soon to be the new prime minister.

He hastened to inform Bahá'u'lláh of the Báb's death, and he expressed to Bahá'u'lláh his hope that the Báb's Cause was finally extinguished.

"If this be true," Bahá'u'lláh replied, "you can be certain that the flame that has been kindled will, by this very act, blaze forth more fiercely than ever, and will set up a conflagration such as the combined forces of the statesmen of this realm will be powerless to quench."

Gobineau echoes this statement, recording in his history that "instead of appeasing the flames, it had fanned them into greater violence."

Judged according to the standards of the world, the life of Christ was a catastrophic failure. Of His chosen Disciples one betrayed Him, another denied Him, and only a handful stood at the foot of the cross. Many years were to pass before the world ever heard of His name. Judged by the same worldly standards, the life of the ill-fated Youth from Shíráz appears to be one of the saddest and most fruitless in history. The works He so gloriously conceived and so heroically undertook seem to have ended in a colossal disaster.

Swift as a meteor, His short, heroic career had flashed across the skies of Persia. Now death had plunged it into the darkness of despair. This was but the last in a series of heartbreaks that had beset His path from the beginning.

At the very outset of His career, the Báb went to Mecca, the heart of Islam, to proclaim His mission publicly. There He was treated to icy indifference. He planned to return to the city of Karbilá in Iraq to establish His Cause. His arrest prevented it. The program He outlined for His chosen disciples—the Letters of the Living—was, for the most part, unfulfilled. The moderation He urged them to observe was forgotten in the first flush of enthusiasm that seized the early pioneers of His faith. His only chance of meeting the king was dashed to the ground by the prime minister. His ablest disciples were struck down one after another. The best of His followers were slain in ruthless carnage all across the land. Then followed His own martyrdom. All of these events, on the surface so humiliating, would seem to have marked the lowest depths to which His Cause had fallen and to threaten the virtual extinction of all His hopes.

Yet burning like a flame through the darkness of all of these setbacks and sufferings was the Báb's constant promise that before the year nine would pass, the Promised One of all religions would appear. There was never a shadow of doubt in the Báb's teaching on this point. He was only the Herald of a greater One yet to come. He knew that the seed had been firmly planted in the fields and meadows of human hearts. He was the Dawn, and the Sun was yet to rise.

Of all those devoted figures who were able to carry on the Báb's message and further His work, not one soul was left alive save Bahá'u'lláh, who with His family and a handful of devoted followers was driven destitute into exile and prison in a foreign land. He was banished from place to place until He reached the "Mountain of God" in Israel, the Holy Land. Bahá'u'lláh was exiled, a prisoner, to the fortress situated on the plain of 'Akká, and those startling words of the Islamic prophecy given several hundred years before about the "last days" of the twin Messengers were literally fulfilled: "All of them (the companions of the Qá'im) shall be slain except One Who shall reach the plain of 'Akká, the Banquet-Hall of God."

Although the Faith of God had been crushed into the ground at an early age and rudely trampled upon, this very process would bring about its germination. Buried in the earth, warmed by the blood of its martyrs, His faith would blossom out in glory at a later date with the brightness of the sun and would fulfill prophecy with the exactness of the stars.

The Dawn would give way to the Sun, and the era promised to humankind since the beginning of time, the Day of the "one fold and one shepherd"* would be ushered in by the sacrifice of that gentle Youth from Shíráz: the Báb, the Gate of God.

* John 10:16.

Glossary

'ABBÁS QULÍ KHÁN The sniper who killed Mullá Ḥusayn.

'ABDU'L-BAHÁ Literally *Servant of Bahá:* the title assumed by 'Abbás Effendi (23 May 1844–28 November 1921), the eldest son and appointed successor of Bahá'u'lláh and the Center of His Covenant. Upon Bahá'u'lláh's ascension in 1892, 'Abdu'l-Bahá became Head of the Bahá'í Faith.

'ABDU'L-KARÍM Follower of the Báb who found Him after receiving a vision in a dream in which a bird warned him in a sweet voice "Lo, the year '60." When he finally encountered the Báb, He spoke the very same words to 'Abdu'l-Karím. 'Abdu'l-Karím became a Bábí and performed secretarial duties for the Báb in Shíráz.

A.D. Abbreviation for *Anno Domini,* Latin for "in the year of our Lord," used to indicate that a time division falls within the Christian era.

A.H. Abbreviation for *Anno Hegirae,* Latin for "in the year of the hegira," used to indicate that a time division falls within the Muslim era.

'AKKÁ A four-thousand-year-old seaport and prison-city in northern Israel surrounded by fortress-like walls facing the sea. In the mid-1800s 'Akká became a penal colony to which the worst criminals of the Ottoman Empire were sent. In 1868 Bahá'u'lláh and His family and companions were banished to 'Akká by Sulṭán 'Abdu'l-'Azíz.

BÁB, THE Literally *The Gate:* title assumed by Siyyid 'Alí-Muḥammad (20 October 1819–9 July 1850) after declaring His mission in Shíráz in 1844. The Báb's station is twofold: He is a Messenger of God and the Founder of the Bábí Faith, and He is the Herald of Bahá'u'lláh.

BÁBÍ Of or pertaining to the Báb, used especially to denote His followers.

BÁBU'L-BÁB Literally *Gate of the Gate:* title given by the Báb to Mullá Ḥusayn, the first Letter of the Living.

BAHÁ Literally *Glory, Splendor, or Light:* the Greatest Name; a title given to Bahá'u'lláh by the Báb.

BAHÁ'Í Of or pertaining to Bahá'u'lláh, used especially to denote His followers.

BAHÁ'U'LLÁH Literally *The Glory of God:* title of Mírzá Ḥusayn-'Alí of Núr (12 November 1817–29 May 1892), Founder of the Bahá'í Faith.

BÁRFURÚSH Town in the northern Iranian province of Mázindarán, home of the Sa'ídu'l-'Ulamá, birthplace of Quddús, also the place of his martyrdom in May 1849. It is located near the Shrine of Shaykh Ṭabarsí.

BASTINADO A form of corporal punishment in which the soles of the feet are exposed and beaten with a stick.

BAYÁN Literally *exposition, explanation, lucidity, eloquence, utterance:* the title given by the Báb to two of His major works, one in Persian, the other in Arabic. It is also used sometimes to denote the entire body of His writings.

CARAVANSARY An inn surrounding a court in which caravans can rest at night.

CHIHRÍQ A mountain fortress in the Iranian province of Ádhirbáyján where the Báb was imprisoned for most of the last two years of His life. He named the place *Jabal-i-Shadíd,* meaning "the Grievous Mountain."

COMTE DE GOBINEAU A French writer and diplomat who held various posts in Iran shortly after the martyrdom of the Báb. In 1864 he published *Les Religions et Philosophies dans l'asie centrale,* in which he gives vivid accounts of Bábí heroism that attracted further study and European attention to the Bábí Faith.

DAWN-BREAKERS Refers to the Bábís and early Bahá'ís, many of whom gave their lives as martyrs.

DERVISH Literally *beggar, poor one:* the name given to one of many orders of religious mendicants and Islamic mystics.

DISPENSATION The period of time during which the laws and teachings of a Messenger of God have spiritual authority. For example, the Dispensation of Jesus Christ lasted until the beginning of the Islamic Dispensation, usually fixed at the year A.D. 622, the year Muḥammad emigrated from Mecca to Medina. The Islamic Dispensation lasted until the advent of the Báb in 1844. The Dispensation of the Báb ended when Bahá'u'lláh received the intimation of His mission in the Black Pit, the subterranean dungeon in Ṭihrán in which He was imprisoned in 1852. The Dispensation of Bahá'u'lláh will last until the advent of the next Manifestation of God, which Bahá'u'lláh asserts is to occur in no less than one thousand years.

GABRIEL In Muslim belief, the angel who brought God's revelation to the Prophet Muḥammad.

ḤÁJÍ Honorific title denoting one who has accomplished the *Ḥajj*, or Muslim pilgrimage to Mecca instituted in the Qur'án.

ḤÁJÍ MÍRZÁ ÁQÁSÍ Prime minister of Iran under Muḥammad S͟háh, he has the infamous title "Antichrist of the Bábí Dispensation." He prevented the meeting of Muḥammad S͟háh and the Báb, ordered the successive imprisonments of the Báb in Máh-Kú and C͟hihríq, and saw to the arrest of Bahá'u'lláh. He fell from power after the death of Muḥammad S͟háh and died, poor and abandoned, in Karbilá, Iraq, in 1849.

ḤUJJAT Literally *Proof:* refers to Mullá Muḥammad-'Alí of Zanján. The Báb bestowed upon him the designation Ḥujjat-i-Zanjání, meaning "Proof of Zanján." After acquainting himself with the claims of the Báb, he addressed his disciples from the pulpit, directing them to turn towards the Bábí Cause. He became the target of persecutions in Zanján in which the town split into two camps, one of Bábís following Ḥujjat, and the other opposing them. He and his companions took refuge in a nearby fort where they faced repeated attacks for a period of nine months. During the final month-long siege that was destined to massacre most of his three hundred companions, Ḥujjat was wounded, witnessed the killings of his wife and child, and was himself killed a few days later. His body was displayed for three days in the public square, after which it disappeared into the hands of the enemy.

ḤUSAYN K͟HÁN Governor of the province of Fárs who was responsible for the arrest and torture of Mullá Ṣádiq and Quddús in S͟híráz. On the eve of his attempt to execute the

Báb his city was visited by a cholera epidemic, prompting him to banish the Báb rather than kill Him.

IMÁM Designates both the religious leader who leads the prayers in the mosque and, in S͟hí'ah Islam, the twelve legitimate, hereditary successors of the Prophet Muḥammad.

IMÁM ḤUSAYN In S͟hí'ah Islam, The Third Imám, son of 'Alí and Fáṭimih, and grandson of the Prophet Muḥammad. He was martyred at Karbilá, Iraq, in A.D. 680.

IRAN Country in southwest Asia whose borders are shared with the Persian Gulf and the Gulf of Oman on the south, Iraq on the west, Armenia, Azerbaijan, the Caspian Sea, and Turkmenistan on the north, and Afghanistan and Pakistan on the east. Iran was formerly known as Persia, and its capital is Ṭihrán. It is the homeland of both the Báb and Bahá'u'-lláh.

ISLAM Literally *Submission to the Will of God:* The religion of the Prophet Muḥammad, upheld by Bahá'ís to be divine in origin.

JAMÁDÍ The fifth or sixth month of the Muslim lunar calendar; Jamádíyu'l-Avval is the fifth month, and Jamádíyu'th-T͟hání is the sixth month.

KARBILÁ Iraqi city where the Imám Ḥusayn, Third Imám of S͟hí'ah Islam, was martyred and where his shrine is located. It was the residence of Siyyid Káẓim.

K͟HURÁSÁN Eastern Persian province that was home to Mullá Ḥusayn.

LETTERS OF THE LIVING The first eighteen people who independently recognized and believed in the Báb. The first Letter of the Living was Mullá Husayn; the last was Quddús.

MÁH-KÚ Fortress, near the village of the same name, in the extreme northwest of Iran, where the Báb was imprisoned for nine months. He gave it the name *Jabal-i-Basíṭ* (the Open Mountain).

MANIFESTATION OF GOD Designation of a Prophet who is the Founder of a religious Dispensation, inasmuch as in His words, His person, and His actions He manifests the nature and purpose of God in accordance with the capacity and needs of the people to whom He comes.

MANÚCHIHR KHÁN Governor of Iṣfahán from 1839 until his death in 1847, he was a Georgian eunuch converted to Islam. He was respected for his administrative ability, and he lent his protection to the Báb. He became a follower of the Báb and endeavored to ensure His safety until his efforts were cut short by his death.

MASJID Literally *place of prostration:* a **Mosque.**

MECCA The most holy city in Islam and home of the Ka'bih, an ancient structure constructed by Abraham as a shrine dedicated to God. Gradually, the Ka'bih became a place of polytheistic worship until the arrival of Muḥammad, who restored it as a site for the worship of the one God. It is the destination for millions of Muslim pilgrims each year.

MEDINA Mecca's sister city to which Muḥammad and His followers fled in A.D. 622, marking the beginning of the Muslim calendar. It was home to the first Muslim community.

MÍRZÁ A contraction of *Amír-Zádih*, meaning son of an Amír. When it follows a name, it signifies "prince"; when it precedes, it means simply "Mr."

MÍRZÁ BUZURG Also known as Mírzá 'Abbás, he was the father of Bahá'u'lláh and a vizier to a son of Faṯḥ-'Alí S̲h̲áh and a governor under Muḥammad S̲h̲áh. He was well respected for his personal charm and intellectual qualities but lost his office through the animosity of Ḥájí Mírzá Áqásí. He died in 1839.

MÍRZÁ ḤUSAYN 'ALÍ See **Bahá'u'lláh.**

MÍRZA TAQÍ KHÁN Prime minister under Náṣiri'd-Dín S̲h̲áh. Determined to eradicate the Báb and His followers, he was involved in the persecution of the Bábís at the fort of S̲h̲ayk̲h̲ Ṭabarsí, at Nayríz, and at Zanján. He was also involved in the execution of the Seven Martyrs of Ṭihrán, and he gave the order to execute the Báb. He eventually fell out of favor with the royal court and was killed by royal decree while bathing.

MOSQUE Muslim place of worship.

MUḤAMMAD The Prophet-Founder of the religion of Islam who lived from A.D. 570–632. Bahá'ís regard Muḥammad as a Messenger of God and His book, the Qur'án, as holy scripture.

MUḤAMMAD 'ALÍY-I-ZUNÚZÍ The youth who was martyred with the Báb.

MUḤAMMAD S̲H̲ÁH S̲h̲áh, or king, of Persia from 1834–48, he sent Vaḥíd to investigate the claims of the Báb. Upon Vaḥíd's conversion, Muḥammad S̲h̲áh summoned the Báb to the royal court, but was influenced by his prime minister and ordered instead that the Báb be imprisoned at Máh-Kú.

MUḤÍṬ Follower of S͟hayk͟h Aḥmad who rejected the Báb's claim at Mecca.

MULLÁ An Islamic cleric, theologian, or judge.

MULLÁ 'ALÍ The first follower to give his life for the Báb.

MULLÁ ḤUSAYN A leading follower of Siyyid Káẓim, he was the first to believe in the Báb as the Promised One, and he received the title *Bábu'l-Báb* (Gate of the Gate). He was the first of the eighteen Letters of the Living and a leader of the Bábís during the siege at the fort of S͟hayk͟h Ṭabarsí, where he was martyred on 2 February 1849 at the age of 35.

MULLÁ ṢÁDIQ A follower of Siyyid Káẓim who eventually became a Muslim doctor of law and later a Bábí. He caused great controversy by adding the Báb's name to the Muslim call to prayer in S͟híráz, after which he was arrested and, along with Quddús, tortured and banished from the city. He participated in the struggle at the fort of S͟hayk͟h Ṭabarsí and was one of the few survivors.

NABÍL Literally *noble, learned:* surname of Mullá Muḥammad-i-Zarandí, who wrote the detailed history of the Bábí Faith titled *The Dawn-Breakers*.

NAJAF A shrine city in Iraq, home to one of the two holiest shrines in S͟hí'ah Islam.

NÁṢIRI'D-DÍN-S͟HÁH Notorious s͟háh of Iran under whose reign the Báb was executed and Bahá'u'lláh was imprisoned and exiled. He was assassinated in 1896.

NAW-RÚZ Literally *New Day:* the Bábí, Bahá'í, Persian, and Zoroastrian New Year's Day. It occurs on the date of the vernal equinox, which, in the Northern Hemisphere, normally falls on 21 March but sometimes on 20 or 22 March.

PERSIA Former name of Iran.

QÁ'IM Literally *He Who Arises:* The Báb.

QAYYÚM Literally *Self-Subsisting, Self-Existent, All-Compelling: Bahá'u'lláh.* Certain Islamic traditions, according to the Shí'ah Imáms, use "Qayyúm" as a reference to the One who would come after the appearance of the Qá'im, the Báb.

QUDDÚS *The Most Holy:* title given by the Báb to Ḥájí Muḥammad-'Alí of Bárfurúsh, the last Letter of the Living, who accompanied the Báb on His pilgrimage to Mecca, attended the conference at Badasht, participated in the struggle at the fort of Shaykh Ṭabarsí, was arrested and tortured in his native town of Bárfurúsh, and was finally martyred in that same town, his body dismembered and burnt.

QUR'ÁN Literally *The reading; that which ought to be read:* the holy book of Islam, revealed in Arabic to Muḥammad. It is comprised of one hundred fourteen súrihs, or chapters.

RAJAB Seventh month of the Muslim lunar calendar.

SA'ÍDU'L-'ULAMÁ Chief cleric of Bárfurúsh who incited a mob against Mullá Ḥusayn and his companions outside of the city, leading to the siege at the fort of Shaykh Ṭabarsí. Caused the martyrdom of Quddús.

SHÁH King, especially of Iran.

SHARIF Literally *noble* or *highborn:* Arabic title of respect. Sharifs originally were heads of prominent families in a town. Later they supplied the local semiautonomous rulers of Mecca and Medina. After the establishment of Ottoman rule, the Ottomans normally recognized the senior representative of the sharifs as prince of Mecca.

SHAYKH Title of respect given to old men, men of authority, elders, chiefs, professors, or superiors of a dervish order.

SHAYKH AḤMAD Founder of the Shaykhí school of Shí'ah Islam, which taught allegoric and symbolic understandings of Islamic scripture and announced the imminent coming of the Qá'im (Promised One). Many early Bábís came from among his followers.

SHAYKH ṬABARSÍ Shrine of Shaykh Aḥmad ibn-i-Abí-Ṭálib-i-Ṭabarsí outside of Bárfurúsh, Iran. It was to this shrine that Mullá Ḥusayn and his companions repaired for refuge when attacked on the road to Sárí. There they were besieged from October 1848 to May 1849. Facing starvation, they were forced to eat grass, boiled leather, and the ground bones of their already slaughtered horses. The siege ended when the enemy prince swore a false oath on the Qur'án that he would spare the lives of the Bábís if they would give up their position. The beleaguered defenders left the fort only to be slaughtered by the prince's army. Mullá Ḥusayn was martyred there along with hundreds of companions.

SHÍ'AH One of the two major branches of Islam, distinguished by its belief in the Imámate as the rightful succession of religious authority in Islam after the death of Muḥammad. The dominant branch of Islam in Iran.

SHÍRÁZ The city in Iran where, in His home, the Báb declared His mission to Mullá Ḥusayn on May 22, 1844.

SHOGHI EFFENDI RABBANI (1897–1957) The great grandson of Bahá'u'lláh and the first and only Guardian of the Bahá'í Faith. He was also related to the Báb through his father. During his Guardianship he established the Administrative Order of the Bahá'í Faith (its elected and appointed bodies), oversaw its spread across the globe, elucidated many of the Faith's teachings, protected the nascent Faith from the relentless attacks of its enemies, wrote voluminously, translated the most important writings of the Faith into English, and oversaw the construction of befitting shrines and gardens to hold the blessed remains of the Báb and Bahá'u'lláh.

SIYYID Literally *lord, chief, prince:* an honorific title denoting a descendant of the Prophet Muḥammad.

SIYYID 'ALÍ-MUḤAMMAD Given name of the Báb.

SIYYID-I-BÁB Name by which Iranians referred to the Báb.

SIYYID KÁẒIM The successor of Shaykh Aḥmad who carried on his work and message, preaching the imminent advent of the Qá'im. He was aware of the identity of the Qá'im and was once in His presence. The Báb attended one of his lectures, and where He sat a beam of light fell on His lap from the window. Siyyid Káẓim fell silent and then said, "Lo, the Truth is more manifest than the ray of light that has fallen upon that lap!" None understood his meaning, but Mullá Ḥusayn answered his call to scatter in search of the Qá'im and became the first to believe in the Báb.

SÚRIH Literally *chapter.* The Qur'án is composed of 127 súrihs.

SÚRIH OF JOSEPH A highly allegorical chapter of the Qur'án that tells the story of Joseph. Mullá Ḥusayn decided that the Qá'im should be able to reveal a commentary on that súrih unlike any that had ever been put forward. The Báb produced that commentary without being asked when he met Mullá Ḥusayn on May 22, 1844. His commentary, entitled the *Qayyúmu'l-Asmá'* and composed in Arabic, "forecast what the true Joseph (Bahá'u'lláh) would, in a succeeding Dispensation, endure. . . ."

ṬÁHIRIH Literally *The Pure One:* title given by the Báb to Fáṭimih Umm-Salamih, also known by the titles *Qurratu'l-'Ayn* (Solace of the Eyes) and *Zarrín-Táj* (Crown of Gold). She was the only female Letter of the Living. She is remembered for asserting the new Revelation by removing her veil at the conference at Badasht. She was a poet and a woman of learning, and declared her belief in the Báb without meeting Him. She was eventually martyred. Her famous last words were "You can kill me as soon as you like, but you cannot stop the emancipation of women."

'ULAMÁ Plural of Arabic *'álim.* Learned scholars; Muslim divines. The Bábí and Bahá'í Faiths found their most devoted believers, heroes and martyrs, as well as their bitterest enemies, among the 'ulamá of nineteenth-century Iran.

YAZD City in southern Iran visited by Vaḥíd which later became a major center of Bahá'í activity and the site of a number of martyrdoms.

Bibliography

Bibliography

Works of Bahá'u'lláh

Epistle to the Son of the Wolf. Translated by Shoghi Effendi. 1st pocket-size ed. Wilmette, IL: Bahá'í Publishing Trust, 1988.

The Kitáb-i-Íqán: The Book of Certitude. Translated by Shoghi Effendi. Wilmette, IL: Bahá'í Publishing Trust, 1983.

Works of the Báb

Selections from the Writings of the Báb. Compiled by the Research Department of the Universal House of Justice. Translated by Habib Taherzadeh et al. Haifa: Bahá'í World Centre, 1976.

Works of 'Abdu'l-Bahá

Memorials of the Faithful. Translated by Marzieh Gail. New edition. Wilmette, IL: Bahá'í Publishing Trust, 1997.

A Traveler's Narrative Written to Illustrate the Episode of the Báb. Translated by Edward G. Browne. New and corrected edition. Wilmette, IL: Bahá'í Publishing Trust, 1980.

Works of Shoghi Effendi

The World Order of Bahá'u'lláh: Selected Letters. Wilmette, IL: Bahá'í Publishing Trust, 1991.

Other Works

Root, Martha L. *Ṭáhirih the Pure.* Introduction by Marzieh Gail. Rev. ed. Los Angeles: Kalimát, 1981.

Younghusband, Sir Frances. *The Gleam.* London: John Murray, 1923.

A Basic Bahá'í Reading List

Basic Bahá'í Reading List

The following list provides a sampling of works conveying the spiritual truths, social principles, and history of the Bahá'í Faith.

Introductory Works

Bahá'í International Community, Office of Public Information, New York. *Bahá'u'lláh*. Wilmette, IL: Bahá'í Publishing Trust, 1991.

Hatcher, William S., and J. Douglas Martin. *The Bahá'í Faith: The Emerging Global Religion*. Wilmette, IL: Bahá'í Publishing, 2002.

Selected Writings of Bahá'u'lláh

Gleanings from the Writings of Bahá'u'lláh. 1st ps ed. Translated by Shoghi Effendi. Wilmette, IL: Bahá'í Publishing Trust, 1983.

The Hidden Words. Translated by Shoghi Effendi. Wilmette, IL: Bahá'í Publishing, 2002.

The Kitáb-i-Íqán: The Book of Certitude. Translated by Shoghi Effendi. Wilmette, IL: Bahá'í Publishing Trust, forthcoming.

Tablets of Bahá'u'lláh revealed after the Kitáb-i-Aqdas. Compiled by the Research Department of the Universal House of Justice. Translated by Habib Taherzadeh. 1st ps ed. Wilmette, IL: Bahá'í Publishing Trust, 1998.

Selected Writings of 'Abdu'l-Bahá

Paris Talks: Addresses given by 'Abdu'l-Bahá in Paris in 1911. 12th ed. London: Bahá'í Publishing Trust, 1995.

The Promulgation of Universal Peace: Talks Delivered by 'Abdu'l-Bahá during His Visit to the United States and Canada in 1912. Compiled by Howard MacNutt. 2nd ed. Wilmette, IL: Bahá'í Publishing Trust, 1982.

The Secret of Divine Civilization. 1st ps ed. Translated by Marzieh Gail and Ali-Kuli Khán. Wilmette, IL: Bahá'í Publishing Trust, 1990.

Selections from the Writings of 'Abdu'l-Bahá. Compiled by the Research Department of the Universal House of Justice. Translated by a Committee at the Bahá'í World Center and Marzieh Gail. Wilmette, IL: Bahá'í Publishing Trust, 1997.

Some Answered Questions. Compiled and translated by Laura Clifford Barney. 1st ps ed. Wilmette, IL: Bahá'í Publishing Trust, 1984.

Selected Writings of Shoghi Effendi

God Passes By. New ed. Wilmette, IL: Bahá'í Publishing Trust, 1974.

The Promised Day Is Come. 3rd ed. Wilmette, IL: Bahá'í Publishing Trust, 1980.

The World Order of Bahá'u'lláh: Selected Letters. 1st ps ed. Wilmette, IL: Bahá'í Publishing Trust, 1991.

Selected Writings of the Universal House of Justice

The Constitution of the Universal House of Justice. Haifa: Bahá'í World Centre, 1972.

Messages from the Universal House of Justice, 1963–1986: The Third Epoch of the Formative Age. Compiled by Geoffry W. Marks. Wilmette, IL: Bahá'í Publishing Trust, 1996.

The Promise of World Peace: To the Peoples of the World. Wilmette, IL: Bahá'í Publishing Trust, 1985.

Index

Index

A

Index

Mírzá Ḥusayn 'Alí as, 226
See also Bahá'u'lláh
Bahá'í, glossary definition of, 290
Bahá'u'lláh (Mírzá Ḥusayn 'Alí)
in 'Akká, 284
and the Báb
correspondence with, 223–24, 231–32, 233, 247
martyrdom of, 283
at Badasht, conference of, 226
birth of, 228–29, 230, 231
coming of, the Báb foretells, 115–16, 224–26, 227–28, 251–52, 284
at fort of Shaykh Ṭabarsí, 148, 242–43
glossary entry on, 290
and Mullá Ḥusayn, 238–39, 241
and Quddús, 241
suffering of, 253–44
and Ṭáhirih, rescue of, 244–45, 245–46
and Vaḥíd, 246–47
Báqir, Mullá (Letter of the Living), delivers the Báb's letter and chest, 223
Bárfurúsh (city of)
glossary entry on, 290
onslaught at, 142–45
Quddús in, 162–64
bastinado, glossary entry on, 290
Bayán, 225
glossary entry on, 290
revelation of, 115
Big, Muḥammad, and the Báb, 103, 232–33
black banner, of Mullá Ḥusayn, 140
Búshihr (city of), 21, 41, 49, 55, 79
Buzurg, Mírzá (of Núr), 238
glossary entry on, 295

C

Caiaphus, 110
caravansary
attack of Bábís at, 146–47
glossary entry on, 291
chief constable, 82–84
Chihríq (prison of)
the Báb in, 110, 119, 123–26, 134
corresponds with Bahá'u'lláh, 233, 247
uncle visits, 211
glossary entry on, 291
cholera outbreak, 83–84
Christ. *See* Jesus Christ
conference of Badasht. *See* Badasht, conference of
Cormick, Dr., examines the Báb after beating, 132–33

D

Dawn-Breakers, glossary entry on, 291

L

See also ‘Alíy-i-Basṭámí, Mullá; Báqir, Mullá; Ḥusayn, Mullá; Quddús; Ṭáhirih

M

Máh-Kú (prison of)
- the Báb in, 101–2, 110, 113–19
  - early days of, 113–14
  - Mullá Ḥusayn visits, 117–19
  - revelation of writings of, 115
- characteristics of, 113
- glossary entry on, 294

Maḥmúd, Ḥájí Mullá, 131
Manifestation of God
- glossary entry on, 294
- *See also* twin Messengers of God

martyrs. *See* ‘Alí, Ḥájí Mírzá Siyyid; Ḥusayn, Mullá; Ismá‘íl, Ḥájí Mullá; Muḥammad-‘Alí, Mírzá; Quddús; Qurbán-‘Alí, Mírzá; Seven Martyrs of Ṭihrán; Ṭáhirih; Vaḥíd
Mashhad (city of), Mullá Ḥusayn in, 117–18
Masih, Ḥakím, 173
masjid, definition of, 114n. 2, 294
May 23, 1844, events of, 26, 251
maydán, definition of, 233
Mecca
- the Báb in, 41–45
- glossary entry on, 294
- Quddús in, 41

Medina, glossary entry on, 294
Messiah. *See* Promised One
miracles, value of, 127
Mírzá, glossary entry on, 295
Mírzá, Prince Farhád, 102–3
mosque, glossary entry on, 295
Muḥammad, Mullá (of Núr), delivers scroll to Bahá’u’lláh, 238–39
Muḥammad-‘Alí, Ḥájí. *See* Quddús
Muḥammad-‘Alí, Mírzá (youth martyred with the Báb)
- and the Báb, imprisonment with, 263–65
- execution of, attempt at, 269
- martyrdom of, 266, 272–74
- remains of, 274–75
- *See also* ‘Alíy-i-Zunúzí, Muḥammad

Muḥammad-Ḥusayn, Mír, death of, 95
Muḥammad (the Prophet)
- glossary entry on, 295
- mission of, 90

Muḥíṭ
- glossary entry on, 296
- meets the Báb, 42–43

Mullá, definition of, 296
Mullá Ḥusayn. *See* Ḥusayn, Mullá
muftí, definition of, 174n. 1

N

Nabíl, glossary entry on, 296
Najaf, glossary entry on, 296
navváb, definition of, 124n
Navváb-i-Raḍaví, hatred for the Báb, 194–98, 200
Naw-Rúz, definition of, 166n, 297
Nayríz
  Vaḥíd in, 202–6
  violence in, 207
Níyálá (village of), Ṭáhirih in, 245–46

P

Persia, glossary entry on, 297
Persian Bayán. *See* Bayán
Pilate, Pontius, 110, 132, 163
prince, betrayal of, at Shaykh Ṭabarsí, 160–61
Promised Ḥusayn, 235–36
  See also Bahá'u'lláh
Promised One
  the Báb claims to be, 129, 133–34
  characteristics of, 23–24
  prophecies of (*see* prophecies, of Promised One)
  search for, 9
  Siyyid Káẓim recognizes, 13–14
  See also Báb, the
prophecies
  of Promised One, 89
    biblical, 228, 229, 248, 278
    Islamic, 15, 21, 35, 89, 125, 133, 140, 149, 183, 206, 228, 229, 248, 253, 259, 262, 269, 274
  of twin Messengers, 15, 228–31, 284
"Pure One, The." *See* Ṭáhirih

Q

Qá'im, definition of, 213n, 297
Qayyúm, glossary entry on, 297
Qazvín (village of)
  'Abdu'l-Karím in, 57, 59
  Ṭáhirih in, 178–81, 244–45
Quddús (Letter of the Living)
  arrest and torture of, 50–52
  and the Báb, 34–35, 42
  and Bahá'u'lláh, meeting of, 241
  in Bárfurúsh, 162–64
  dust from grave of, 166, 246
  at fort of Shaykh Ṭabarsí, 149, 156, 243
  glossary entry on, 297
  martyrdom of, 162–64
  in Mecca, 41
  and Mullá Ḥusayn, 154
  in Sárí, 139–40, 148
  in Shíráz, 49–52
  wounding of, 151
Qum (city of), 100
Qur'án
  glossary entry on, 297

U

V

W

Y

Z

About the Bahá'í Faith

In just over one hundred years the Bahá'í Faith has grown from an obscure movement in the Middle East to the second most widespread independent world religion after Christianity. With some 5 million adherents in virtually every corner of the globe—including people from every nation, ethnic group, culture, profession, and social or economic class—it is probably the most diverse organized body of people on the planet today.

Its founder, Bahá'u'lláh, taught that there is one God, Who progressively reveals His Will to humanity. Each of the great religions brought by the Messengers of God—Abraham and Moses, Krishna, Buddha, Zoroaster, Jesus, Muḥammad, the Báb—represents a successive stage in the spiritual development of the human race. Bahá'u'lláh, the most recent Messenger in this line, has brought teachings that address the moral and spiritual challenges of today's world.

The Bahá'í Faith teaches that there is only one human race and that religion should be a source of unity; condemns all forms of prejudice and racism; upholds the equality of women and men; confirms the importance and value of marriage and the family; establishes the need for the independent investigation of the truth; insists on access to education for all; asserts the essential harmony between science and religion; declares the need to eliminate extremes of wealth and poverty; and exalts work done in a spirit of service to the level of worship.

Bahá'ís believe that religion should be a dynamic force that raises the individual, family, and community to new spiritual heights. To this end Bahá'ís all around the world work to create an atmosphere of love and unity in their own lives, in their families, and in their communities.

About Bahá'í Publishing

Bahá'í Publishing produces books that reflect the teachings and principles of the Bahá'í Faith, a worldwide religious community united by the belief that there is one God, one human race, and one evolving religion.

For more than a century, Bahá'í communities around the globe have been working to break down barriers of prejudice between peoples and have collaborated with other like-minded groups to promote the model of a global society. At the heart of Bahá'í teachings is the conviction that humanity is a single people with a common destiny. In the words of Bahá'u'lláh, the Founder of the Bahá'í Faith, "The earth is but one country, and mankind its citizens."

Bahá'í Publishing is an imprint of the Bahá'í Publishing Trust of the United States.

Other Books Available from Bahá'í Publishing

The Hidden Words
by Bahá'u'lláh

A collection of lyrical, gem-like verses of scripture that convey timeless spiritual wisdom "clothed in the garment of brevity," *The Hidden Words* is one of the most important and cherished scriptural works of the Bahá'í Faith.

Revealed by Bahá'u'lláh, the founder of the religion, the verses are a perfect guidebook to walking a spiritual path and drawing closer to God. They address themes such as turning to God, humility, detachment, love, to name but a few. These verses are among Bahá'u'lláh's earliest and best known works, having been translated into more than seventy languages and read by millions worldwide. This edition will offer many American readers their first introduction to the vast collection of Bahá'í scripture.

The Bahá'í Faith: The Emerging Global Religion
by William S. Hatcher and J. Douglas Martin

Explore the history, teachings, structure, and community life of the worldwide Bahá'í community—what may well be the most diverse organized body of people on earth—through this revised and updated comprehensive introduction (2002).

Named by the *Encylopaedia Britannica* as a book that has made "significant contributions to knowledge and understanding" of religious thought, *The Bahá'í Faith* covers the most recent developments in a Faith that, in just over 150 years, has grown to become the second most widespread of the independent world religions.

"An excellent introduction. [*The Bahá'í Faith*] offers a clear analysis of the religious and ethical values on which Bahá'ism is based (such as all-embracing peace, world harmony, the important role of women, to mention only a few)."—Annemarie Schimmel, past president, International Association for the History of Religions

"Provide[s] non-Bahá'í readers with an excellent introduction to the history, beliefs, and sociopolitical structure of a religion that originated in Persia in the mid-1800s and has since blossomed into an international organization with . . . adherents from almost every country on earth."—*Montreal Gazette*

Marriage beyond Black and White: An Interracial Family Portrait

By David Douglas and Barbara Douglas

A powerful story about the marriage of a Black man and a White woman, *Marriage beyond Black and White* offers a poignant and sometimes painful look at what it was like to be an interracial couple in the United States from the early 1940s to the mid-1990s. Breaking one of the strongest taboos in American society at the time, Barbara Wilson Tinker and Carlyle Douglas met, fell in love, married, and began raising a family. At the time of their wedding, interracial marriage was outlawed in twenty-seven states and was regarded as anathema in the rest.

Barbara began writing their story to record both the triumphs and hardships of interracial marriage. Her son David completed the family chronicle. The result will uplift and inspire any reader whose life is touched by racial injustice, offering an invaluable perspective on the roles of faith and spiritual transformation in combating prejudice and racism.

Refresh and Gladden My Spirit: Prayers and Meditations from Bahá'í Scripture

Introduction by Pamela Brode

Discover the Bahá'í approach to prayer with this uplifting collection of prayers and short, inspirational extracts from Bahá'í scripture. More than 120 prayers in *Refresh and Gladden My Spirit* offer solace and inspiration on themes including spiritual growth, nearness to God, comfort, contentment, happiness, difficult times, healing, material needs, praise and gratitude, and strength, to name only a few. An introduction by Pamela Brode examines the powerful effects of prayer and meditation in daily life, outlines the Bahá'í approach to prayer, and considers questions such as "What is prayer?" "Why pray?" "Are our prayers answered?" and "Does prayer benefit the world?"

Seeking Faith: Is Religion Really What You Think It Is?

by Nathan Rutstein

What's your concept of religion? A 2001 Gallup Poll on religion in America found that while nearly two out of three Americans claim to be a member of a church or synagogue, more than half of those polled believe that religion is losing its influence on society. *Seeking Faith* examines today's concepts of religion and the various reasons why people are searching in new directions for hope and spiritual guidance. Author Nathan Rutstein explores the need for a sense of purpose, direction, and meaning in life, and the need for spiritual solutions to global problems in the social, economic, environmental, and political realms. Rutstein also discusses the concept of the Spiritual Guide, or Divine Educator, and introduces the teachings of Bahá'u'lláh and the beliefs of the Bahá'í Faith.

A Wayfarer's Guide to Bringing the Sacred Home

by Joseph Sheppherd

What's the spiritual connection between self, family, and community? Why is it so important that we understand and cultivate these key relationships? *Bringing the Sacred Home* offers a Bahá'í perspective on issues that shape our lives and the lives of those around us: the vital role of spirituality in personal transformation, the divine nature of child-rearing and unity in the family, and the importance of overcoming barriers to building strong communities—each offering joy, hope, and confidence to a challenged world. Inspiring extracts and prayers from Bahá'í scripture are included. This is an enlightening read for anyone seeking to bring spirituality into their daily lives.

Advancement of Women: A Bahá'í Perspective

by Janet A. Khan and Peter J. Khan

> "All should know . . . Women and men have been and will always be equal in the sight of God."—*Bahá'u'lláh*

Advancement of Women presents the Bahá'í Faith's global perspective on the equality of the sexes, including the meaning of equality; the education of women and the need for their participation in the world at large; the profound effects of equality on the family and family relationships; the intimate relationship between equality of the sexes and global peace; chastity, modesty, sexual harassment, and rape.

The equality of women and men is one of the basic tenets of the Bahá'í Faith, and much is said on the subject in the Bahá'í writings. Until now, however, no single volume created for a general audience has provided comprehensive coverage of the Bahá'í teachings on this topic and its many aspects. In this broad survey husband and wife team Janet and Peter Khan address even those aspects of equality of the sexes that are usually ignored or glossed over in the existing literature.

Tactfully treating a subject that often provokes argumentation, contention, polarization of attitudes, and accusations, the authors elevate the discussion to a new level that challenges all while offending none.

Visit your favorite bookstore today to find or request these titles from Bahá'í Publishing.